England, France and Aquitaine

England, France and Aquitaine

From Victory to Defeat in the Hundred Years War

Richard Ballard

Pen & Sword
MILITARY

First published in Great Britain in 2020 by
Pen & Sword Military
An imprint of
Pen & Sword Books Ltd
Yorkshire – Philadelphia

ISBN HB: 978 1 52676 859 9
PB: 978 1 52676 863 6

Typeset by Mac Style
Printed and bound in the UK by TJ International Ltd,
Padstow, Cornwall.

MIX
Paper from
responsible sources
FSC® C013056

Pen & Sword Books Limited incorporates the imprints of Atlas,
Archaeology, Aviation, Discovery, Family History, Fiction, History,
Maritime, Military, Military Classics, Politics, Select, Transport,
True Crime, Air World, Frontline Publishing, Leo Cooper, Remember
When, Seaforth Publishing, The Praetorian Press, Wharncliffe
Local History, Wharncliffe Transport, Wharncliffe True Crime
and White Owl.

For a complete list of Pen & Sword titles please contact

PEN & SWORD BOOKS LIMITED
47 Church Street, Barnsley, South Yorkshire, S70 2AS, England
E-mail: enquiries@pen-and-sword.co.uk
Website: www.pen-and-sword.co.uk

Or

PEN AND SWORD BOOKS
1950 Lawrence Rd, Havertown, PA 19083, USA
E-mail: Uspen-and-sword@casematepublishers.com
Website: www.penandswordbooks.com

Contents

Preface and Acknowledgements

This book has its origin in a conversation with M. Marc Seguin, historian of South-West France, at Jonzac in 2013 during which he suggested that the origin of my family's name might be found among emigrants from Gascony after the French conquest of Bordeaux in the mid-fifteenth century. He recommended that I read the 19th century study of those events by Henri Ribadieu. I found it on the website *Gallica* of the *Bibliothèque nationale française*, and it has had a great deal to do with the structure of this book.

Soon afterwards, Mme Véronique Martin, then responsible for the Jonzac site of the Departmental Archives of the Charente-Maritime, introduced me to M. Alain Paul, a retired archivist, who invited me to walk over the battlefield of Castillon in the company of a group engaged in revising an older account of the battle. It was he who pointed me in the direction of Malcolm Vale's work. I had already heard the *recoltants* at Saintes market who announced that their wine from Castillon had been 'nourished by the blood of the English.'

The acquisition of books and articles began and I met other interesting people, such as my neighbour M. James Pitaud, also an historian of the region which at the time was changing its name to Nouvelle Aquitaine. Mme Martin and her team made their resources available to me, as did the staff of the Municipal Library of the Haute-Saintonge, also in Jonzac. Members of the Municipal Council encouraged me in the production of an illustrated guide to their town – the castle at Jonzac, in an older version, was sometimes occupied by the English in the Hundred Years War – but they did not mind an Englishman involving himself in such an enterprise.

It was often pointed out that, historically, the Haute-Saintonge looked more towards Bordeaux than Paris, so I was led to the newly opened and glorious building which houses the *Archives Métropole de Bordeaux* where medieval documents are found, both in their original form and printed in bound volumes, edited by historians of the Third Republic and after, which their guardians welcomed me to investigate on several occasions. I was guided to several French websites, such as Cairn and Persée, which reproduce learned articles from recent and not so recent journals, comparable with the English and American ones like Wiley and Jstor. Then the Gascon Rolls Project was suggested, and there was no going back. British History Online made its appearance.

Memories of lectures by E.F. Jacob and K.B. McFarlane revived themselves, as well as the fascinating tutorials with Vivien Green, whose *The Later Plantaganets* had not long been published at the time, and of which my most vivid relevant memory (after sixty years) is his explanation of the mystique which surrounded medieval kings.

In personal terms, my thanks are due to the many people who have helped this book see the light of day. Tom Edlin, who teaches this period for A Level students at Westminster School, read the entire text in its (longer) draft form in his Christmas holidays wishing me a festive season 'more Edward IV than Henry VI.' Henrietta Hopkins also read it, since she is my style guru and offered indispensable assistance over proof-reading. All my family in two generations encouraged me, as did my dear friend Lucie.

There are many others who helped me in this enterprise as they came and went in the last six years to whom I owe my gratitude, among them Martin Ableman, who found me several treasures in book sales around England. I owe much to Dr. Lester Crook who, on this occasion and on two others previously, has taken up what I have offered and ensured its publication.

Richard Ballard
Jonzac, Versailles, 2013–2019

Introduction: Interests in Common

The story begins with a committee of bishops meeting at Beaugency in March 1152 to announce the nullity of Eleanor of Aquitaine's marriage to King Louis VII of France. They had been married for fifteen years – seven as king and queen – and had two daughters. She thought she had married a monk. He thought she was too feisty and there were rumours about her and her uncle Raymond at Antioch on their ill-fated crusade. They were separated by the churchmen on grounds of consanguinity since they were both descended from King Robert II of France, she in five degrees of it and he in four.

Eleanor had met Henry Plantagenet before, and he held lands bordering on hers in Poitou. She was nine years older than he. Whether there was love kindled between them or not, it would be a very suitable match. He would protect her from the marriage-market predators and she would unite her southern lands with his. It only took two months for them to be married in Poitiers. They visited Aquitaine together, and saw how independent-minded the indigenous nobility was. Two years later, he would inherit England by his treaty with Stephen of Blois. They would have the sons that Eleanor did not have with Louis. Louis was reluctant to give Aquitaine up, but by 1153 he had, and Henry was Duke of Aquitaine before he became king of England.[1]

Their son John, early on as a joke called 'Lack-land' by his father, lost everything except Aquitaine by the battle of Bouvines in 1204 to Philip Augustus, King of France. Aquitaine was presumed to be an *allod*, that is, independent as a duchy, and Philip's claim stopped short at the mouth of the Gironde. At the same time, Alfonso VIII of Castille wanted to expand his kingdom northwards, at first by diplomatic effort and then by siege. He started by demanding Bayonne but the Bayonnais said they would only surrender to him if the Bordelais did and they didn't.

Duke John thanked the citizens (*prud'hommes*) of Bordeaux, Bazas and Saint-Emilion in a letter of 29 April 1205 for their resistance to French and Castillian diplomatic intrigues. Bordeaux was besieged by the Castillians in either 1205 or 1206. The Bordelais successfully organized resistance by their own efforts, there being no one else to turn to. They seem, on the basis of 'liberties' offered them in 1199 by Eleanor and John, to have had a municipal assembly of some kind. John wrote to 'the *jurats* and the bourgeoisie of Bordeaux' on 4 February 1200, recognizing the existence of such a political entity. Faced with the Castillians' siege, this body seems to have transformed itself, so that by 30 April 1206, when he wrote again, John refers to 'the mayor, *jurats* and loyal subjects of Bordeaux' over the appointment of a seneschal, and the need for foreigners in the town to take an oath of fidelity to the king and to the *commune*. He sent another letter to the mayor, the *commune*, the seneschal of Gascony and the royal bailiff. So the town (using the French term rather than calling it a city) had at the time of the siege some kind of autonomous municipal organisation. The town had no royal charter, but necessity and danger were the cause of its coming onto being. It was to this *de facto* government that John wrote his letter but added the royal seneschal to the structure of government.

After Richard I's death, John and Eleanor had given charters to several towns in Poitou-Aquitaine based upon the twenty-eight clauses of a document called the *Etablissements de Rouen*, a sort of model for civic charters. Because the substantial people of Bordeaux had drawn up their own system in response to the crisis of a siege, and it was already in being, no charter was issued to them, nor does one appear in the Bordeaux *Livre des Coutumes*, while every other document they possessed does. The rapid expansion of the town during the thirteenth century puts any doubt about its institution beyond dispute.[2] The tacit recognition by the king of the status of Bordeaux, even without a charter, encouraged the townspeople to enlarge their terrain with another area enclosed by a new rampart to the south of the original one.[3]

In 1224 several Gascon towns around Bordeaux, Bazas, Langon, Saint-Macaire, as well as several landowners, surrendered to Louis VIII and it was reported to Henry III that Saint-Macaire and La Réole would not have let in the enemy if they had had enough troops to defend themselves.

It was evident that Bordeaux was defended well enough, because the count of La Marche did not follow up his conquests of the other towns and soon left Gascony altogether. Bordeaux had saved Gascony for the king/duke and given ample proof of loyalty to the king of England.

Henry III appointed Henry of Thouberville as seneschal and requested the Bordelais to maintain their extraordinary tax for two more years. The seneschal's task was complicated by factional disputes between bourgeois families which led to an insurrection in 1228. This appears to have been suppressed by the time Henry III in person crossed Poitou without hindrance and laid siege to Mirambeau in the Saintonge in 1430 requesting assistance from the mayor of Bordeaux. It was given, but the expedition was not in any sense successful in reducing a French threat to the Bordelais. Nevertheless, when Bordeaux renewed a defence pact with La Réole in the same year, the two towns re-affirmed their loyalty to Henry III.

A spirit of independence was self-evident in Gascony. The Gascons at this time of commercial expansion were loyal to the king of England as the best way of resisting the king of France. They put up with English authority while rejecting the French sort. There was an attempt at greater autonomy in 1246 in an interregnum between two royal seneschals when the mayor wanted to assume the Entre-deux-Mers into the orbit of Bordeaux, keeping back taxes that should have been paid to the king/duke in order to do so. Henry III responded quickly by appointing a new seneschal, putting an end to what the Bordelais had taken to be a concession. In 1235, the position was made clear by the charter which the king issued on 14 July. This confirmed the Bordelais in the right to have a mayor and *commune* with all the liberties and free custom they already had.

This seems to have been done in reaction to the seneschal at the time having been too severe, and there was a redressment of grievance from England. When a truce of three years had been concluded with France in 1435, the seneschal held court at Langon in order to promulgate it. The archbishop of Bordeaux, several other ecclesiastics, barons and town councils, including that of Bordeaux, were at this meeting in August and demanded the setting free of certain residents of La Réole who had sided with the king of France in 1224. The seneschal refused. The Bordelais protested 'with shameful words … not to be uttered in a royal presence,' even to the extent of threatening to kill him. Back in Bordeaux, they went to the Ombrière Palace, seized the king's revenues, and sent the sergeants packing, inviting other towns to do the same.

The residents of Saint-Bazeille did not co-operate, and denounced the mayor of Bordeaux to the king, adding that the best part of the *prud'hommes* of Bordeaux did not agree with the mayor, and that the seneschal was only doing his job. Certain among the Bordelais themselves wrote to the king to say that 'the bourgeois of Bordeaux have usurped, and do usurp, the king's rights every day.' The factions were clearly divided between those who wanted direct royal control and those who wanted more autonomy, with the taxes raised in the Bordelais remaining in their hands to implement policy in the king's name but not by the king direct. The 1235 royal charter was intended to settle this situation, and the king affirmed his supremacy while confirming the privileges.

With the fall of La Rochelle to Louis VIII, Bordeaux had become the sole producer of wines for the king of England and the wines were no longer to be from further afield than Gascony itself. That brought the Gascons an increase in prosperity enduring for two centuries until the actions on the part of the Valois monarchy that form the central interest of this book.

Henry III saw the prosperity of Bordeaux and the importance of its customs for himself when he came to Bordeaux after his defeat by Louis IX at the battle of Taillebourg in 1442 and stayed for several months. The English crown was to make systematic use of the customs to maintain its power in Gascony and to share in the new-found prosperity, even to the extent of financing a crusade in 1470. Often, the income from these taxes was farmed out to the king's preferred creditors to repay the sums that he had borrowed from them.[4]

As time went on, Bordeaux under English domination extended control of the wine trade to the hinterland, what is called the *Haut-Pays*, and the wines produced there: Cahors on the Lot, the higher valley of the Garonne, and the valley of the Tarn. The county of Toulouse became incorporated into France in 1271 and there were subsequent negotiations between the Bordelais, led by the seneschal Jean de Grailly, and the merchants of Toulouse and its dependencies leading to a commercial treaty made at Perigueux at the end of 1284 which incorporated them into the system of customs payable in Bordeaux. Other towns associated themselves in this tendency: Agen, Villeneuve-sur-Lot, Bayonne, Nérac, Condom.

When they crossed to England the Gascon traders had a privileged position. They were not foreigners, they were subjects of the king of England and, when they were in London, they were considered as Londoners. Even when the London vintners in a xenophobic moment wanted to limit the time they could stay in any one visit to twelve weeks, Edward I had protected the Gascons by an act of Parliament in 1302. The preamble to it relates that it was the king's response to requests made by the traders of the duchy of Gascony, with a view to maintaining the prosperity of their commerce. They were to accept the king's regulation of their trade but they were allowed to stay in the kingdom as long as they liked. The right on the king's part to take two units of wine from each cargo that arrived in England was abolished, and payment was to be henceforth immediate: the price was fixed according to market forces, not by royal officials. There was to be a tax of two pence on each unit of merchandise brought ashore, but once it was paid, the wine could be transported anywhere in the kingdom.[5]

Reciprocally, English traders settled in Bordeaux, and not only traders but artisans of all sorts, who, after three generations, were thoroughly integrated and had adopted Occitan versions of their surnames. There were some who had successfully climbed the social and economic ladders, and some who had slid down a few snakes since their grandfathers arrived. Pockets of English residents were found in two places: in the shadow of the ducal Palace of Ombrière if they felt they needed protection, and in the Sainte-Colombe quarter, within the new ramparts to the south of the town centre where the trading was done. Others were dispersed generally around several quarters as the evidence in the Departmental Archives of the Gironde makes clear.

Semequin Sportaly can be mentioned as a bourgeois resident of the Saint-Pierre quarter, the best known Englishman of his time because he was deputy controller of the Ombrière and close to the king/duke's seneschal. As such, he was sent to Cadillac in 1408 in a delegation to arrange a truce with the count of Armagnac. He provided wine for the use of the *jurade* and was part-owner of a ship, the *Margarida*. When the ship was taken by Breton privateers (a constant risk), its cargo was valued at three thousand *livres* for forty-two tuns of wine destined for Rouen. In reprisal, the *jurade* impounded two Breton ships in the harbour and proposed that they be exchanged for the *Margarida*. There are plenty of other examples of integrated *Angles* like him.

The inventory of trades is all-inclusive: shoemakers, at least one carpenter, a coach builder, a pastry-cook, soldiers, notaries, minor clergy, and office clerks: a complete social mix. People left money in their wills to help poor Englishmen. Only temporary residents and their servants who came and went with the wine fleets were regarded as foreigners and they remained under the jurisdiction of the Ombrière while their stay lasted. If any of these stayed longer than a year and a day, they were given status of residents, and foreigner status over time became obsolete when a common bond grew between English and Gascons fighting against Frenchmen in periods of active conflict during the Hundred Years War.

The English bourgeoisie co-operated with ardour with the *jurade*, whose apogee was in the most dangerous period after Charles VII had begun his intervention southwards in the 1440s. The *commune* of Bordeaux was dominated by a plutocracy of thirty or so families who shared the principal offices among themselves, with the exception of the mayor who was nominated for a period by the king/duke. This was the body which, whenever no king's lieutenant had been appointed, organized defence. Gascons seem not to have been very concerned to speak English, so English settlers were on significant occasions used to convey communications to the government in England about conditions in the town: men like Johan Beterdeyna, in 1406, and Janequin Brixtona in 1420. Other English residents provided goods and services, like Arnaud de Feulias,who provided firewood, Janequin, an English carpenter, Johan Folc, an English cutler, who also ran a ferry. The payments made to people like these are all meticulously recorded in the town's registers.

Doubtless, consciousness of an interest in common, of belonging to the same political and economic entity, explains the English settlers' involvement in the affairs of the Gascon capital, they were known for taking the side of Bordeaux when the failing power of the king/duke let them down and so upheld the Anglo–Gascon alliance in their own way.[6]

When it finally came, the French conquest of Gascony was a heart-rending matter for English and Gascon families alike. Coming, as it did, in 1453, the same year as Christendom lost Constantinople, it takes its place as one of the turning-points in European history. On the eve of the discovery of new worlds in west and east, the old world was re-arranging its political affinities. Kingdoms began the long development into defining themselves in terms of territorial boundaries. No wonder that history and geography are taught by the same people in French secondary schools.

Chapter One

The Road to Agincourt

The deposition, then mysterious death, of Richard II in 1399 brought about a crisis in Bordeaux. The new king, Henry IV of the house of Lancaster, the son of John of Gaunt, the former – and unpopular – Duke of Aquitaine, had to impose his authority in England against the supporters of the king he had replaced. Bordeaux showed no less a tendency to maintain Richard II's cause: after all, he had been born within its walls, and had heaped privileges on his birthplace. For a time, the Bordelais resisted Henry IV as a usurper. He won them over, however, by renewing their ancient privileges, and affirming that the city would never be separated from the English crown.[1]

The Duchy of Aquitaine had been greatly reduced in area by this time. The Bordelais, the Médoc peninsula, the coastal strip of the Landes, the Bayonnais and some towns on the River Adour, were the only remaining elements of the Anglo-Gascon duchy which had been agreed upon with the French by Edward III's ambassadors at Brétigny in 1360. The extent of Aquitaine agreed at that time comprised not only Gascony, but also Poitou, Saintonge, Angoumois, Perigord, Limousin, Quercy, and Rouergue, besides lands in the Pyrenees.[2] It resembled the duchy held by Henry II in virtue of his marriage to Eleanor, duchess of Aquitaine, at his accession in 1154. John Lackland did not lose it in 1204 when the rest of his Angevin heritage was assumed into the kingdom of France. Louis IX reduced it greatly after he had humiliated Henry III at the battle of Taillebourg in 1242 and imposed the River Charente as the boundary between Aquitaine and his kingdom in the treaty of Paris in 1259. In the century and a half between then and the seizure of the throne of England by Henry IV, the frontier was constantly being modified, and the latest incursion had been in 1377 by the Duke of Anjou and General du Guesclin, meaning that the Brétigny agreement was a dead letter.

The duchy was still a viable entity, however, sustained by the production and export of wine and the import and entrepôt trade in dyes from the Toulosain. There was the great port at Bordeaux on the River Garonne where it is 600 metres wide, approached from the Gironde Estuary by two great convoys of English ships that each year took the new wine for immediate use. English traders had commercial contacts with Gascon winegrowers. Similar conditions operated in the port at Bayonne and the transport of trade goods from there was dominated by its own ships and mariners. The system worked well for the landowners, vinegrowers and traders of the duchy. The king/duke continued to command their loyalty because he kept his distance in the matter of government and paid properly for the regional product. The English monopoly was by no means resented. Besides, English armies arrived from time to time at need to repulse French encroachments from the north and east. Usually, the conditions prevailing during the Hundred Years War – though, of course, nobody called it that at the time – of alternate warfare and truces did not disrupt the established pattern of trade.

Henry IV achieved a certain 'precarious strength'[3] in the duchy by making concessions to the outlook of its ruling classes, while maintaining his support for the English nominated officials, and assuring the various *communes* that he did not intend to rule in the overbearing way that his father John of Gaunt had in the previous century, for which the older men among the clergy, the nobles and the powerful bourgeoisie, still harboured resentment.

Two days after Henry IV's coronation, in October 1399, his son, the Prince of Wales, future Henry V, was named as Duke of Aquitaine. Since he would inherit the throne, the Gascons could not complain that they had been separated from the king as they had previously done when Richard II had made his uncle John of Gaunt the Duke, who never felt welcome enough to take up residence in the Ombrière Palace. It was even possible that the prince would soon lead a military expedition there while his second cousin, the Earl of Rutland was seneschal,[4] though it was his brother, Thomas, just before he was created Earl of Clarence, who would actually be sent by Henry IV as lieutenant on an expedition in 1412 after the king had become suspicious of his heir's precocious ambition as a member of his council.[5]

There were several incursions into Gascony by the French: attacks from its northern frontier with the Saintonge, to the western towards the Perigord and the southern in the Agenais, at the beginning of the fifteenth century. From 1406 to 1407 the Duke of Orleans' expedition to the southern extremity of the Gironde Estuary proved abortive,[6] but a passing glance at how those who lived there reacted to it will lift the lid on assumptions they made about the need to defend themselves.

Preparations for the Duke of Orleans's invasion began in June 1406. Several French nobles expressed confidence that the English could not maintain their duchy and that several Gascon lords were keeping an open mind about their own continued loyalty – men like Archimbaud de Grailly, Count of Foix, who said that he was always loyal to the king of England, but would never write it down in case the paper fell into French hands.[7] Louis of Orleans, King Charles VI's brother, began his journey south, bearing the *Oriflamme* – the French battle standard that denoted a major offensive operation – in the second half of September. He raised this standard at Saint-Jean d'Angély on 15 October accompanied by 5,000 men-at-arms and a plethora of noblemen. A French fleet, including a squadron from Brittany, was already at La Rochelle. Orleans' plan of campaign was to attack towns and fortresses on the north bank of the Dordogne, with ready access for naval operations on the wide reach of the Gironde. One target was the huge fortress of Fronsac which dominates the valley and was recognized as the key to taking Bordeaux. His proclamation to the people of Libourne, Saint-Emilion and Bourg claimed that 'they owed no allegiance to their regicide king'[8] who was responsible for Richard II's death. This makes us sit up and take notice because Louis of Orleans was one of the French lords who befriended the future Henry IV in France when he was exiled by Richard II nine years before.[9]

The invaders hoped that Blaye, the town upon the east bank of the Gironde where the estuary begins to narrow for its approach to the Dordogne and the Garonne, would allow them to pass unopposed. The *chatelaine* there was a young woman called Marie de Montaut, daughter of the lord of Mussidan,[10] whose relations were, for the most part, supporting the duke's invasion if not actually taking part in it. As would happen later also, it was hoped that a relief force from England was on its way but, when it was evident that it was not, Marie avoided committing herself to the French or the Anglo–Gascons, refusing equally an oath of allegiance to Henry IV and support to the Duke of Orleans.

Blaye was garrisoned from Bordeaux with troops under the command of Bertrand de Montferrand, an associate of the seneschal, Gaillard de Durfort. Marie shut Montferrand out from the town and sought protection from the count of Foix who, on condition that she should marry his third son, also called Archimbaud, so as to gain her lands, sent the freebooting captain Jeannot de Grailly to protect her and the town. Orleans knew that the loyalty of the Grailly family was doubtful, and began negotiations with Dame Marie and Jeannot. Seneschal Durfort crossed the Gironde on 23 October with men-at-arms, crossbowmen and English archers and occupied the town for five days, but Jeannot did not let him into the castle, or allow him directly to approach Mlle de Montaut. So she continued to negotiate with the Duke of Orleans.

Eventually, Durfort and Marie de Montaut did meet, and Durfort's attitude to her was uncompromising, demanding that she swear allegiance to the king/duke, which she refused on the advice of her council. Durfort threatened to burn the town if she did not accept his offer that she could exchange her *seigneurie* for that of Blanquefort, on the Bordeaux side of the Gironde. He ordered Jeannot to desist from his negotiations, but Marie left the town, riding pillion on the Count of Armagnac's saddle, and was taken to Orleans's headquarters in a nearby abbey. Durfort, so as to escape being trapped on the wrong side of the estuary, returned to Bordeaux.

Marie de Montaut made a bizarre agreement with the French commander. She agreed to surrender the town and the castle to the count of Foix, but only while Orleans' campaign lasted, and Jeannot was to continue to hold the castle. If Bourg, the next town on the estuary, were to fall to the French, then they should have Blaye as well. For the moment, her town was to remain neutral. She reaffirmed her agreement to marry Archimbaud. The French commanders were optimistic about their eventual success, and moved on to Bourg.

Bourg resisted stalwartly under the command of the seneschal and the municipality of Bordeaux. Bordeaux raised the necessary funds to pay mercenaries and shipping, as well as for provisions already brought from England, and cannon and ships' guns from resources previously stocked in the city. Bertrand de Montferrand led the operations with the garrison of regulars in Bourg and the Bordeaux militia.[11] Despite Louis of Orleans' energetic siege action, Bourg resisted and his repeated attacks were repulsed. The effects of a prolonged siege were soon apparent. The attackers could not be provisioned, the weather turned cold with the approach of winter, their camp was waterlogged; then dysentery broke out and troops began to desert. The Gascons took advantage of all this, and when the count of Foix came to his castle at Cadillac to marry his son to Mlle de Montaut, he waited in vain for her to arrive.

The La Rochelle fleet was prevented from supporting the attackers when the annual English wine fleet arrived, heavily armed against Breton raiders. They kept the access open to Bourg from Bordeaux by the waterways, in company with the ships and barges already in the port. Their patrols up the estuary to Talmont prevented the French fleet from approaching Blaye or Bourg. The seneschal was in charge of all these movements.[12]

Orleans ordered the Admiral of France to be more aggressive in December, and he did take action. But the English merchantmen, ready to leave laden with the year's wine, put it ashore again and, together with other ships from Bordeaux and Bayonne under Bernard de Lesparre, confronted the eighteen French supply ships in the mist among the sandbanks, which they knew and the French did not, on 23 December. The Anglo-Gascon naval victory was complete, and the French survivors retreated. Two of their captured ships were set alight in front of Bourg. After trying to negotiate with Bertrand de Montferrand, Louis of Orleans gave up and dismantled his camp on 14 January. Jeannot de Grailly handed Bourg over to English officers, Marie de Montaut married someone else, towns and strongholds on the Dordogne were recovered. 'The most serious threat to the duchy since 1377 had failed.'[13]

Certainly, the wine fleet had turned into a vital military force, but there had been no specifically military expedition from England to meet Orleans' challenge to the duchy. The Anglo-Gascons had managed their own resistance – even the seneschal at this time was Gascon born and bred. The claim made in 1452, after the French conquest, by the Bordelais delegation to Charles VII, that taxation for the armed security of the province of Guyenne was unnecessary because the Gascons could defend themselves, had some basis of truth in the light of this episode from nearly half a century before. Moreover, the importance of this incident was to demonstrate that, six years after Henry IV had usurped Richard Plantagenet's throne, the substitute king/duke could count upon the loyalty of the Gascons.

*   *   *

Before we go any further, some aspects of tensions existing in France have to be considered. We have to look backwards to the onset of King Charles VI's mental illness in the last decade of the fourteenth century to understand how French internal politics had come to be so detrimental to the national interest by the opening years of the fifteenth century.

Charles VI came to the throne in 1380 at the age of twelve, in succession to his father, Charles V. His uncle Philip, Duke of Burgundy, held the reins of power before he came of age. With the king's mental illness preventing his own assumption of power even when he had attained his majority, Philip became not only the power behind the throne, but the power instead of it. The king's younger brother, Louis, Duke of Orleans, challenged his position, and the conflict between the two dukes came out into the open. Burgundy appealed to the Paris *Parlement* for an arbitration, since the body of magistrates was then in process of assuming more authority over legal decisions concerning state policy.[14]

From 1392 onwards, Charles VI's instability, most likely inherited from the consanguineous marriage of his great-grandfather, Philippe VI with Jeanne of Burgundy,[15] showed itself in a crisis after he had been ill with either typhoid or encephalitis and in what appears to be a clinically obsessive state. He left Paris with a retinue to take revenge upon the Duke of Brittany, one of whose protégés had unsuccessfully plotted the assassination of his favourite adviser, Olivier de Clisson. He was approaching the forest of Le Mans near a leper colony, when a roughly dressed man emerged from the trees, took hold of his horse's bridle and shouted that he must turn back or be destroyed. The king was visibly disturbed by what had been said. As the cavalcade emerged from the forest into the hot open plain, one of the king's pages, half asleep because of the heat, dropped his lance which made a noise as it fell on someone else's helmet. The king drew his sword, shouting, 'Forward against the traitors! They wish to deliver me to the enemy!' He struck out at those around him and continued in this delusion until he was exhausted. His madness was plain for all to see.[16] Other incidents followed to demonstrate his suffering from schizophrenia. Aeneas Sylvius Piccolomini, who was to become Pope Pius II, wrote that 'he sometimes believed that he was made of glass and could not be touched; he inserted iron rods into his clothes and in many ways protected himself lest he broke in falling.' Sometimes he did not recognize Queen Isabeau, though he had had twelve children with her in twenty-one years. Eventually, she left his bed and was replaced by Odette de Champvilliers, a horse-dealer's daughter, whom he called his little queen, and their daughter Marguerite de Valois was legitimized later on by Charles VII in the same way as he also legitimized his own daughters by Agnes Sorel.[17]

From 1404 onwards, the king's brother, Louis, Duke of Orleans (whom we have already seen being worsted by the Anglo-Gascons at the towns of the southern end of the Gironde), and his nephew, John the Fearless, now Duke of Burgundy, both born within a year of each other, vied for domination over the incapacitated monarch as much as they had when he was a minor. The inheritance of the former comprised the duchies of Valois and Luxembourg together with the counties of Blois, Porcien and Vertus, while that of the latter was increased by the counties of Flanders and Artois. Neither of them could replace the king, since the rules of succession were well understood, and Charles VI had three sons in their way at the time. That did not, however, stop them from vying with each other for a claim on the royal finances.

John the Fearless (so-called because of his reputation gained at the disastrous battle of Nicopolis against Sultan Bajazet I in 1396 when he was in his early twenties) was looking for support from the great bodies of the state, from the University of Paris and from the leaders of the bourgeoisie, in the cause of political reform. On 26 August 1405 in the Paris *Parlement* in the presence of the Dauphin Louis of Guyenne and the Duke of Berry, he announced his intention to treat Charles VI in the most honourable manner, but to re-establish justice, and to govern the royal domain and military expenses better than was being done at present. He warned that if the royal administration were not improved 'a very great commotion' would ensue. An urgent priority was that the king be better advised.

His proposals amounted to offering himself as the defender of the crown and its subjects. A few days later, the Duke of Orleans made a counter-claim, opposing Burgundy's 'brutal conduct' by officially presenting himself instead as the defender of the king and the royal family. John the Fearless in turn countered this move by resorting to the weapon of a marriage alliance. Since Louis of Guyenne was already engaged to his daughter Marguerite, he arranged the engagement of another daughter, Agnes, with the three-year-old count of Ponthieu, who would, after his brothers' deaths, become the Dauphin Charles and then Charles VII.

Then Louis of Orleans was set upon and murdered by a gang of armed men as he went home from the queen's lodgings on the evening of 23 November 1407 in the vieille rue du Temple. All fingers pointed to John the Fearless as the instigator of this crime. He had not been in Paris when the murder happened, so he arranged for a scholastic conference to be held in the hall of the Hôtel de Saint-Pol, the royal residence, on 8 March 1408 in order to exonerate himself. During it, a Norman theologian whose name was Jean Petit, argued that Orleans had been disposed of in an act of justifiable tyrannicide.

By August, according to the future archbishop of Reims Juvenal des Ursins, it was the queen, Isabeau of Bavaria who presided in the council and had become the actual government of the kingdom. John the Fearless returned to the capital on 28 November, covered in glory after his victory over the Liegois at Othez on 23 September. The result was 'intestinal strife', as the contemporary commentator Christine de Pisan called it.

Attempts at reconciliation between the Orleans faction and the Burgundians were unsuccessful, but they were part of the of the six-year-old Charles of Ponthieu's political education. He would have been present when Charles VI, enthroned in Chartres Cathedral on 9 March 1409, attended by Queen Isabeau, Louis of Guyenne, then dauphin, Louis II of Anjou, the Dukes of Berry and Bourbon, and count Charles of Albret, then constable of France, tried to smooth away the enmity between the late Duke of Orleans's heir, the seventeen-year-old Duke Charles, and John the Fearless. John's son-in-law, the Dauphin Louis of

Guyenne, in spite of his sympathies with Orleans, spontaneously offered him the kiss of peace.

Queen Isabeau had already formed the pact of Melun in November 1409 with John the Fearless, and brought him to the threshold of power by making him guardian to Charles of Ponthieu, housed in his fortress of Loches. A clear-cut division was from then on made between the two factions of the ruling class. Charles Duke of Orleans married Bernard VII of Armagnac's daughter. In a recent historian's words:

> It was in 1410–1411 that, in a derisory manner, the Duke of Burgundy's adversaries were called Armagnacs by his supporters: 'foreigners,' with an incomprehensible language, a despicable way of conducting themselves, more brigands than military men. This injurious label came into being … and it was carried on, with highs and lows, until 1445.[18]

Charles Duke of Orleans, along with his brothers, Philippe, count of Vertus, and Jean, count of Angoulême, met at Jargeau on 18 July 1411 to send letters of defiance to the Duke of Burgundy as their father's murderer. The Duke of Burgundy ignored them and entered Paris on 3 November to enjoy his popularity there. Pope Pius II, the renaissance intellectual, sided with the Burgundians to denounce the bands of Armagnacs as illegal and impious assemblies.

Orleans was accused of wanting to oust the king completely. During violent outbreaks, the Abbey of Saint-Denis was pillaged by the Armagnacs, and Bernard VII would gladly have made his son-in-law king. Burgundy had Berry's château at Bitrex pillaged at the same time as he opened relations with Henry IV of England and so it came about that Henry IV and the Prince of Wales, the future Henry V, became involved in French civil strife. In 1411, the Prince was a leading member of his father's royal council with a certain autonomy of action.

The prince and his father agreed on the importance of persuading the government of France to implement the terms of Edward III's 1360 treaty of Brétigny with France. This treaty had taken advantage of the weakened state of France after the English victory at Poitiers in 1356, with the capture of the French king, Jean II and his gilded incarceration in London at the Savoy Palace until his death in 1364, the bids for power made by Charles of Navarre against his son the regent the future Charles V, and the insurgence of rural France in the *Jacquerie* and the ravaging of the countryside by freebooting soldiers known as *routiers*.

By not asserting his claim to the throne of France again, Edward III had gained the assent of the French negotiators, at their meeting place near Chartres, to great sacrifices against their own interests. France would give up Guyenne, Gascony, Saintonge, Angoumois, Poitou, Limousin, Quercy, Rouergue, Périgord, Bigorre, and Agenais in the south-west, Ponthieu, Calais, Guines, Boulogne-sur-Mer, in the north, and all the islands off the Atlantic coast, without the need to pay homage for them. This, had it been maintained, would have brought about a mutilation of France, since it would have lost its maritime frontier and the mouths of all its rivers except the Seine. Could that be a viable France?

Once Charles V had eventually become king, however, he overcame the problems of his time as regent of France. With the aid of his formidable Constable, Bertrand du Guesclin, he was able to renounce the treaty and pay off his late father's enormous ransom.[19] However, as we have seen, the regency for, and reign of, Charles VI followed from 1380, with further disaster for the Valois monarchy. We return now to the conclusion of the reign of Henry IV of England.

John the Fearless offered a marriage alliance with his fifth daughter to Prince Henry, and this made sense, since Burgundy at present controlled Charles VI and was effective ruler of Flanders (which could help resolve commercial disputes resulting from trade with Calais). The prince was warden of the Cinque Ports and captain of Calais, the latter often being threatened by the Duke, and so, for him, Burgundy was preferable as an ally than an adversary.

An English delegation was in discussion with Burgundy to ascertain whether Burgundy would help the English to recover lands held by the Armagnacs which they were claiming as theirs under the terms of Brétigny. It was planned that Henry IV would lead an expedition to recover the larger Aquitaine. Ships were prepared to transport it, but the king's illness prevented him from leading it. The commander sent instead was Thomas, Earl of Arundel, but without the king's authorization. Arundel was a close associate of the prince.[20]

The Brut Chronicle records that 'The same year, came the ambassadors of France into England from the Duke of Burgundy, unto the prince of England, King Harry's son and his heir, for help and succour of men of arms and archers against the Duke of Orleans.'[21] The Chronicle of London is more explicit:

Also in that year came ambassadors to the king from the Duke of Burgundy for to have men out of England to help him in war against the Duke of Orleans; but the king would no men grant, for which the ambassadors spoke thereof to the prince; and he sent to the Duke of Burgundy the Earl of Arundel and Lord Cobham with other lords and gentlemen with a fair retinue and well-arrayed people … also in this year the Duke of Burgundy , with the help of Englishmen, slew much people of the Duke of Orleans at the battle of Saint-Cloud.

In this way a precedent was set for Henry, once he was king, to associate himself more closely with the Burgundians and to impose the settlement he opportunistically made concerning the future government of France in 1420.

Nevertheless, it was the Duke of Berry for the defeated Armagnacs who took a new initiative towards the house of Lancaster after the king had dismissed the prince from the council, desiring to reassert his own authority after his son had acted independently in supporting the Burgundians. What Berry offered him was Aquitaine in free sovereignty, the cession to him of twenty named towns and castles while the French should hold several fiefs on their own territory from him. There was even talk of yielding Poitou to him if he were to do homage for it to the Duke of Berry. Under the power of these blandishments, Henry IV elevated Prince Henry's younger brother Thomas as Duke of Clarence, thus outmanoeuvring Prince Henry,[22] and sent him, via Cherbourg, accompanied by Edward, Duke of York, with 1,000 English men-at-arms and 3,000 archers, in support of Berry and the Armagnac faction.[23] These troops were established as far south as Blois on the Loire, and were given concessions of land by Berry and Orleans.

John the Fearless, bringing Charles VI with him, laid siege to Bourges, Berry's capital, in June 1412. A sort of peace was established, however,

by the middle of July. A royal mandate was issued on 7 September to put
an end to disorders and divisions. The king's council met at Chartres,
with both Orleans and Burgundy present, and called the nobles of France
to arms on 8 October in order to resist the English, hatred for whom
on the part of Charles VI was deeply rooted. Financial straits prevented
this happening, however, and Clarence was persuaded to leave only when
Orleans gave him his brother Angoulême as a hostage, not to be freed
until thirty-three years afterwards. Clarence did not take the shortest
route home after he had been handsomely paid to go away (the sum
offered was 210,000 gold crowns with immediate security in jewels and
plate): he had been appointed the king's lieutenant in Guyenne on 11
July 1412 and, taking his time, being unopposed, he reached Bordeaux
on 11 December where he took up residence in the archbishop's palace.
He threw his weight about a bit, raising a special tax on wine to feed his
troops because no one else in Bordeaux offered to do it. This journey 'had
demonstrated the weakness of a divided France and that it was possible
for an English army to march unscathed and without resistance from
Normandy to Aquitaine. If nothing else, he had provided his more able
brother with a model for the Agincourt campaign.'[24]

Clarence summoned Bernard VII of Armagnac to do homage to him
as Henry IV's representative while he was in Bordeaux for the four
castellanies which he held in the Rouergue. There is no confirmation that
he actually did so, but an alliance was made between Clarence, Bernard of
Armagnac and Charles of Albret on 14 February 1413 witnessed by the
English lords accompanying Clarence, Gaillard of Durfort, still in office
as seneschal, Bertrand de Montferrand, and one Fortaner de Lescun (a
small town in the approaches to the Pyrenees), seneschal of the Landes.
If they were to be attacked by France, English aid would be forthcoming.
Furthermore, any aid England might in future offer to the Duke of
Burgundy was not to be funnelled through Gascony, which underscores
the short-lived nature of the Armagnac/Burgundian reconciliation that
had just taken place back in Paris.[25]

The Estates-General met at the Hôtel de Saint-Pol, the king's
residence, on 13 January 1413, during which remonstrances drawn up
by the university of Paris identified 'dysfunctionality, inefficiency and
corruption' in the government. Programmes for reform were set in hand,

in which the heir to the throne, the Duke of Guyenne, and the Duke of Burgundy assumed leading roles. But Paris descended into the chaos of the Cabochien movement which took its name from its leader, Simon le Coutlier, known as Caboche, a skinner and son of a merchant who sold tripe in the *parvis* of Notre-Dame Cathedral. Burgundy tried to profit from this murderous disorder by issuing an ordinance in *Parlement* on 26–27 May, but it bounced back at him, when the Armagnacs and Paris bourgeoisie united against him. He left the capital on 22 August, and did not return there for five years, though he did try to.[26]

Henry V's coronation took place at Westminster Abbey on 9 April 1413 with unseasonable snow falling outside. He was twenty-six years old, 'an intelligent and unscrupulous politician in the full force of his age, endowed with an iron determination, a remarkable capacity for work and a great deal more experience of war and government than most newly crowned monarchs'. All this after what amounted to a conversion experience which led him to renounce the wildness of his youth in order to become a private man who kept his own counsel deliberately concealing his personal life and parting company from his former companions. From now on, he had a 'forbidding public presence', even known to rebuke close associates from looking straight at him. Like his son after him, he had 'a certain prim rectitude,' and a French diplomat thought the king 'fitter to be a priest than a soldier'.[27] Because Henry V already understood the prevailing political situation in France from his membership of his father's council until he was dismissed from it a year before his accession; he was able to insert himself as king into its tensions and exploit them.

In November 1413, Louis of Anjou, titular king of Sicily and Jerusalem, changed sides from Burgundy to Armagnac, ostentatiously breaking off the engagement between his son and John the Fearless's daughter. Instead, his daughter Marie was betrothed to Charles of Ponthieu, the future Charles VII who was not yet dauphin, since his two elder brothers were still alive. Thus began Charles's lasting association with the Angevins which was to stand him in good stead for years to come. The ten-year-old prince moved with his fiancée and his influential mother-in-law Yolande of Aragon, from Loches to their capital at Angers.[28]

Henry V took advantage of having kept the door open between himself and Duke John of Burgundy after the military action of 1411 for which he had been responsible. In August 1413, the Duke was banished from Paris and an alliance with Henry V against his Armagnac rivals would suit him. Besides, commercial cooperation between England and the Low Countries under Burgundian rule was mutually desirable. Henry had been captain of Calais since 1410, and the hinterland of Calais needed a friendly Burgundy for its security. This was a reversal of the father's policy by the son once he had inherited the crown. The keeping of the seas was an important consideration too. The Armagnacs had used the French northern ports, Harfleur and Dieppe, to dispatch aid to Glyn Dŵr's rebellion when Henry as Prince of Wales was campaigning against him ten years before. Harfleur in particular had been the port from which English shipping could be continually threatened. Restriction of its piratical activity was about to become a priority for Henry V.

Henry V sent Bishop Chichele of St David's and Richard Beauchamp, Earl of Warwick, to make an alliance of perpetual friendship with Burgundy as well as to conclude a truce to avoid conflict with the Armagnac government of France. The truce was made at Leulinghem, on the outskirts of Calais on 23 September 1413 and renewed into 1415, the eve of hostilities.

When John the Fearless of Burgundy had been expelled from the capital he met Henry's ambassadors at Bruges for four days of negotiation after which, he offered a marriage alliance between Henry V and one of his daughters, but this excited no interest in London. There was a similar lack of interest in England on the part of the Armagnacs now that they were back in power. They were intent only on preventing an alliance between England and Burgundy by making Charles VI's remaining unmarried daughter, the thirteen-year-old Catherine, attractive as a future marriage prospect for Henry. At the same time, the Duke of Bourbon – one of their number – went south to the Saintonge and Poitou on the marches of Bordeaux to expel the English occupants from towns of which they had allowed Henry IV to take possession. All three parties, Armagnacs, Burgundians and English were devising double games around each other.

By now a pretext for war was being found behind the appearance of a desire for peace. This was represented as 'a matter of justice', inasmuch as the terms of Brétigny were still the basis of negotiation and there was still the ransom for King John II, captured at Poitiers, outstanding. A marriage alliance with Catherine of France would have been a way for Henry to integrate himself into the French ruling class without the need for war and was being discussed: he undertook not to marry elsewhere until a given date, but made sure he was taken seriously by looking towards a different alliance with an Aragonese princess as well. Then he entrusted several courtiers with exploring the offered Burgundian marriage, before renewing the undertaking not to marry except with Catherine. Further diplomacy was carried on to neutralize Brittany for ten years by means of a truce. Ambassadors were also sent to the emperor-elect, Sigismund, to make a pact with him. These approaches on Henry V's part 'constituted an attempt to rally some of France's closest allies to himself should he ever choose to attack that country'. An additional consideration was that it might turn out that by allying himself with John the Fearless he might end up by losing his freedom of initiative.[29]

John of Burgundy was eager to return to Paris and the seat of power which was always in the anointed king's presence. He tried to negotiate his way back to Paris but was on a hiding to nothing. When emissaries from Charles VI made impossible demands upon him at Lille on 14 November 1413, he took horse and rode away without replying and broke utterly with the Armagnac party. A month later, at Antwerp, he produced successive authentic looking letters purporting to come from the queen and the Duke of Guyenne (then dauphin) calling upon him to bring an army to Paris to free them and the king from the captivity in which they were held in the Louvre Palace by the Armagnacs, though there was no discoverable evidence for that being true. John the Fearless made it true, however, and he gathered troops to do what he claimed had to be done.

Charles VI was suffering from a recrudescence of his mental incapacity and Queen Isabeau of Bavaria had assumed authority in his place, presiding over a meeting at which the Armagnac princes and the dauphin, the chancellor and representatives of the university and the city were present. The chancellor assumed that the letters upon which Burgundy was taking action were genuine and said so in public. The queen confronted the seventeen-year-old dauphin in private and found that they had been written and given the appearance of authenticity by young men who were Burgundian sympathisers in his household, one of whom, Jean de Croy, was put in prison, while the rest were sent away. The dauphin soon overcame his resentment at his privacy being invaded by his mother, and joined in preparing the capital against an attack from his father-in-law John the Fearless and his army. He repudiated the letters.

Charles VI's incapacity came and went several times during 1414 as he moved about between the Paris basin and Picardy in Bernard of Armagnac's shadow. English delegations were sent to both parties before Henry V decided for certain upon his expedition to Harfleur in early 1415. On 4 March 1414, three English ambassadors, Lord Scrope, Hugh Mortimer and Henry Ware were welcomed at the Saint-Denis gate by the Armagnacs with great ceremony, but all that interested them was the year's truce that they had already obtained, because they did not want the English interfering in their civil war. The ambassadors stayed for long enough to take stock of how things were, with the king once more relapsing into folly, and they could plainly see the preparations being made for combat as they made their way back to Calais afterwards.

John the Fearless made overtures to Henry V requesting a military alliance with troops sent to aid him at English expense, in return for his own military support for any English action taken against the count of Armagnac in the south-west, in his own territories, or those of Charles d'Albret in the county of Foix, or in Angoulême, a fief of Charles of Orleans, all of which had frontiers with English Guyenne. Then he could attack lands held by Berry and Bourbon north of the Loire to disengage the king and the dauphin from them. The spectre of being compromised arose again for Chichele and Scrope, the English negotiators on that occasion. There could be no agreement with John the Fearless on the basis of the terms he was offering.

Scrope and a different colleague, Hugh Mortimer, arrived in Calais to negotiate again with Duke John, who met them at Ypres in July 1414, but then left immediately for Lille to discuss his next moves with the Duke of Brabant his brother and the countess of Hainault his sister. The siege of Arras by the Armagnacs began, while John returned for his meeting with Scrope and Mortimer, whom he had restricted to Ypres, knowing full well that other English ambassadors were talking to the Armagnacs, as he was himself. His own people were talking to the dauphin's at Douai and Lille. He agreed nothing with the English and they returned home to see what would happen, while another set of English ambassadors came in processional pomp into Paris from Saint-Denis where they had been met by Armagnac counterparts. The Duke of Berry was the only Armagnac prince left in Paris, and they were to confer with him. Bishop Courtenay of Norwich made conciliatory noises, but Brétigny was still Henry V's agenda, without feudal obligations of homage to the French king. There was still the question of King John's ransom at 1,600,000 écus (he had been dead for fifty years by then) and a dowry for Catherine of 2,000,000. Berry dismissed most of what was asked, saying he had no authority to negotiate, but told the English that the ransom would be linked to any territorial settlement that might be made, and that Catherine's dowry would be a more realistic 600,000. Courtenay went home.[30]

Archbishop Guillaume Boisratier of Bourges in Berry's fief was sent to negotiate again when the English preparations for an expedition somewhere in France were known about, hoping to delay the channel crossing until it was too late in the year to sail. Henry made his final demands through his spokesmen Archbishop Chichele (promoted to Canterbury) for the territories he wanted and the hand of Princess Catherine, and said if they were not met, he would achieve them by invasion. When this did not produce the required result, he continued his preparations, keeping the French archbishop's delegation in England so that they could not inform the Armagnacs until it was too late for them to know where he was going to land (whether at a northern port or at Bordeaux) and take additional defensive measures. It was important for Henry not to lose the initiative. At the same time the future cardinal archbishop, John Kemp, at present bishop of Rochester, was sent to the court of Aragon to continue negotiations for a marriage alliance there with Princess Mary to keep the Armagnacs guessing.[31]

Invasions are costly affairs. From early 1415 onwards, at the time that the decision to attack France from Normandy rather than Gascony was made, the king issued indentures to captains for the implementation of his plans, and made many pledges from the royal treasury of plate and jewels so that they would be able to pay the men-at-arms and the archers they undertook to bring with them for the second quarter of the campaign. The treasury would pay the money value of these pledges at a later date and the valuables would be returned. The leaders of large retinues, like Edward, Duke of York, were pledged elaborate pieces of precious metals and jewels, in York's case 'a great gold alms dish in the shape of a ship (a *nef*), known in England as the Tiger because of the miniature tigers in the castles at prow and stern'. The irony was that this piece had been the gift of the Duke of Berry to Charles VI in 1395, who had given it to Richard II of England the year after, whence it had passed into the Lancastrian kings' treasury. York was killed at Agincourt, and it took until 1437 to afford to recover the *nef* for the treasury. On the other hand, the esquires who were indentured for a handful of archers received much less in the way of bejewelled pledges, sometimes, even, a broken piece of plate with a jewel or two clinging to it. In this way the king provided himself with a war chest of 'around £33,000 and very likely much more.'[32]

Before the king could give the sailing orders, a plot to assassinate him led by Richard Earl of Cambridge was uncovered. All sorts of suggestions were made for the origin of the plot: something conceived by the Armagnacs, or by the Lollards, or by the northern lords who did not like the Lancastrian settlement, or a dynastic plot by the Mortimer family? It was too complicated a plan to be kept secret, and, once it had been uncovered, the king acted swifty to arrest the conspirators at Porchester Castle. After judgement by the Duke of Clarence, Cambridge and his associate Lord Scrope were executed despite the latter's loyalty to the king as a soldier and diplomat for which he had been made a Knight of the Garter. In fact, the king's vindictiveness towards Scrope 'went beyond the law'.[33]

A week later, the fleet sailed and the closely guarded secret of the choice of landing place was revealed as Harfleur on the Seine Estuary, energetically defended by Raoul de Gaucourt against Henry's cannon, until dysentery decided the inevitable surrender on 22 September. The colonization of Normandy began, with Henry's uncle, Thomas Beaufort, being appointed as captain of the town backed up by an English garrison of 2,000.

If Henry were to make good his claim to be king of France, then he had to treat the people of Harfleur with justice and mercy, so his English troops were kept under strict discipline. He expelled a great many of the population to Rouen, but he provided them with an escort. These people had denied him entry and therefore they were rebels and their goods and property were confiscated. For contemporaries this was part of the laws of war, and it seems that professed ideals of chivalry did little to soften such blows. English merchants and victuallers were invited to live in Harfleur and take over the empty houses, becoming permanent residents to develop the port as a second Calais or a replacement for Cherbourg which Richard II had abandoned twenty years before. The taking of Harfleur was the first stage in an occupation which was meant to be permanent.[34]

*   *   *

Henry V's hundred-and-fifty-mile march from Harfleur in October 1415 to return home via Calais need not take up much space in a book whose intention is to tell the story of the English loss of Gascony. Agincourt has received so much attention from so many dedicated scholars[35] down the six centuries that have succeeded it and it too can be rapidly passed over.

The dauphin and the Armagnacs had held back at Rouen, as they gathered their army from all over France, to see what the English would do once Harfleur had fallen. They most likely expected a set-piece progress, known as a *chevauchée*, on the model of those conducted from Bordeaux by the Black Prince through the Midi towards Carcassonne in 1355 and the Auvergne towards Bourges in 1356. In these marches over considerable distances the invader's purpose was to demonstrate to the local populations, by destroying their homes, farms, livestock and harvests, that their own rulers were not taking appropriate steps to defend them.

Henry V intended instead to conquer and settle the duchy of Normandy, expelling those of the indigenous population who would not take an oath of allegiance to him, and then governing it with high officials appointed from England, the church establishment being respected. It was to be self-financing by local taxation so as not to be a drain on the English exchequer subsequent to conquest. This was what would begin after he had returned to England to prepare for it.

His brother, Thomas, Duke of Clarence, did not agree with this proposed return to England via Calais and, after discussions in the council of war, was given permission to return directly to England by sea with the many wounded. When Henry used his usual argument that his march to Calais was God's will and that He could save by many or by few, 'in an age of faith it was unanswerable'.[36] It was estimated that it would take eight days to complete the march if there were no obstruction, and the troops had to take adequate provisions with them, under strict instructions not to pillage the countryside which it was intended should soon become territory loyal to the English Duke.[37] The grape-harvest was in progress, wine was plentiful (the new vintage was always available for drinking straight away, not laid down to mature in casks), and 'with wine, the English soldier could march to the end of the world.'[38]

There had been an accord patched up between the Armagnacs and the Burgundians in a peace treaty made at Arras in September 1414, but it was precarious since John the Fearless objected to the 500 Cabochiens arrested in Paris by the Armagnacs after their revolt being unilaterally excluded from a general amnesty. He accepted the treaty only after the English had begun their siege of Harfleur in July 1415. The Armagnacs had their justifiable suspicions that Duke John had agreed with the English not to resist their invasion. The treaty was ratified, but no one on the Armagnac side could be sure that the Burgundians were committed to it. When the former took Soissons from the latter in May 1414, it was an English contingent that was accused of letting them in. John wrote to the nobles of Picardy instructing them to take up arms against the invader, but only if the final order were given by him and he were to be in command of them in person. 'If the Duke really had made a non-interference pact with Henry V, then he needed to to prevent his own men from rising in defence of their homeland.'[39]

Henry V and his army reached the Somme, hoping to cross it between Abbeville and the estuary by a ford with a wide causeway previously used by Edward III at Blanche Taque. It was learned from a captured Gascon gentleman that Charles of Albret, in his capacity as constable of France (commander-in-chief) was already there with 6,000 men, along with Marshal Boucicaut, the count of Vendôme, the admiral of France, and Arthur of Richemont, and had obstructed the causeway with sharpened stakes. Henry decided to march upstream to look for another crossing which was found on 19 October, having repaired causeways broken down by the passing French. The day after, they were visited in their encampment by heralds from Albret, Orleans and Bourbon who issued their challenge to battle. It was remarkable that the challenge came from them and not from the Dauphin Louis of Guyenne, but he had not responded to Henry V's challenge to personal combat and, for the French army commanders to do so was a matter of honour. Albret and Boucicaut had gone from Peronne to choose a site for battle. They found it and blocked the way to Calais with the huge force that had assembled from Rouen.[40] It was only after the battle that Henry V gave the battlefield its name from a nearby fortress.

The archers prepared the stakes that they had been carrying with them for days to protect themselves from the expected cavalry charge. This technique was a Turkish invention found by the international European force on the occasion of their overwhelming defeat at Nicopolis in 1396. The report of it was widespread among western military commanders originated by – guess whom – Jean the Fearless who was a combatant in the battle and received his sobriquet there.[41]

Then followed the rain on the night before, the waterlogged battlefield that slowed down the French cavalry charge, the *mêlée*, the captures, the attack on the baggage waggons, the order given by Henry to kill most of the prisoners, the burning of the stripped bodies, the attribution of the victory to the judgement of God. The main problem for the French army was that they did not have a unified command against a force that was, in tactical terms, 'supremely well led'.[42]

English patriotism has regarded Henry V's victory at Agincourt as representing the glory days of the second Lancastrian king's reign. This is a view strongly held among some British historians. Malcolm Vale, the historian of English Gascony, for example, in his review of the fourth volume of Jonathan Sumption's all-encompassing study of the Hundred Years War,[43] objects to 'recent (and not so recent) attempts by historians to cut the victor of Agincourt down to size, to make him yet another "common man"', and asserts that they 'have failed.' Dr. Vale's own recent book about the king emphasises his innovative skill in administration, his support for the adoption of the English language in official documents, his concern for the arts – especially for music, and his capacity to deal with a heavy workload.[44] From this point of view, Henry V's treaty of Troyes, with its establishment of the Lancastrian dual monarchy, is admirable, because, as long as Henry V lived, it represented an ideal of 'a durable Anglo-French peace settlement'.[45]

This was understandably not the view of historians on the other side of the English Channel. Edouard Perroy's academic stability had been interrupted by the 1939–45 War and he wrote his book in which Henry V had a rôle to play 'in a single burst,' as he said in the preface, 'thanks to precarious periods of leisure … during hide and seek with the Gestapo'.[46] Professor Perroy (he taught history at the university of Lille), after speaking well of Henry V's undoubted abilities, had this to say of him:

> His bigoted hypocrisy, the duplicity of his actions, the claim to serve justice and put wrongs right when he sought solely to to serve his own ambition, the cruelty of the vengeance he took, all *that* announced a new age. Henry is certainly of his own century, the century of Italian tyrants and of Louis XI, a thousand leagues away from the chivalric kings whose inheritance he claimed or whose projects he made his own.[47]

Perroy stood within his own inherited tradition. Jules Michelet, the 'father' of modern French history-writing in the 1840s, made the same criticism of Henry V in his account of what happened after the battle at Agincourt, reproducing information from the chronicler Monstrelet, who was a contemporary of the events he related – and participant in some of them – as an adherent of the house of Burgundy. The worst thing for the French prisoners after the battle was to endure the moralizing of this 'king of priests'.[48] Standing amid the bodies of the slain – many of whom had been slaughtered on his orders after they had surrendered because he heard that the French had revived the battle – Henry pointedly announced to Montjoie herald of France that the victory belonged to God who had pronounced judgement on the sins of the French.

On the road to Calais, Henry heard that one of his principal prisoners, Duke Charles of Orleans who, the day before, had been pulled out from under a pile of his dead countrymen, had not eaten anything. He rode alongside him and asked him why not. The Duke replied that he was fasting. This – Michelet quotes Le Febvre de Saint-Rémy, a Burgundian knight who was a participant in the battle – evoked the hardly sensitive observation from the king:

Good cousin, don't trouble yourself. I know well that, if God has had the grace that I should win the battle against the French, it is not because I am worthy, but it is, I firmly believe, because he intended to punish them ... It is said that he has never seen such disorder, such voluptuousness, such sinfulness and bad vices that are seen nowadays in France. It is pitiful to hear, and horrifying for those who hear it. If God is incensed at it, no wonder.[49]

K.B. McFarlane's lecture on Henry V delivered to the Oxford branch of the Workers' Educational Association in 1954 puts a hand on the other side of the scales. He cites the passage from Edouard Perroy translated above and demolishes it, referring to it as a 'baseless immoderate indictment' coming from 'a determination to judge Henry by standards inapplicable to his time'. He denies the idea that the king's piety was a pretence, citing his reforming spirit as an orthodox churchman and his determination to eradicate the views professed by the Lollards while he did his best to limit the consequences for them. But the most telling riposte is over his diplomacy where Perroy compared him to the universal spider, Louis XI.

Henry's diplomacy was thoroughly tortuous and those who were deceived cannot escape the jibe of being fools. But he was not the one Macchiavelli in an innocent world; he merely played the usual game with unusual skill. In war one hopes to deceive.[50]

The riposte also asserts that, while modern French writers are not prepared to admire Henry, his contemporaries among French chroniclers did. The killing of the prisoners at the end of the battle was an instant decision taken to prevent them escaping when a new attack seemed likely to develop, and it was 'condemned neither by contemporaries nor by the laws of war'. French chroniclers in particular emphasize the king's respect for justice 'and their admiration is ungrudging. This justice may have been roughly applied, but it was fairly and indifferently at the disposal of the conquered.' For them he was 'an honourable opponent', 'an honest man, upright in his dealings, temperate in his speech and action, brave, loyal, uncomplaining in adversity, God-fearing. This judgement is universal, and coming from his victims has greater force than when it came from his fellow-countrymen who agreed with it.'[51]

Yes, but from the point of view of those who were booted out of Normandy in 1450 and Bordeaux three years later, is it the French historians or the English ones who hold the balance of the argument about the success or failure of Henry V's great design for the dual monarchy of England and France which he engineered out of the raw material of a French power vacuum five years after Agincourt? Was the treaty of Troyes of 1420 statecraft, or was it opportunism?

Chapter Two

Death of Two Kings

The 1360 treaty of Brétigny made by Edward III, although it was abrogated by Charles V of France in 1369, remained the basis of Henry V's diplomacy with the factions in France until well after Agincourt. John the Fearless and Queen Isabeau came to Meulan in person in June 1419 to talk with him after he had made major inroads into Normandy, bringing Princess Catherine with them, expecting to offer him Normandy in full sovereignty and Aquitaine as it had been understood in 'the Great Peace' (by which they meant Brétigny). But all three parties realized that this would not work. Isabeau explained why in a subsequent letter: the Armagnac lords were advising her that she should support her son, the Dauphin Charles (her two older sons now having died) and, if she had concluded an agreement with Duke John and King Henry, she would have lost the support of the French nobles, the cities and towns, who, siding with the Dauphin, would have made war on her. This was something like what did happen eventually, but Henry V changed his diplomatic tactic because a new set of circumstances arose: what we would call a gamechanger.

The Dauphin Charles and Duke John agreed to meet and settle their differences but, as the arrangements were being made, it was plain to see that neither party trusted the other. The meeting was arranged to take place at Montereau-sur-Yonne on 10 September 1419. Fences had been erected on the bridge to keep the meeting secret. John the Fearless passed a wicket gate that was then shut behind him. Tanguy de Châtel, the dauphin's close associate who had saved him from the Cabochiens in Paris in 1413, struck the blow that killed Duke John, while the dauphin was not far away. There seemed no doubt that this action was the Armagnacs' revenge for the murder of Louis of Orleans fifteen years before on Duke John's orders. Moreover, nothing 'could disguise the fact that John of Burgundy had died under the dauphin's safe conduct at the hands of the dauphin's men'. The enormity of the crime led to the exclusion of the dauphin from the throne for *lèse-majesté* and having him declared illegitimate. It was said that when King Francis I visited John the Fearless's tomb at the Carthusian house in a suburb of Dijon in 1521, and wanted to see John the Fearless's skull, one of the monks showed him the wound in it, remarking, 'Sire, this is the hole through which the English entered France.' Yet the consequences of the murder had been realized by members of Dauphin Charles's entourage straight away. One of them, immediately upon learning what had happened, said, 'This has greatly imperilled the crown of France.'[1]

The English were making rapid advances in Normandy in 1419 and, having already taken Caen, they were soon to take Rouen, its capital. Queen Isabeau wrote to Henry V to condemn Burgundy's murder and offer her co-operation. Charles VI showed favours to Philip, the new duke, soon known as 'the Good', especially since he was his son-in-law. He displaced the Dauphin Charles by making Philip lieutenant of the kingdom. The only winner in all this was Henry V. Philip of Burgundy and the Queen signed the Treaty of Troyes with him in the cathedral there on 21 May 1420 with a certain amount of theatrical pomp. Charles VI, now out of his mind again, did as he was told. Henry was to become his heir when he was dead, and regent for him while he lived. Henry married Catherine on 2 June. By the treaty, any male child they produced would be king of France and of England, each country having its own administration and separate laws. Charles VI disinherited his only surviving son because he had 'rendered himself unworthy' by his part in John the Fearless's assassination, and Queen Isabeau disclosed no details of a suspected liaison with Louis, Duke of Orleans, but agreed to have Charles of Ponthieu declared illegitimate.[2]

The treaty document opened by the statement that, because Henry V had married his daughter, Charles VI had taken Henry to him as his son, and that Henry V would honour him and Queen Isabeau as his parents. Henry was to assume the title 'heir of France' at once. The validity of the treaty was not to rest upon the authority of the mentally handicapped king, nor was the crown private property to be transferred at will, but the change was to be ratified in the *Parlement* of Paris and in the English Parliament. Only in this way would it carry legality. Oaths to abide by it were taken by the French nobles, so to abrogate it would be treason.

The treaty applied to England, Burgundy and the parts of France still under the authority of Charles VI, but there were vast swathes of territory in France not under his authority to the south and south-east of the Loire. These maintained allegiance to the disinherited Dauphin Charles and fought for his cause. The war against him was to continue, and any lands taken from him were to be added to the French part of the dual monarchy. There was a real problem with the Treaty of Troyes: the Anglo-Burgundian alliance was 'thoroughly unnatural' ... 'precipitated by the act of naked aggression which ended John the Fearless's life at the bridge of Montereau'. The Burgundian council in 1419, before the treaty, accepted an alliance with Henry V, in their own words, as the lesser of two evils. They regarded it as a short-tem solution to a passing emergency. As long as support for the dauphin remained, it could not bring peace.[3]

When Henry died at Vincennes on 31 August 1422, after contracting dysentery at the siege of Meaux in the spring, the Burgundians began to look for and find legal loopholes in the treaty, so as to break it when the alliance between Duke Philip and the Duke of Bedford broke down fifteen years later. Another commentator has asserted that, rather than a peace treaty, it condemned Henry VI's England and Charles VII's France to perpetual warfare until one of them lost.[4] It could be concluded, then, that the origins of the loss of Normandy in 1450, and of Gascony only three years afterwards – the preoccupation of this study – were in the treaty of Troyes of 1420.

Charles VI fell ill too. He recovered somewhat after a diet of oranges, but died on 21 October. The infant son of Henry V and Catherine inherited his kingdom and, in all likelihood, his illness. War continued between the English, governed by a regency of Henry V's brothers, Bedford in France and Gloucester in England (Clarence had died in battle at Beaugé in 1421), and with his uncle Beaufort, bishop of Winchester – the richest bishop in England – sometimes acting as paymaster and no longer prevented, as he had been by Henry V, from accepting his cardinal's hat.[5] John of Bedford married Philip of Burgundy's sister Anne, and the Anglo-Burgundian alliance lasted while she lived. In 1435 Philip and Charles VII concluded the treaty of Arras from which Bedford excluded himself. Bedford's death soon followed, and Charles was able to take Paris.

*   *   *

The heir to the Treaty of Troyes was a nine-month old baby, born at Windsor on 6 December 1421 while his father was in France and so never saw him. From 21 October 1422 he was king of the double monarchy of England and France. As the monk of St Albans, Thomas Walsingham, was to remark in his Great Chronicle in a fit of depression,[6] 'Woe to the nation whose king is a child.'

He was the third Lancastrian king after his paternal grandfather's usurpation of the throne from Richard II in 1399, and the last twenty-two years had seen a 'Lancastrian' tradition developing, with sufficient supporters to provide an establishment from which the regency council for the infant and adolescent king could be formed. They decided upon the legal fiction of a public personality for the child, so that collective decisions made by the council were made in the king's name as if he were already of age. They did this in order to prevent his uncles Bedford and Gloucester or his great-uncle Beaufort from assuming any personal power in England during his minority.[7]

Fifteenth-century English society could not function without an active king whose directives were taken as the genuine initiatives of national policy at home and in the arena of international politics. The king was not above the law, but he had his function in the making as well as in the application of it. As John Watts has said,

> Service to the common weal had to be focused upon the crown and was concentrated and directed by the will of the king. Even though this will was to be wholly responsive to the common interest, it had to exist apart from and above the mass of individuals who made up the *communitas*. Only this way could common interest be preferred before that of any group or individual. Fifteenth-century advice-writers recognised that their polity required direction, but were careful to restrict the freedom of the royal will to the purposes for which it was required ... Only a single independent will, rooted deep in the king's own person, could guarantee a single common interest and the unity of the realm with which it was so closely associated.[8]

How was such an understanding to be implemented when the king was a minor or, later, when the king had succumbed to an inherited malady?

It was in these conditions, particularly in the minority, that the attempt was made to make Lancastrian principles operate. What were these Lancastrian principles?

The Tudor myth asserted that the deposition of Henry VI in 1461 was retribution for the sin committed by his grandfather in 1399 of deposing Richard II.[9] Shakespeare, who dramatized the myth, has Henry V on the eve of Agincourt praying that his soldiers' hearts will be steeled for the fight, but makes him add:

> Not today, O Lord,
> O not today, think not upon the fault
> My father made in compassing the crown.
> I Richard's body have interréd new,
> And on it have bestowed more contrite tears
> Than from it issued forcéd drops of blood.
> Five hundred poor have I in yearly pay
> Who twice a day their withered hands hold up
> To pardon blood. And I have built
> Two chantries, where the sad and solemn priests
> Sing still for Richard's soul ...[10]

However, behind this Tudor myth was what might be called the Lancastrian justification. In 1415, Henry V did indeed found two new religious houses, the Carthusian monastery at Sheen with forty monks which provided confessors for the king's courtiers, and the Bridgettine convent at Syon, modelled on practice at Vadstena in Sweden. These were part and parcel of the Lancastrian religious orthodoxy which Henry V imposed upon England.[11]

The origin of these Lancastrian principles pre-dated the usurpation of 1399 but were more fully elaborated during the reigns of Henry IV and Henry V. After the death of these two kings, they were applied by the regency council to the way in which it was hoped the dual monarchy would work out in England. There were also supporters for it in France: the treaty of Troyes, ratified in the *Parlement* of Paris, envisaged the separate evolution of two nations under one ruler.

The originator of Lancastrianism was Thomas, second Earl of Lancaster, Edward I's grandson who led the baronial opposition to Edward II, presenting grievances to the king about the way government and finance was being handled. These complaints led to Ordinances being issued in 1311 in favour of good government envisaging baronial restraint on the king's power. Earl Thomas eventually lost the struggle in his military defeat at Boroughbridge on 6 April 1322, deserted by many of his followers. He was executed six days later. But, as steward of England, and in Parliament, he had embodied a political programme of good government as opposed to Edward II's tyranny. After his execution at Pontefract, Thomas's tomb became the scene for reported miracles, and Edward III from his accession in 1327 onwards promoted his cause as a reformer. The way in which people prayed for his soul revealed 'a nascent political programme' to which the name Lancastrianism would be appropriate. It was claimed that he had died for the liberty of England's laws, for justice and for the whole realm of England. The pope never officially regarded him as such, but he was a saint in the eyes of those who came to his tomb as pilgrims until the Protestant Reformation put a stop to it.[12]

Richard II recognized in Thomas the same kind of opposition as he faced in the Lords Appellant in 1388, but for his adviser and uncle, John of Gaunt, Duke of Lancaster, the memory of Thomas was ambiguous, and he did not deny the benefits of his reforming legacy in sponsoring a Lancastrian version of history in the chronicle known as the *Brut* which was currently being translated from Latin into English. While Gaunt was pursuing his ambitions in Spain, his son, Henry Bolingbroke, supported Thomas's programme and joined the Lords Appellant against Richard II, thus incurring his vindictive wrath in banishing him from England for ten years. When Gaunt died, Richard II denied Earl Henry his inheritance as Duke of Lancaster. Bolingbroke was in Paris and made a secret treaty with Louis of Orleans while his brother Charles VI was incapacitated and then landed at Ravenspur in Yorkshire on 4 July 1399 while Richard II was in Ireland.

Richard II came back to England, met the new Duke of Lancaster at Flint castle and submitted to him in return for the promise of his life. He was lodged in the Tower of London at the end of September 1399, and the

Lords and Commons heard it announced that he had resigned the throne 'with a cheerful expression'. Lancaster had supplanted him, claiming to be God's choice in a realm that was 'at the point of ruin for lack of governance and destruction of good laws'. Parliament accepted his claim to be King Henry IV, but the acceptance of this insecure claim needed to be re-confirmed four times by Act of Parliament. Lancastrian principles of good government were asserted to justify Henry's usurpation of Richard's throne after the tyrant had starved to death. So 'the dominant theme of political discourse during the ensuing two decades was ... to establish the legitimate foundations of Lancastrian rule.'[13]

Writers and poets like Thomas Hoccleve, John Gower, Thomas Chaucer and John Lydgate were motivated by their princely patrons to give their support which was widely appreciated by their Lancastrian readers. The English language was used to record government proceedings so there was an element of popular appeal in all this. It was of importance that

> In the wake of Richard's deposition an appeal to the Commons both mitigated the act of usurpation itself and nullified the suspicion that Henry had come to the throne at the head of a narrow political faction. Yet it introduced a degree of debate into the business of kingship, forcing the Lancastrian kings to submit their rule to the approbation of their servants and of the wider political nation to a far greater extent than their predecessors.[14]

An appeal was also necessary to the Church for its support, since there could be no stability without it. Because Lollardy (the programme of the Oxford theologian John Wyclif) at the beginning of the fifteenth century had such a popular appeal, the attitude towards it for the first fifteen years of Lancastrian rule was ambivalent, despite the Act of Parliament for the burning of a heretic (*de heretico comburendo*) being passed in April 1401. Nevertheless, Lancastrians wanted to be seen on the side of orthodoxy. This went along with Henry IV's condemnation of such clergy as preached that Richard II was still alive, and 'linked sedition with heresy'.[15] Nevertheless, the Lancastrians did not allow condemnation without an attempt to persuade the Lollards to leave their mistaken ways. Prince Henry spent many hours with one John Badby who was eventually burned in 1410 for refusing to accept the doctrine of Transubstantiation.

Lancastrian orthodoxy was neither static nor reactionary but expressed itself in progressive new forms of worship under the aegis of certain members of the royal households of Henry IV and his son. The Chapel Royal fostered new polyphony in music and was certainly a priority. Malcolm Vale has pointed out the frequent references to 'conscience' in Henry V's letters dictated under the signet in which there is 'a ring of authenticity and immediacy'.[16] Henry V's personal involvement in episcopal appointments for suitable candidates has also been noted. The Lancastrian kings had a particularly 'hands-on' approach to the Church in England, although it was nothing like the emergent Gallicanism that Charles VII was later to favour in his Pragmatic Sanction issued at Bourges in 1438. It is no wonder that Henry VI, the third Lancastrian King, should have responded so eagerly to the advice of his bishops over his royal ecclesiastical and educational foundations at Eton and Cambridge.

*   *   *

One of the terms of the Treaty of Troyes stated that Normandy, the *pays de conquête* must be returned to the kingdom of France when Charles VI died. Nevertheless, Bedford kept the province separate from the rest of France and maintained its administrative and judicial capital at Rouen. Henry VI's councillors in France undertook to legitimize his rule there by the minting of a new coinage. The principal French coin was the gold *salute*, and the new version showed an angel bearing the English shield with leopards announcing the coming of the saviour to the Virgin who carries a shield bearing the fleur de lys.[17] Could this heavy-handed symbolism have convinced many Frenchmen of the rightness of young Henry's entitlement to rule over them?

At the same time, Bedford, as Henry's regent in France, commissioned a poem from an Anglo-French notary called Lawrence Calot in which the new king's descent from the ancient French and English ruling houses would be set out. The poem went with elaborate genealogical paintings which were displayed in churches tracing his ancestry back to Saint Louis IX[18] who had defeated Henry III at Taillebourg in 1242. The irony of this imagery cannot have escaped many French men and women (particularly one young woman) who were increasingly ready to accept the Dauphin Charles as King of France. Nevertheless, the new order was accepted by several influential French cathedral chapters and, to some extent, by the even more influential University of Paris.[19]

There were reservations in England: the Parliament of 1420 expressed fears that the treaty would at some future time lead to the domination of England by France which explains the reluctance of parliaments before 1429 to grant supply for further warfare. Richard Beauchamp, Earl of Warwick (too early for the Kingmaker) commissioned an English translation of Calot's poem in French from John Lydgate. David Grummitt comments upon the debate this would have opened among the literate public, unavoidably leading to anxieties about the Lancastrian regime's priorities. The poem's survival in forty-six manuscripts, however, suggests that it was taken seriously. Lydgate himself followed his commissioned translation of Calot with an original prose work of his own called *The Serpent of Division*. Its thesis was that only the unity among the lords could save Henry's crowns. The poet seemed to have accepted the inevitability of failure since his work is full of paradoxes and ambiguities. Peace in England and France could be brought about only by prosecuting war, the union of the two realms only by the 'besy peyne' of that exemplar of active kingship, Henry V. Lancastrian principles of government were now embodied in a small child and however much his council might plan, 'it was "pitous fate" that would ultimately decide the fortunes of the dual monarchy.'[20]

When Henry V was on his deathbed at Vincennes, he had given instructions to be followed about the future in both kingdoms but, of course, at that time Charles VI was still alive and not expected to die so soon after him. He laid stress on the importance of the English alliance with Burgundy, the necessity of keeping Normandy, and of not releasing the French prisoners taken at Agincourt until his son had come of age. Philip of Burgundy was offered the regency in France but, when he refused, John of Bedford took it on and arrangements were made in the Paris *Parlement* on 19 November 1422. With his marriage to Anne, Philip of Burgundy's sister,

Bedford was perfectly placed to make the Dual Monarchy a political reality. He epitomised the cosmopolitan international princely pretensions of the House of Lancaster. He was thoroughly Francophone, patronising French monasteries, artists and poets and when he died in 1435 he chose to be buried in Rouen cathedral.[21]

Just under three weeks before Bedford's ceremonial assumption of authority in Paris, on 30 October 1422, the dauphin struck his own blow on the political anvil by having himself proclaimed as King Charles VII at Mehun-sur-Yévre.[22] He had heard of his father's death on 24 October. He sent a circular letter to the towns of his kingdom to announce his accession to them and moved back to Bourges. The war against the English was obviously his preoccupation. Charles VII soon showed that he was his own man with undeniable self-confidence. From Bourges as dauphin, he had been working on building up foreign support. So, at his accession, not highly regarded by his enemies, he had acquired the support of Savoy and Castille, and disarmed the hostility of Pope Martin V in whom the Great Schism in the western Church had been ended. His father-in-law of Anjou was gaining ground in southern Italy and prestige for the large part of France that was loyal to him. The northern Italian princes were taking notice of him.[23]

Charles VII did not move from Bourges. He had presided over the Estates-General that met there in January, and the only time he left his base was to go to Selles in August to preside over another meeting. News came that Meulan had capitulated to the English on 1 March. There was a major setback at Cravant near Auxerre on 31 July where the French and Scots under the count of Vendôme and the Earl of Buchan had been cut to pieces by an Anglo-Burgundian army commanded by the Earl of Salisbury. This Scottish force was almost completely wiped out (but there would be others), and Salisbury's skills as a general were confirmed,[24] though he had no more than six more years in which to demonstrate them.

But there was better news for Charles VII by 9 October when he wrote to the residents of Tournai to announce that the count of Aumâle had gone into Normandy and had fought a battle near La Gravelle in Maine on 26 September against more than 2,000 English, who were all killed except their captain and between eighty and a hundred of his men. The greater part of the English force had taken flight and were soon captured or killed. The French lost only eight or ten gentlemen, and 'a few varlets'. Aumâle claimed he had found the means to overcome the English archers' longbow.[25]

Charles wrote that he expected more good news from Aumâle. There had also been a 'great robbery' made on the border of the Maconnais by Admiral Culant and other commanders, where about three hundred Burgundian officers had been taken prisoner (Think of the ransoms!). The king, buoyed up by all this, stated that his intention for the next battle season was to go with a large force from Macon to Reims for his coronation (Charles VII had this idea himself while Joan of Arc was still a child at Domrémy) and then to reduce all his rebel subjects – the Burgundians – with the help of his '*beau cousin*' count Gaston IV of Foix and another contingent of 8,000 Scots who were expected to arrive soon. 'All this,' he told the inhabitants of Tournai, 'to take away from you and others the dangers you are in.' He had more good news to tell the towns on Saturday 3 July: a son (*un très beau fils*) had been born to Queen Marie of Anjou. The future Louis XI, had come into the world, with all that that entailed.

Charles VII's mother-in-law, Yolande of Aragon, turned up in Bourges from Tarascon in Provence to re-assume her role as his confidante and adviser (*son rôle de mère vigilante*). The royals had taken over the archbishop's palace, hung with tapestries offered by the Duke of Orleans. A sumptuous baptism ceremony was arranged. Louis had John II, Duke of Alençon and Martin Gouge, bishop of Clermont-Ferrand, for godfathers, and his godmother was one of the queen's ladies, the countess of Tonnerre.[26]

There followed a progress in the Touraine, to the Estates-General at Selles, then to Loches, and a joyful entry at Tours. On the road again through Vierzon, Selles and Bléré, and then there was an alarm signal: rumour – which turned out to be false – had it that the English were threatening Tours and were already occupying Le Lude. This did not prevent more celebrations in Tours, or the town's bourgeoisie presenting the king and queen with ten pipes of wine to wet Louis' head again, along with ten measures of barley, a hundred fatted sheep, a hundred wax torches and two *livres tournois* from each of them. The king was received at the abbey of St Martin of Tours on 8 November and made an oath before the canons there.[27]

The itinerant court moved on after two months to Chinon for yet another meeting of the Estates-General, and then to Bourges for Christmas. The English were all this time threatening the central provinces and the king took measures to protect the towns in the Berry that were on the frontier with the Nivernais. At the end of January there were complaints made at Selles to the royal council that the recruited French soldiers were disorderly. In reply the king issued an ordinance in which he sent all his French soldiers home and announced that he would only pay wages to his Scottish and Lombard soldiers. Ten thousand more Scots arrived soon afterwards on 8 March under the command of the Earls of Douglas and Buchan and other lords. This army was made up of 2,000 knights and squires, 6,000 trained archers, and 2,000 highlanders (*escos sauvages*) armed with axes. Charles also had 2,000 heavy cavalry from Milan at his disposal (those Lombards whose wages he would continue to pay). Milanese armourers were famous in all Europe, and Milanese steel was the best hope of resisting English arrowheads.[28]

Once more at Selles, the Estates-General heard the king give his assessment of his kingdom, and repeat his intention to pursue the war more actively. The Estates voted an aid of a million livres, and agreed to recall the army that had been sent home to be ready on 15 May 1424. Jacques and Charles de Bourbon were appointed lieutenants-general: one in Languedoc and the other in the Maconnais. Ambassadors were sent to bring about a rapprochement with the Duke of Brittany. In ordering the army to assemble on the banks of the Loire, Charles VII announced with formality that he would use all his powers to repulse the enemy, and to be present in person as the need arose.

With Yolande of Aragon's return, factions revived with as much force as they had when Charles VII had been dauphin. The Chancellor, Bishop Martin Gouge, seconded by Yolande, wanted peace and actively promoted a reconciliation with Philip of Burgundy on the basis of what was actually accepted in the Treaty of Arras twelve years later. The other party wanted foreign alliances, and hoped for armed assistance from Spain, Lombardy and, above all, Scotland to fight against the Anglo-Burgundian alliance and free the kingdom from the yoke of the captains [known as *écorcheurs* (literally, 'strippers')] who were dishonouring the king's cause by their excesses.[29]

Then came the Duke of Bedford's 'Second Agincourt'[30] at Verneuil on 17 August 1424 where Scots led by Douglas and Buchan were 'cut to pieces'.[31] Bedford had held his council of war in Paris in June to plan the conquest of Anjou and Maine and of Picardy. His Anglo-Norman force had recently been reinforced by the Earl of Warwick, Lord Willoughby and Sir William Oldhall with men on short contracts. Bedford had called up all who held lands from the crown and were used to bearing arms, whether English or Norman. They were to meet at Vernon on 3 July. He also took 2,000 men from the Norman garrisons, but some of these had to be disciplined for fraud since, having received their wages until November, they left their units and enrolled in the castles so as to receive double pay.

The Earl of Suffolk was besieging the fortress of Ivry south-west of Paris and after three weeks it was ready to capitulate, having arranged 14 August as a 'day of battle' on which to surrender if an Armagnac relieving force did not arrive. This force was on its way, but Aumâle and Alençon, who had been dispossessed of their lands in Normandy, decided not to proceed to Ivry, but to occupy Verneuil, thirty miles further to the south-west. Bedford arrived before Ivry in person on the day before and regarded their failure to encounter him there as a breach of chivalry.[32]

Charles VII had also realized how important the campaigning season of 1424 was to be and, aware of the dissensions between Bedford, Gloucester and Philip of Burgundy, decided to set the recovery of Normandy in hand. With an estimated 15,000 men, assembled between Le Mans and the Loire, and sufficient resources from the Estates to pay them and the Scots, Lombards and Aragonese who were with him, he decided upon resolute action. The French contingents were from the Auvergne, the Limousin, Anjou, Languedoc, Dauphiné and from Brittany. It was a heterogeneous force.[33] There were half-a-dozen commanders but no concerted battle plan. Charles VII had wanted to lead the army himself, but his council persuaded him against taking the risk. On the English side, however, there was a unified command, disciplined, sure of itself. Bedford was in total control, with Salisbury, Suffolk, Talbot, Falstolf and Scales as his subordinates, who knew how to make the best use of their smaller numbers. When the time was ripe and conditions permitted, Charles VII would learn from the malfunction of the French armies during these years.

The French army did, however, organize some crafty dealings at Verneuil. Aumâle, Alençon and Narbonne had made their rendezvous with Douglas and Buchan at Chateaudun, intending to advance to the relief of Ivry, but they decided it would be better to take Norman frontier towns one after the other instead, starting with the nearest which was Verneuil where there was an English garrison. They took advantage of the fact that the Scots with them spoke English. They tied them facing backwards on their horses roped together as if they were prisoners and spattered their clothes with theatrical blood as if they were wounded. They led them in front of the town walls and made them utter loud lamentations in English, saying that Bedford had been beaten at Ivry and that they were the remnants of his army.

The English garrison believed what they were hearing, closed the gates and manned the towers. Then the Armagnacs brought Guillaume d'Estouteville, the seigneur of Torcy, and handed him over to them, tied up like the others. He told them that all the English cavalrymen had died that very day before Ivry. They believed him, opened their gates and surrendered to the French and Scots, not knowing that this Norman lord had changed sides to serve the dauphin. Estouteville died in the battle that followed. An anonymous contemporary source calls this action of Estouteville's 'treason'.[34] There were several Norman defectors who took the serious step of leaving Bedford. They were willing to risk everything, which shows that 'they must have been confident that the French intended to fight and their chances of victory were high.'[35] The ruse worked and Verneuil was taken. They were not so lucky later on: even if they survived the battle, their lands were confiscated by the English.

Bedford by this time had taken Ivry, and went off to Evreux, leaving Suffolk to watch the French army's movements. When he knew that Verneuil had been taken, he resolved to take it back, angry at the ruse which the French had used. The question of chivalry was important to him. He had heard about the approaches Philip the Good had been making towards Charles and sent de L'Isle Adam with his three thousand Burgundians away to Picardy, reducing his army to eight thousand men. He reached Damville, twenty kilometres north-west of Verneuil, on 16 August.[36]

Aumâle and Alençon now had the advantage of choosing where the battle should take place. The flat fields to the north of Verneuil were ideal for an action by the Lombard heavy cavalrymen, and the plan was to have them ride down the English archers before they could let off any of their famous volleys from the safety of their embedded stakes that had been so successful at Agincourt. The English fought on foot, and tethered their horses together in the rear by the wagons, with a reserve force to guard them, while they themselves could act as a protection against attack.[37]

In mid-afternoon, the Milanese began their advance, brushed the archers aside, and separated Bedford's division from Salisbury's. They did not regroup from behind, but stopped to pillage the baggage wagons. The disciplined English rallied and advanced in their turn against the French men-at-arms. Whether the archers used their longbows or not (the sources seem to be silent about this), this movement decided the battle. For Bedford, the Scots who were fighting under Douglas and Buchan were oath-breakers. Their king, James I, had recently been released from captivity in England and his officers had sworn not to ally themselves with England's enemies, so Bedford had ordered in advance that no quarter was to be given, and the combatants did as they were told: discipline was good in his army. The Scots were hounded to death on the field of Verneuil-sur-Avre.[38]

'Bedford completely routed the dauphin's forces.'[39] The death-count on the Franco-Scottish side was 7,262, among them the French commander, the count of Aumâle, and both the Scottish ones, Douglas and Buchan. Alençon was a prisoner, held for a ransom of 200,000 gold *saluts*,[40] together with his half-brother, the bastard Pierre, and the Marshal Lafayette. Bedford claimed that the English had lost two men-at-arms and 'very few' archers.

The victory had a symbolic value for the dual monachy. The Duke wore a surcoat which bore the French white cross combined with the English red one to represent it, over which he put on a blue velvet robe when he was not fighting, representing his status as a Knight of the Garter.[41]

By depicting himself as a chivalric knight, commanding a brotherhood of knights certain of the justice of their cause, Bedford claimed the moral high ground against the Dauphin whose councillors had advised him against taking the field in person. Indeed, the unjust nature of the Dauphin's cause was underlined in the battle's aftermath: the body of one of the French commanders, the count of Narbonne, who had been killed during the battle and who had been implicated in the murder of John the Fearless, was strung up on Bedford's orders and later quartered in front of the Anglo-Norman army.[42]

Charles VII put his plans for his coronation at Reims on hold, and, for a time 'abandoned himself to a life of indolence in his kingdom of Bourges'. Bedford returned as a hero to Paris. Salisbury and Suffolk went on to seize Senonches and Nogent-Le-Rotrou, while the French general La Hire agreed to evacuate other fortresses. The first wave of conquest ended when the English had taken Maine and Anjou. The only objective not taken was Mont Saint-Michel.[43]

The importance of Bedford's victory at Verneuil is reflected in the decision of many in Normandy that further resistance to English occupation and the implementation of the Treaty of Troyes would be futile. Nicolas le Jendre had been at the head of a priory outside the walls of Ivry and had accepted English rule from 1419 onwards when Rouen had been taken. But renewed hostilities meant that income from pilgrims' offerings to his priory dried up, and he went to live in the town after the Armagnacs had captured it. He was elected abbot of Saint-Germain-de-Truite, and went on to be consecrated by the bishop of Evreux, but refused to take the oath of allegiance to Henry VI because he feared how the Ivry garrison wound react toward him. He was in Ivry when he heard of Bedford's advance and fled into English Normandy. Once Ivry was no longer in French hands, he took his oath after receiving a pardon for not having done so before.

Other residents of Ivry also received Bedford's pardon for supplying the Armagnacs during their occupation of the place, as was also the case with those who had believed Aumale's ruse with the Scots at Verneuil and opened their gates to him. The non-combatant attendants who had run off as soon as the Lombard cavalry crashed through the English formations spread the rumour that Bedford and his lieutenants had lost the battle. There was, as a result, a Norman rebellion against Bedford.

When the truth was known, the rebels, who had killed a few of the fugitives, submitted.[44]

*   *   *

During and after the time of Verneuil, Henry VI's younger uncle, Humphrey of Gloucester, was branching out on an adventure of his own which was to rock Bedford's boat to say the least. He had fought and been wounded at Agincourt but he was no statesman and regarded the possibility of eventual peace with France as 'casting a slur on the memory of a brother whom he had revered'. His fame as a soldier whetted his appetite for more of it.

He had been 'Guardian of England' during some of Henry V's absence in Normandy and it was argued that Henry V's wish from his death-bed was that Gloucester should be regent again. The Regency Council, as has been noted, had other ideas. There were other restrictions placed upon him as well: his powers of patronage in England were limited to the nomination of officials with the council's consent. He was interested in literature and scholarship as expressed in his patronage of Oxford University with his famous library. He fostered the anti-foreign feelings of the Londoners. But 'nothing can hide his factious irresponsibility' which is best seen in his relationship with Jacqueline, countess of Hainault, Holland and Zeeland.

This 'unfortunate lady' was daughter and heiress to William, count of Holland, had considerable wealth, and had been married twice, firstly to the French Dauphin Jean de Touraine, and then, at his death, to John, Duke of Brabant, a marriage contrived by his cousin, Philip the Good, Duke of Burgundy, to increase his own power. This second husband was 'a feeble debauchee'. She could tolerate neither him nor the way he handled her property. She fled to London, to seek Henry V's help. Gloucester fell in love 'either with her or her possessions, possibly with both – though love of the latter endured the longer'. Gloucester bigamously married her in January 1423 (he obtained a dispensation from the last of the anti-popes of the Great Schism, Benedict XIII at Avignon), and then arranged an expedition to recover her lost possessions. The couple arrived in Calais in October 1424 with an English army and set up headquarters at

Mons. He was successful in Hainault itself, but he over-reached himself when he decided to attack Jacqueline's erstwhile husband in Brabant and actually approached the town walls. This could have sabotaged the Anglo-Burgundian alliance entirely only three months after his brother's victory at Verneuil. Philip the Good issued orders to his nobles – Jean de Luxembourg and the Croy brothers – to be ready go under arms to the Duke of Brabant's assistance. Brabant was his cousin after all and his lands were important for the consolidation of the Burgundian state.

Philip responded to a letter from Gloucester with a challenge to personal combat, a trial by battle, 'a deadly serious affair'[45] for which he went into strict training and spent large sums on equipping himself. However, the pope intervened to prohibit it and Bedford arranged a chivalric court in Paris to declare that honour had been satisfied without the duel taking place. Gloucester abandoned Jacqueline to the Duke of Burgundy and, accompanied by her lady-in-waiting, Eleanor Cobham, whom he made his next duchess (she was later imprisoned on suspicion of having used witchcraft to the detriment of Queen Margaret), he returned to England.[46] With this loose cannon bumping about on deck, it was no wonder that Lydgate expressed misgivings about the possibility of co-operation between the English royal dukes to make the dual monarchy effective for any length of time.

The cause of Bedford's decision to send de L'Isle Adam and his Burgundian troops away from his army was that it was becoming known that Philip was making approaches to the court at Bourges on the basis of Gloucester's insult to the Duke of Brabant. But now, in defeat, Charles VII was given concessions by Duke Philip, and they signed a treaty to avoid war between them in the county and duchy of Burgundy, the Bourbonnais, the Maconnais and Forez, and then regularly renewed truces between themselves.

Gloucester's folly had more serious results, inasmuch as Duke Philip made 'tentative concessions' to the dauphin when he signed a treaty of abstinence from war with him in September. The treaty was limited in scope, since it did not include areas where Bedford was interested in further conquest, but it was the first in a series of such agreements and, in signing it, Philip acknowledged the dauphin as King Charles VII of France:[47] another one in the eye for the dual monarchy, to which he had been a signatory.

This dispute between Gloucester and Burgundy also damaged another of Bedford's projects. Before the campaign which led to Verneuil, he had signed a tripartite treaty at Amiens with Burgundy and Brittany, committing the signatories to 'true fraternity' and the preservation of their honour, sealed with marriage alliances. Bedford married Anne of Burgundy, and Jean IV of Brittany's brother, Arthur de Richemont, married her sister Margaret. Richemont had been a prisoner in England after Agincourt for seven years, but had been released upon taking an oath to Henry V, served in France with Suffolk and was made lord of Ivry. After Verneuil, Charles VII offered him the post of Constable of France. Because of the offence he had been given by Gloucester's activities, Burgundy advised Richemont to accept, which he did in a spectacular about turn. Burgundy then married his sister Agnès to Charles of Bourbon, an Armagnac, whose father was still an Agincourt prisoner. The Duke of Brittany himself then revoked the treaty he had made at Amiens with Bedford and, in October 1425 signed the treaty of Saumur with Charles VII expressly to expel the English from France.[48]

Humphrey of Gloucester had by no means finished his tergiversations. Another source of danger for the stability of the English monarchy during the minority, let alone the implementation of the Treaty of Troyes was the acrimonious dispute that broke out between him and the bishop of Winchester, Henry Beaufort. During Gloucester's absence from England, Beaufort was exerting the influence of being the wealthiest diocesan bishop in England to 'mould the personnel and policies of the government in his own interests'.[49] Since the death of his nephew Henry V, Beaufort had gained in influence, helped on by his elder brother, the Duke of Exeter, being appointed the infant king's guardian. His continued ability to make loans to the government for the expenses of warfare during the period of two years 1422–1423 when parliament made financial difficulties allowed Bedford to make his campaigns in Normandy leading to Verneuil. Beaufort proved invaluable to the work of the king's council and the minority government, to the extent that he was re-appointed to the post of chancellor of England in July 1424, where he tried to 'balance the welfare of the king and the realm with the ambitions of the Duke of Gloucester.'[50]

Gloucester sent a message to the newly-elected mayor of London, one John Coventry, a mercer, on 29 October 1425 to gather a force of armed men to protect London Bridge from the menace of men-at-arms and archers gathered in Southwark by Bishop Beaufort from Lancashire and Cheshire and from the garrison at Windsor Castle, along with a mob of lawyers' apprentices. Gloucester was popular in London for his support of the merchants there against the Flemings who were present to facilitate the cloth trade. They, of course, owed allegiance to the Duke of Burgundy, who was also the count of Flanders. Beaufort was not popular among the citizens because he had recently had some of them arrested. The presence of household servants from Windsor with Beaufort was worrying to Gloucester because he feared that it was part of a plot to take the boy-king from nearby Eltham to Windsor, the better to influence and educate him as his great-uncle might wish. The mayor did as Gloucester asked. The bishop's men were kept at a distance, and the Londoners restrained from attacking Southwark.

Gloucester was exasperated by developments that had taken place in London while he was away in Hainault and Brabant. Bishop Beaufort, the chancellor of England, had been alarmed by anonymous threats to the Flemings posted up in the city and suburbs on 13 February 1425 and even nailed to Beaufort's own door, which led him to make Richard Woodville custodian of the Tower of London on 26 February. It was then that he had made the arrests on charges of treason among the Londoners, charges made by someone alleged to have been paid by him, while it was also claimed that he was favouring the interests of the Flemings against theirs. This animosity had led to a demonstration against Beaufort at a wharf not far up-river from his lodgings at Southwark including threats to throw the bishop/chancellor himself in the river. Reports were brought to Bedford in Normandy and he in turn was anxious, especially as he was trying to repair relations with Philip of Burgundy, still smarting under Gloucester's attack on his cousin Brabant as well as the offence offered to his Flemish traders.

Richard Woodville seemed the ideal candidate for the task of restoring stability: he had served in Normandy under Henry V, been captain of Caen and elsewhere, and treasurer-general for Bedford in the province. When Gloucester returned from Brabant, intending to take lodgings in the Tower by virtue of his office as protector and defender of the realm, Woodville would not let him in, a decision which Beaufort supported.

'These annoyances ... brought to flash-point the fierce animosity that existed between Beaufort and Gloucester.'[51] The Londoners saw him as a fellow-citizen, with his residence in the city at Baynard's Castle, and they manned the embankment in his cause in case Beaufort's men should attack him. When Gloucester tried to make Woodville set free a prisoner he was interested in (Friar Randolph, imprisoned since 1419 for implication in necromancy and witchcraft), he, Woodville, consulted Beaufort, and Beaufort, considering Gloucester to be setting himself up against the regency council, supported Woodville's refusal to let Gloucester reside in the Tower without a warrant from that same council.

Despite having been out of England for the last six months, Gloucester considered that Beaufort was attempting to keep him away from Henry VI, also without any authorisation from the council. Gloucester had never been allowed to be the king's guardian, which rankled with him, but nor had Beaufort – as we saw earlier, the regency council was a collectivity to prevent the king being influenced by his uncles or great-uncle – who was being accused of lodging in Southwark to be closer to Eltham as a stage in a move toward securing his protection by having the king under his control. Gloucester returned to England in April 1425, and the violence in London in October occurred when these tensions burst out into the open.

Archbishop Chichele of Canterbury did all he could to contain the 'extremes of resentment' between the disputants, along with the Earl of Stafford and the Portuguese Duke of Coimbra who was Gloucester's cousin, then a guest in the bishop of London's palace. It was Beaufort who took an initiative drastic enough to lead to the suppression of the dispute: he wrote urgently to Bedford, who was the only one with sufficient authority to impose a solution. He concluded the letter with, 'For your wisdom knows well that the prosperity of France stands in the welfare of England.'[52] At least he had his eye on the dual monarchy, which Gloucester seemed to be ignoring in his egocentric behaviour. Bedford left Normandy in the care of Salisbury and Suffolk and was in England, accompanied by Anne of Burgundy, in January 1426 when he issued writs for a parliament to be held at a distance from turbulent London in Leicester which opened on 18 February.

Delays in opening the business of the parliament were the result of the refusal of Gloucester to attend a meeting of the king and the great council at St. Albans, as they were on their way to Leicester, and again at Northampton. He was sent a 'peremptory royal letter'[53] on 18 February to make sure that he was present at Leicester for the parliament itself. Gloucester would have been protector and royal lieutenant in parliament had Bedford not been summoned by Beaufort, and his proper pride (the name that used to be given to self-respect) made it difficult for him to submit himself to judgement by parliament. The commons sent a delegation to Bedford to emphasise the dangers inherent in such a dispute between magnates and the urgency of resolving it by bargaining for a compromise. Bedford reacted positively, and on 7 March Gloucester and Bedford agreed to submit their dispute to a panel of arbitrators and adhere to its decision. This panel was headed by Archbishop Chichele, and included four bishops (one of whom, Stafford of Bath and Wells, was the treasurer), and four lords (one of whom was the keeper of the privy seal): virtually all of the regency council without the two protagonists in the dispute.

The Duke of Gloucester and the bishop of Winchester were required to forgive and forget their actions against each other made before 7 March 1426. Gloucester must be a good lord to the bishop, and the bishop would undertake to serve him as he should. They would forgive each others' followers for their past actions also. Beaufort had to swear an oath of loyalty in the presence of the king and Bedford and the lords and commons, and this was embodied in an act of parliament. Gloucester was required to do no more than accept Beaufort's declaration of good will towards him. Bedford accepted that his uncle Beaufort had exceeded his responsibilities and accepted that, once he had returned to Normandy, Gloucester would once again be protector of England and his dignity as such must be preserved.

So, a few days later, Beaufort resigned the chancellorship, which was transferred to Archbishop Kemp of York. Bedford made new appointments to offices of state avoiding members of Beaufort's retinue and, on 14 May, Beaufort himself was given leave to go on pilgrimage, 'probably to Rome'.[54] This tempestuous assembly was known as the 'Parliament of Bats' because the members were ordered to leave weapons of any kind at their lodgings and they secretly carried bats with them. When this in turn was noticed and forbidden, they carried large stones in their capacious sleeves so as not to go unarmed.

Bedford had to act against other rivalries during his stay in England. One of them concerned Lord Talbot (the future commander of the force that would re-take Bordeaux from France in 1452 and lose it again at Castillon in 1453) and the Earl of Ormond. He also took steps to raise known Lancastrian supporters to higher status: Norfolk and Cambridge were elevated from earls to dukes, and sufficient rewards were given to men who had distinguished themselves in France in the form of knighthoods. It was also decided to elevate the five-year-old king's own position in knighting him as well, and having him dub as knights the heirs of magnates – and other magnates themselves – as well as military commanders who had served Bedford. Sir Richard Woodville was one of these.[55]

Once Bedford was back in France, new ordinances assured that the whole regency council would be engaged in decisions, so as not to allow magnates to enter into disputes damaging to the kingdom's interests. Gloucester truculently commented that when his brother had gone, he would govern as seemed good to him, but he soon backed down.[56] As for Beaufort, he was allowed to receive the cardinal's hat which Henry V had refused him, fearing that he would favour the pope's interests above those of England at the time of the Agincourt campaign. Bedford himself invested him with it in St. Mary's church in Calais on 25 March 1427, a week after his return to France.[57]

During Bedford's absence, most of the action had been directed against the Duke of Brittany after his Treaty of Saumur with Charles VII, in response to which the English had made a formal declaration of war in January 1426. Sir Thomas Rampston (fifteen years later prominent in the Bordelais) as Suffolk's lieutenant, had attacked as far as Rennes, which subdued the duke. The duke made a truce which turned into an alliance signed on 8 September 1427. He became Henry VI's liege man in life and limb.

But this coin had its reverse side. The future count of Dunois, then known as the Bastard of Orleans, and La Hire had defeated Suffolk and Warwick at Montargis, where they had been besieging the Armagnacs.

The earls had to abandon their artillery and baggage. John Talbot was made governor of Anjou and Maine, and he would make good the losses and impress his adversaries.

Talbot was now one of the richest men in England, having married the Earl of Warwick's elder daughter. He was a Knight of the Garter, and was an expert in speed and surprise, skills learned in Wales and Ireland. He had come to France after Agincourt, and returned with Bedford in March 1427 for what was supposed to be a six-month contract. He began his campaign in early 1428 by a punitive raid at Laval. Le Mans had been lost to La Hire, but Talbot began a siege of the castle in which the English garrison had remained when the town surrendered. Talbot's rapid advance from Alençon led to a violent exchange with La Hire's troops in which the English garrison joined. The prisoners taken were so many that a special court of chivalry had to be set up under Lord Scales to decide about ransoms, which led to judgements in the Paris *Parlement*, and one of the cases concerned Talbot himself. After that, Talbot, because of his punishments meted out to those who had earlier betrayed the town to La Hire, became known to both sides in the conflict as 'the English Achilles'. Bedford valued this 'soldier's soldier', endowed him with lands, and often called him to his council in Paris.[58]

Chapter Three

Three Coronations and a Marriage Alliance

Humphrey Duke of Gloucester looked to his associate, Thomas Montagu, Earl of Salisbury who had come from Normandy to recruit a new army for action, perhaps in a different part of France, to provide him with another continental project. Parliament voted a direct tax on churches and knights' fees for Salisbury's expedition. Bedford decided to deploy this force to take Angers in a siege expected to last four months in accordance with his policy of gaining Normandy piece by piece. Gloucester and Salisbury on the other hand decided upon direct action nearer to the dauphin's stronghold at Bourges south of the Loire and Salisbury set out for Orleans. Bedford's own comment was that the decision to attack Orleans instead of Angers was taken 'God knows by what advice'. But it was taken, despite the chivalric principle of not attacking the domains of prisoners whose revenues ought to be used to provide their ransoms: Charles, Duke of Orleans had been captive in England since Agincourt, and would not be released for another eleven years.[1]

In a study about events in Aquitaine, we will pass quickly over the siege of Orleans, the taking of certain strongpoints by its defenders, the killing of Salisbury by a cannonball, the 'battle of the Herrings' at nearby Rouvray where Sir John Falstolf defended a supply train so successfully that a major French and Scottish army sent to intercept it was utterly defeated, and the eventual raising of the siege already decided upon before Joan of Arc burst on to the scene.

* * *

Charles VII took Chinon on the north bank of the Loire in spring 1428 as a counter-measure to the English advance into Maine and the threat posed to Anjou. It was from there that he heard of Salisbury's advance against Orleans. He sent the Bastard of Orleans and La Hire, with Poton de Xaintrailles and the Count of Clermont, to undertake the defence of Orleans as Salisbury, and then Suffolk, occupied positions on the south side of the Loire. He stayed back at Chinon sixty miles to the south-west. Then there were newcomers at Chinon, a girl called Joan from Bar-Lorraine in the east of France and her little bodyguard.[2]

Charles VII's mother-in-law, Yolande of Aragon, was responsible for having her introduced to the court. Yolande's second son was René of Anjou who had been adopted by his uncle, a cardinal who was also Duke of Bar-Lorraine, where Domrémy, Joan's birthplace, was situated, and René had been adopted as his heir. Yolande's late husband, Louis of Anjou, and these Angevins were the most influential people in young Charles' life since his parents had disowned him.[3] It was Yolande who had established Charles at Bourges in the Duke of Berry's territory, and then left for her other important domain of Provence where her elder son Louis was duke, to return in 1423 when her daughter gave birth to the future Louis XI:[4] '... there could be no doubt that any communication between the duchy of Bar and the royal court in the Loire, especially concerning a matter as weighty as a message from heaven, would come to the attention of René's mother Yolande.'[5] It was certainly she who certified that Joan was a virgin when other courtiers were anxious about the veracity of her claims. Joan's claim to be God's messenger was thoroughly examined by members of the university of Paris who had sided with the Armagnac/Orleanist cause and were now to be found at Poitiers.

Joan was given military training, a horse, a suit of armour, a banner, and a sword found where she said it would be. She dictated her challenge to the English: 'King of England, and you, Duke of Bedford, who call yourself regent of the kingdom of France, you, William de la Pole, count of Suffolk, John, lord of Talbot, and you, Thomas, lord of Scales ... you will never hold the kingdom of France from God ... but King Charles, the true heir, will hold it.' She was allowed to go in the company of John II, Duke of Alençon (who had given her the horse) to Orleans. The best proof of whether her claims were authentic or not was to let her relieve Orleans and take the dauphin to his coronation at Reims: if it worked it would be justified.

It did work. Joan and Alençon came to one of the bastilles that the English had constructed on the east side of Orleans, took it, and then took the stronghold called the Tourelles which gave access to the city, where the bastard of Orleans welcomed her amid general rejoicing. Then there were the mopping up operations at Jargeau, up river from Orleans where Suffolk's force was defeated and he was taken prisoner. From there, they turned westwards and took Meung and Beaugency downstream. With Falstolf's approach from the north, there was the engagement at Patay, where Talbot and Scales were taken prisoner but Falstolf got away. The kingdom of Bourges was extended to the northern bank of the Loire. The first part of Joan's mission was accomplished.

Charles himself and Joan led the army into Anglo–Burgundian territory together for the second part. Her letter sent into Troyes on the shaft of an arrow was eventually enough to overawe the garrison there into surrendering, and so the town where the loathesome treaty had been signed in 1420 was in Charles VII's hands. Once Troyes had opened its gates to their lawful king, the population of Reims opened theirs, and the chancellor of France, Regnault de Chartres, also archbishop of Reims, entered his cathedral from which he had been excluded by the Anglo–Burgundians. Charles VII was anointed with the holy oil of Clovis, then crowned and acclaimed with Joan beside him. She knelt before him and called him 'noble king.'

[Joan] had been an exceptional leader in an exceptional moment – a miraculous anomaly who, by the will of heaven, had transformed the landscape in which she stood. She knew that God was with her, and how much work still lay ahead. But what if those around her believed the moment of miracles had passed?[6]

* * *

Meanwhile the alliance between England and Burgundy had been re-affirmed by the Duke of Bedford. Despite the point of their meeting in Paris being sharpened by a masque re-enacting the murder of his father on the bridge at Montereau in 1419, Philip was increasingly passive in the alliance. All energetic resistance to Joan's dauphin now acknowledged as legitimate king was left to Bedford. Philip sent representaives to Reims for Charles's coronation.

Philip left for Arras where he cautiously received Charles VII's chancellor, Regnault de Chartres, and his general Raoul de Gaucourt to discuss future possibilities, which Bedford knew all about from Duchess Anne. Bedford had Cardinal Beaufort with him who had arrived with a contingent of soldiers intending to make for Bohemia to help King Sigismund put down the Hussite rising, but he left his troops with Bedford instead. Bedford set about putting the Paris defences in order with thirty foot walls and improved moats, doing his best to reassure the regency council in Engand that all was well between England and Burgundy: there was at least no open breach in the alliance for another five years.

Bedford denounced Charles as an imposter and Joan as a sorceress to the people of Paris. Charles VII took Bedford's words as a challenge, and advanced with his army nearly to Senlis, reaching to within sight of Bedford's troops in Paris. Their opposing armies dug in in front of each other. The next day they faced each other in the August heat but avoided any major engagement. Under cover of night, Bedford withdrew behind his strengthened walls into Paris.

Charles was free to wander about around Paris and take over in Compiègne and in Beauvais. He met Regnault of Chartres and Gaucourt near Arras with the result of their mission to Duke Philip who had accepted Charles's admission of his participation in the Montereau murder and his offer to repay the value of jewels that had been stolen at the time. Philip would keep the lands the English had allowed him, and he would not have to do homage to Charles as king of France. Nevertheless, Bedford's mystery play in Paris had had its desired effect upon Philip, and he agreed to no more than a truce in towns north of the Seine. Paris was not to be one of them, and its future was left undecided.

Joan set out from Compiègne intending to take the capital accompanied by Alençon. She took Saint-Denis, with its ancient abbey without opposition. She waited there for two weeks for Charles to arrive and then reconnaissances began of the new fortifications that Bedford had established. When Bedford heard that they were there, he mustered his Norman troops at Vernon to return. Joan decided to attack Paris before he could arrive. The Burgundians in the city were determined to resist her sacrilegious attack on 8 September, the feast of the Nativity of the Virgin.

Joan advanced into the moat towards the evening and shouted up her familiar challenge to the men on the machicolations who replied in a brutal and licentious manner. One of them hit her in the thigh with an crossbow bolt, and another killed her standard bearer.[7] The Armagnacs carried her out of harm's way and retreated. With Bedford likely to arrive soon, Charles VII decided to return south of the Loire to prepare further action, leaving Clermont to hold what possessions he had north of the river.

As for Joan, the theologians behind the walls of the city which she had tried to take now pronounced against her, asserting that her motivations were heretical, and that those who followed her had rejected the Church's authority. Bedford soon arrived in Paris and reproached the people in Saint-Denis for having harboured the Armagnac army. Duke Philip joined him, as did Cardinal Beaufort once more. It was agreed to leave Paris in Burgundian hands and Armagnac ambassadors agreed to a six-months' truce

Those around Charles VII were evidently keeping the impetuous and aggressive Joan away from the king. She found herself stranded at La Tremouïlle's castle at Sully. All she could do was write letters to encourage the governors of Reims against the Burgundians, and to the Hussites in Bohemia to tell them to renounce their heresy or she would march againt them. But then she was permitted to range around in the Paris basin again involving herself in skirmishes, until Duke Philip decided to take Compiègne. Accompanied by Poton de Xaintrailles, she rode north to oppose him, and then, surrounded by Burgundians on a boulevard, she surrendered to their captain, Jean de Luxembourg. After Philip had come from his headquarters to look at the captive, she was taken to her captor's castle at Beaulieu-les-Fontaines, expecting to be ransomed or exchanged as any other knight would have been. Personally speaking, her captor agreed, but Armagnac advice, particularly that of Archbishop Regnault, the Chancellor, was that Charles VII must dissociate himself from her or risk having charges of heresy and sorcery sticking to him.

The Paris university theologians and the inquisitor of the faith in English France requested Duke Philip to give her up to the Church for judgement. When he did not reply, they suggested she should be handed over to the custody of the bishop of Beauvais, since she was at present held in his diocese. The bishop was Pierre Cauchon, a scholar who had justified Duke John the Fearless over the murder of the Duke of Orleans. After the coronation at Reims the Armagnacs had taken over his diocese and ejected him. He had long been in the ruling councils of English France and he was eager to have Joan put on trial. The English ought to pay her ransom to Jean de Luxembourg and then hand her over to the Church as a heretic so that Cauchon himself would be her judge. They did and he was. The *universitaires* wanted her tried in Paris, but the English regency council thought it was risky to send her there, and so she was brought to Rouen in December 1430.[8]

* * *

Because of Joan's assertion, widely accepted among his French supporters in 1429, that Charles was the divinely appointed king of France, the rulers of England hastily arranged what amounted to counter-coronations for Henry VI in England and in France. Bedford and his council in Rouen were the instigators of this decision. Henry VI would be crowned at Westminster and then brought to France during a military expedition, of which he would notionally be the commander, for his other coronation there. Preparations began as early as October 1429.

Henry VI was taken to the Abbey on 5 November by his tutor, Richard Beauchamp, Earl of Warwick, for his coronation. After that, he presided at the banquet in Westminster Hall, seated between Cardinal Beaufort and Catherine of France, his mother. Ten days afterwards, he presided in the Parliament when Humphrey Duke of Gloucester relinquished his title of Protector of the Realm.

The king was not quite eight years old, but he was acknowledged as the sovereign of England. The same acknowledgement had to be made in France, and that meant raising the finance for the military expedition which may well have been required to fight in the present circumstances. Parliamentary business and the recruiting of the army was not over until the end of February 1430, and it took until 23 April for Henry VI, Cardinal Beaufort and this military force to reach Calais.

Duke Philip of Burgundy had agreed to support the project and was promised the county of Champagne in recompense because it still seemed intended that the coronation would happen in Reims. When it was realized that the English army was the only force that could be relied upon, the venue was changed in favour of Paris. Henry VI's party reached Rouen in July 1430, and remained there until November 1431. The Burgundians had captured Joan in May 1430 and handed her over to the English for her trial in Rouen. She was burnt at the stake in May 1431. More troops came from England during that time and they secured the route to Saint-Denis and thence into Paris. Joan's removal seemed necessary before the purpose of this journey could be accomplished.

The coronation at Notre Dame de Paris took place on 16 December 1431. The Frenchmen who were there were not impressed by the ceremony itself nor the food served at the banquet, nor the behaviour of the English in the cathedral. But more importantly:

> ... the fact that Cardinal Beaufort presided (and crowned Henry with a brand new crown purchased especially for the occasion) and the notable absence of the Duke of Burgundy from the ceremony underlined the fact that Lancastrian kingship was contested and that Henry was only one of two individuals claiming to be the rightful king of France.

It is doubtful whether a crown that had been used before, a French archbishop presiding and a Burgundian presence would have made any difference. Henry had little or no contact with the French nobility, and it was seen that he did not speak French, since his tutor spoke for him at the banquet. He left for Rouen after only ten or eleven days in Paris, and he was back in England in February. 'He would never again set foot in his kingdom of France.'[9]

* * *

In August 1433, there was a significant change in the personnel of the king's entourage: William de la Pole, Earl of Suffolk, assumed office as Steward of the royal household. He had served in France from 1422 onwards and been captured during the battle of Jargeau in 1429. He was freed after a few months having paid a large ransom. His new position in the royal household brought him into close contact with the eleven-year-old king, which would eventually facilitate their policy of peace with Charles VII and excite fierce opposition. This close relationship was developed independently of the royal uncles or the council.

Bedford came to England in July 1433 for a parliament which met at Westminster to discuss further action in France. The commons requested Bedford to stay in England from where he could exercise good government in both kingdoms and also 'the welfare of the king's noble person,' as expressed in Henry V's dying wishes. He remained in England until June 1434 by which time Henry was beginning to assert himself over the members of the council, though they resisted his will to rule on his own authority without them.[10]

Duke Philip was increasingly sure that he had little to expect from his alliance with the English. The Flemish cloth traders were turning away from their English suppliers and looking towards the Mediterranean for stocks of Merino wool. The war between England and France was inhibiting transport from Bruges. These considerations pushed Philip towards an approach towards the king of France. This explains why he had not opposed Joan of Arc's gallop through his territory to Reims for the coronation of her dauphin, why he was not present in Paris for Henry's, and why he concluded a truce with the court at Bourges where the peace party in his favour gained the upper hand after the disgrace of Georges de La Tremouille in 1433.[11]

A week after Bedford died at the age of forty-six in Rouen in September 1435, Philip made his separate treaty with the French at Arras. The civil war was over, and reconciliation had taken place between Valois and Burgundy. Dieppe was taken by France in December. The French had more successes in early 1436, and, on 17 April, the English garrison in Paris surrendered to Charles VII's army. The signing of the treaty of Arras provoked an initiative by the English council to raise loans from towns, religious houses and certain individuals for the defence of Calais. Henry VI emerged as an active and participating ruler in these measures. There was even a brief suggestion that he should lead a military expedition to

Calais himself, but it was a force led by Edmund Beaufort, destined for elsewhere in France, that was diverted there in the summer months of 1436 which broke the Burgundian siege on 29 July.

When the council met at Clerkenwell in November 1437 Henry was well on the way to having assumed full kingship in fulfilment of Lancastrian principles of consulting with his council. He was exercising patronage and distributing grants by himself by then. The minority government was at an end. 'The dominant theme in English politics over the next decade or so was the extent to which Henry VI listened to counsel and exercised discretion in making his royal will felt.'[12]

* * *

A particular sphere of government important at the time that Henry VI was beginning his period of adult kingship was his religious and educational foundations in England. Such foundations were endemic in the Lancastrian system of government as in the case of Henry V's Carthusian house founded at Sheen from 1417 onwards and in his confirmations of earlier foundations in Normandy and France made by kings of England.[13] Henry VI was providing the royal initiative in these foundations that was observably not present in other areas of government. He was engaged single-mindedly in the projects for his colleges at Eton and Cambridge and he showed his determination that they should be lodged in buildings that were incomparably magnificent. Part of the financial endowment for Eton was found in the resources of the several French alien priories in England, such as Stogursey in West Somerset, founded by William de Falaise and his wife Geva in 1109 as a dependency of the Norman abbey at Lonlay,[14] confiscated by Henry V before the Agincourt campaign but not used for it on account of certain scruples about using church money for bloodshed.[15] These resources were still in hand for religious purposes in 1440. The buildings at Eton had to be truncated. College Chapel is no more than the quire of the great church that the king conceived and re-designed several times even after building had taken place on the scale of the greatest cathedrals,[16] but that does not detract from the grandeur and conviction of faith that the king injected into it. A similar magnificent concept applied to the chapel of King's College, Cambridge with all its wonders of undercut carving and perpendicular and lateral spaciousness. That the foundations were seen as linked, with schoolboys educated in the one proceeding to being undergraduates in the other, is evidence of a spirituality in the monarch in the early years of his majority that does not entirely coincide with the great K.B. McFarlane's quip that he passed from first to second childhood without the 'usual interval' in between.[17] Others were making similar foundations: Cardinal Kemp at Wye College in Suffolk and at Ewelme, and Lord Cromwell at Tattershall.[18] Archbishop Pey Berland's foundation of the university of Bordeaux in the king/duke's domains must not be overlooked, nor his College of Saint-Raphaël to train indigenous clergy. Transcendent otherworldliness was certainly part of the spirit of the age in the Lancastrian epoch.

After Bedford's death, there was less opposition to Suffolk developing his peace policy for France at the king's naïve instigation, and less positive direction for an aggressive policy. The treaty of Arras had a double significance for Henry VI: Philip the Good had recognized Charles VII as his rightful king and was no longer England's ally against him. 'The return to normalcy under an adult monarch'[19] was accepted in the meeting of the English great council which took place over three days between 12 and 14 November 1437. The declaration in which this was embodied referred back to the relationship established between Henry IV and his councillors of whom Henry Beaufort was one and could remember because he was there when it was set up in 1406. The king had just reached his sixteenth birthday. He was not prevented from making decisions on his own, and the councillors could not make decisions without him in matters concerning the kingdom of England or the duchy of Aquitaine. The king was less limited in his decisions and actions than nineteenth-century historians had maintained.[20] Also writing in 1981, Bertram Wolffe was in agreement with R.A. Griffiths about the normal process of government being resumed: 'The record of his childhood and adolescence ... suggests physical strength, normal but not excessive piety and the natural ambition of a young monarch to become king, in fact as well as name, just as soon, if not sooner, than his advisers approved.'[21]

Henry VI had no intention of leading an army of his own in Normandy and for three years there was great hesitation about who should take command. Richard, Duke of York, with John Talbot's assistance, had consolidated the English presence in upper Normandy and Picardy between May 1436 and the end of his two-year commission. After a good deal of hesitation in council, the king reluctantly re-appointed the duke for a five-year term from July 1440, but he did not arrive in Harfleur until June 1441, after his lengthy negotiations for powers comparable to those held by Bedford. Charles VII was pushed back to the gates of Paris, but there was not enough impetus to finalize the conflict, especially since Gascony was now in such great need of financial and military assistance.

Charles VII had profited from the presence of the Castilian freelance *routier* Rodrigo de Villandrando ravaging up from Agenais, Armagnac and Béarn as far north as Soulac at the northern tip of the Médoc. He had the support of French officers such as Poton de Xaintrailles, the bastard of Bourbon and Charles II of Albret. Then came the 'Day' of Tartas, 24 June 1442, when no English army appeared to challenge Charles VII's occupation of the town on the Adour river, and his subsequent advance to Saint-Sever and Dax.

Gloucester was vigorously drawing attention to Charles VII's undeniable intention to advance into English Gascony at the same time as condemning the release of the Duke of Orleans from his captivity in England in 1440. The policy of obtaining peace in France through negotiation remained Henry VI's over-riding interest, despite the failure of the earlier conference at Gravelines in 1439 where the two cardinals, Beaufort and Kemp had conducted negotiations. The hope that the Duke of Orleans, once released, would be a spokesman for peace came to nothing when Charles VII persistently ignored him.[22]

A delay in the peace process towards France was tolerated when, in the early 1440s, Jean IV of Armagnac was hoping for an alliance with England in order to resist the expansion of the Valois monarchy towards the Pyrenees. He had deliberately not prevented his heir, the Viscount of Lomagne, from enrolling under the banner of Charles VII, hoping to turn away the king's suspicions about himself while he continued in his double game, begun in July 1437 when he and Charles d'Albret had made a truce with Henry VI.[23] This truce, made on the count's own initiative, would last until 1 November 1438, that is, for the first full year of Henry VI's majority. It gave Armagnac and his vassals free access to Guyenne and the subjects of the king/duke could enter his lands. Armagnac was not to give aid during this time to Charles VII.

With the king's majority there arose the question of his future queen and what alliance that would make possible.[24] Jean IV of Armagnac raised the possibility in May 1442 for a marriage alliance between the king of England and one of his three daughters: Bonne, daughter of his first marriage to Blanche of Brittany, or either of Eléonore and Isabelle, daughters of Isabelle of Navarre.[25] A marriage alliance with England seemed to be the best guarantee of safety from the inroads of Charles VII. Armagnac left the English to make the first step and then sent as his ambassador Jean de Batut, archdeacon of Rodez, who was well-received in London with his numerous entourage.[26]

Henry VI entrusted the negotiations for his part to Thomas Beckynton, future bishop of Bath and Wells (who was close to him in the Eton project), Sir Robert Roos and Sir Edward Hull. Beckynton left Windsor on 5 June in company with Batut. The two clerics met up with Roos and Hull on the way to Plymouth and set sail in the *Catherine*, a Bayonne ship, reaching Bordeaux on 16 July. Batut left to report to his master at Lectoure.

The Englishmen found the military situation around Bordeaux very worrying. The seneschal, Sir Thomas Rampston, had been taken prisoner at the head of troops sent into combat against French forces. Batut found no better encouragement on his arrival at Lectoure. Jean IV realized that, if Charles VII did not know already about his plans, his son Lomagne would soon inform him of them. In the circumstances of French military gains and Anglo-Gascon losses, Jean IV naïvely believed that 'in offering his daughter to one of the kings and his son to the other, he could be friend to both and wait the outcome of hostilities without disquiet.'[27] He wrote to Roos, apologizing for the delay, and explained that a safe-conduct from the king of France to go into Armagnac territory to meet the princesses would obviously be difficult to obtain. He added that he would have liked to have found a portraitist to send the girls' likenesses to Henry VI, but suggested it would be easier for the ambassadors to find one. A month later, Batut regretted that it would no longer be possible for them to make the journey since French troops were occupying the Landes. Roos's reply was full of tight-lipped irony, amounting to a threat to call the whole thing off.

In the middle of September, Batut wrote a letter from Auch which was so full of intricate arguments that a reply in book form would have been needed. Beckynton was as well-trained in scholastic subtleties as the good archdeacon but, in the end, to reply was not worth the candle. Nevertheless the ambassadors did put pressure on Batut to hurry up with the portrait since Edward Hull, who had briefly returned to England, had brought a painter called Hans (too early for Holbein) back with him. Hans had been sent off to Lectoure with secret orders hidden in his measuring stick. Batut claimed that Hans was four days away from completing one likeness out of the three, but his pigments had frozen in the cold weather. The ambassadors saw through all this to the bad faith of Count Jean, so on 10 January 1443, Beckynton was on board ship in the Gironde, leaving his colleagues behind. Roos caught up with him bringing final letters from the count and Batut. Beckynton did not meet the king at Maidenhead until 21 February. The conclusion of all this was that the count and his astute councillor had wasted a whole year on a rather hopeless project. Henry VI never forgave Jean IV for the affront he had shown him, and Charles VII never forgave Henry VI for his approach to one of his enemies.[28]

*   *   *

Henry VI had emerged as the long awaited adult monarch but those around him experienced disappointment. Now that we have reached the 1440s, we have to ask once more the question of how effective the government of the king was when he was in his twenties. For this, Christine Carpenter developed ideas put forward by John Watts in meticulous detail in articles and a magisterial book.[29] Henry VI was Charles VI of France's grandson, and the possibility that he had inherited his mental incapacity was worrying: 'all the evidence points to the idea that, some time between 1437 and 1443 or 1444, it was realized that the king would never become an adult except in name, and that the nobles, directed by Suffolk, decided to shoulder the burden of rule, just as they had done under Bedford in the minority.'[30]

The king listened to his advisers, and a pretence was maintained that the decisions made were the king's own, expressed by those close to him.

Historians talk of over-mighty subjects from among the nobility, but this was more a case of a less-than-mighty king. Henry VI's indecisiveness was undeniable as was particularly observable in the administration of justice where 'royal powers ... in the localities could be manipulated with impunity by those who enjoyed Henry's access and favour'.[31] A tranche of Gascon trouble during this decade illustrates this assertion with considerable clarity. It resulted directly from the failed embassy for the alliance with the count of Armagnac, when a personality of considerable force and genuine rectitude presented himself in the king's presence and brought about a positive outcome in a set of really difficult circumstances.

Archbishop Pey (Pierre) Berland of Bordeaux had welcomed Beckynton and the other ambassadors into the town, and it was during their visit, menaced by French activity in the hinterland, that the mettle of this most able supporter of the English presence in Gascony was understood and acted upon.

Berland was a native Gascon, born to a family of free graziers at Saint-Raphaël in the Médoc, three miles from Castelnau. He had been noticed for his potential as a boy, brought to Bordeaux for his schooling and sent to the university of Toulouse from which he emerged as a theologian and a doctor of canon law. The then archbishop of Bordeaux made him his secretary, and he travelled with him for the international conferences that ended the Great Schism. He was presented to a canon's stall in the cathedral of Saint-André, and became archbishop himself in 1430, admired for his educational and philanthropic projects, and his resistance to Charles VII's ecclesiastical policy in France manifested in the Pragmatic Sanction of Bourges, whereby the king intended to control the appointments of all bishops in his kingdom regardless of the pope's authority.[32] Being acquainted with Eugenius IV from his earlier career, Pey Berland gained his support for the foundation of the University of Bordeaux.

Berland resisted Charles VII's encroachments in south-west France where he was the metropolitan and inheritor of the role instigated in the late Roman empire whereby the archbishop was the defender of the city and its people against all and any of its oppressors. Pey Berland became a Gascon *homme politique*. He accepted the position he was offered by his fellow Gascons as their director of policy and was regarded in England as the third power alongside the seneschal who administered the duchy and the mayor and *jurats* together who governed the town of Bordeaux.[33] The seneschal of Gascony, the constable of Bordeaux, and the other king's officers in the duchy were ordered to protect the archbishop, 'one of the king's councillors in the duchy of Aquitaine ... because of the archbishop's good service and the negotiations he often carries out for the king'.[34] When Jean IV of Armagnac wanted to make his truce with England, Pey Berland and the constable, Walter Colles, were named for the drawing up of the conditions.[35] That was from above. From below, when Rodrigo de Villandrando was making his ravages in the countryside in 1438, the country people came into Bordeaux and Pey Berland, who was from the same stock as they were, gave them bread, wine and subsistence, and bought extra supplies of grain at scarcity prices to distribute to them.[36]

Now in 1442, Pey Berland accepted a particular function. French forces had entered the Saintonge, the Agenais, and the Perigord. Royan on the Gironde estuary and Clairac on the Lot had been taken, and strongpoints on the tributaries of the Dordogne were under threat.[37] Roos and Beckynton reported that when they arrived on 16 July 1442 they found 'as sorrowful a town and as greatly dismayed and discouraged as any might be in the earth, as people desolate and cast out of all comfort of any succour to be had from your majesty against your enemies that had been in this country in great puissance'. Charles VII had 'won and subdued all the country of the Landes except Dax and Bayonne,' although the siege of Dax was going on at the time the letter was being written with bastilles being constructed around it.

That no hope could be expected from England was announced in letters that had been brought in 'by one that calls himself Francis, whose name is in fact John Gore and delivered to divers estates here the Sunday before our arrival when he had come by boat to Castillon and thence rode overland into Bordeaux'. The city was full of rumour and sorrow on account of being 'abandoned and cast away for ever'.

The envoys appealed to the king to send help quickly since 'Your duchy of Guyenne is one of the oldest lordships belonging to your crown of England.' They then tell the worst news: 'In taking of Saint-Sever, Sir Thomas Rampston, your seneschal, is taken prisoner and, as it is said, the seal which he had ... under my Lord of Huntingdon is taken also.' So the reason for the false letters brought in by John Gore being accepted as real by the Bordelais was explained.[38]

Roos and Beckynton had produced the king's authentic letters that had reached them at Plymouth before they left, and Pey Berland had translated them into the Gascon dialect to read out from the cathedral pulpit. These spoke of 'the good and tender zeal' which the king had 'to the conservation and welfare of this your city and of all your true subjects in these parts, and putting them out of doubt of succours to be had in right brief time'. The letters encouraged the people to do all they could in the meantime for the city's defence and safeguard, which had been done and was being done daily 'in the strongest wise'. Bulwarks, guns, engines and all other necessary habiliments had been put in place. The king/duke's letters had not said when English help would arrive, nor how powerful it would be. The clergy, nobles and bourgeoisie of Bordeaux decided that Pey Berland should go to England to represent the true state of the country and to plead for efficacious support.[39]

The day before he left, a body made up of all who had most influence went on a tour of inspection of the state of readiness of the town's defences. The archbishop went on board ship in the afternoon of 25 July, seen off on the quay by the mayor, the *jurats*, the notables, Roos and Beckynton. A doctor of canon law and a herald called Robert travelled in the same ship. The herald was carrying letters from the ambassadors to Henry VI and to members of his council.

The archbishop arrived in London at a time that was least favourable to his enterprise. He met the Duke of Gloucester and Cardinal Beaufort, preoccupied with their own dispute. Gloucester was likely to favour sending armed help but he had little influence at the time, and Beaufort, who then dominated the council, was still preoccupied with peace proposals. But there was a third person, Ralph, Lord Cromwell, Lord Treasurer, and it was to him that the herald Robert had brought a secret letter from Roos and Beckynton under a separate cover from the other letters. They criticized the town's government, but had important things to say about Pey Berland. They saw the qualities of a diplomat in him but said he was too reticent to volunteer much information. He needed to be 'well groped and throughly examined' so as to reveal the true state of affairs in the duchy because he was uniquely placed to show things in great depth out of his own experience.[40]

Pey Berland, after frustrating delays, approached Henry VI himself. So the strong-minded prelate, such as this conventionally pious king would warm to, was listened to when he stated the Gascon cause. This resulted in two letters and ordinances from the king, one dated 21 September, and the other 7 March. The first was written during Berland's stay at court so that he knew what it said. He had shown the king that Charles VII was carrying out his invasion with an unusual number of forces and that the loss of the whole duchy was a real possibility.[41]

The king of France entered the Adour Valley with Gaston IV at his elbow. Jean Bureau's guns had made short work of the walls of Dax, making an approach to Bayonne possible. Other armies intervened from Agen westwards, and from the Saintonge southwards, taking Royan which was well inside the Gironde Estuary. Pirates on the Gironde were siezing Gascon ships and preventing all commercial activity. On the night of 1–2 August, a hundred and thirty French soldiers from Royan came into the port of Bordeaux with six *gabares* (flat-bottomed river boats) and captured two ships laden with wine and wheat. They would have taken them to Royan had they not been caught off Blaye by several boats crewed by local people who knew the currents, gave chase and recovered the ships.[42] Using such information, Pey Berland succeeded in persuading Henry VI to take a greater interest in the region and winning the attention of the council. It was decided that the Earl of Somerset would be sent there with an army of 10,000 men.

The king wrote to inform the people of Bordeaux himself of this, in French, dated 21 September 1442:

Dearly and well beloved, we have learned and it has been certified, as much by letters as by messages and especially by the very reverend father in God, our beloved and faithful counsellor the archbishop of Bordeaux, of the great hardships, evils and oppression, losses and injuries, that you have had to suffer during a certain time, and from which you are still suffering by cause of the continual war which our adversary Charles of Valois makes ... We have also been informed of the true obedience, love, union and concord in which, to maintain your loyalty towards us, you always maintain yourselves with our officers sent there, awaiting very patiently the support and aid which you have so humbly sought and requested. And, dearly and well beloved, because, in great bitterness of heart, pain and compassion, we sustain your grief, evils and oppressions, and nothing will make us desist from the cause which has belonged to us for such a long time, and which our predecessors have so dearly loved and carefully guarded, to lose it, as we know will happen if there is not very soon a great remedy and support, and so on and so on ...[43]

Pey Berland seems to have had doubts about the power of this letter to reassure his people, and realized that he could influence the king as much as anyone, so he asked for the dispatch of the letter to be delayed until it was possible to send a first reinforcement to Gascony along with it. And so it arrived in Bordeaux a month after it was written, together with ships from England disembarking a small contingent of troops commanded by Sir Edward Hull, who had been in Gascony earlier and whose return had been eagerly awaited. Pey Berland, a man wiser than had been presented in Thomas Beckynton's letter, stayed in England so as to be reassured that the great army which Henry VI had promised was actually being sent.

After the fall of Dax, the French took the castle at Orthez, then, instead of attacking Bayonne, they had turned north and by the end of September had progressed as far as Langon.[44] They took a number of small forts on the right bank of the Garonne into the Perigord area, into Sarlat and on the right bank of the Dordogne. On 3 October, Charles VII was at La Réole, where the town capitulated, but the great fortress of Quatre-Sos held out against him. Another French force went into Entre-Deux-Mers, taking Saint-Loubes on the road that led to Libourne.

Fear had returned in Bordeaux with the French now so close. Pey Berland was still in England, and no other home-grown leader emerged; so the Englishman Robert Roos was chosen as commander, and he found himself as the superior of the mayor who was not gifted with any great initiative despite a high opinion of himself. A sense of defeatism was growing, even expressed in public by the dean of the cathedral as Somerset's force was awaited. However, when Hull arrived with Henry VI's letter of encouragement, spirits rose when it was announced that Hull's force was the advance guard for an army 'as the memory of men had not seen in Gascony' which was soon to arrive.[45]

Then the tide turned. Early in October, the Anglo-Gascons of Bayonne re-took Dax, which had been left defended by a force of only thirty men-at-arms. On 26 October, troops gathered by Robert Roos found the courage to re-take Saint-Loube and emptied it of gangs of freebooters who had been ravaging it. The captal de Buch, Pierre de Montferrant and other Gascon nobles were part of this force. Archers had recently arrived from England to support this mission, and Roos returned triumphant to Bordeaux. November saw other successes: three boats from Agen loaded with supplies of bread for the French troops besieging the Quatre-Sos fortress at La Réole were siezed by soldiers from Saint-Macaire; three hundred men-at-arms and as many archers, led by Roos and Hull, took Langon back from the French; those besieged at Quatre-Sos were reinforced when newly-arrived armed men managed to get inside; troops also set off to take back Sainte-Foy.[46]

The French put more effort into the siege of the Quatre-Sos fort at La Réole under the personal direction of Charles VII with intense artillery bombardments against the fortress's immense walls. One Sunday, while Mass was being said, one of the largest guns exploded after being continuously fired, but it was replaced by two mortars which lobbed in 500- and 700-pound gunstones, so that the fortress surrendered. At the same time as that happened, Pey Berland disembarked at Bordeaux with more contingents of Somerset's army led by Sir William Bonville, a disputacious landowner from Crewkerne in Somerset.

The house where Charles VII was lodging at La Réole caught fire on 4 December, and he escaped in his shirt with the help of his Scottish bodyguard. His sword – presumed to have belonged to St. Louis in the thirteenth century – was destroyed in the intense heat. Besides, the winter came early and was harsh: no provisions for the army could come from Toulouse along the frozen Garonne. A substantial number of horses perished from cold and lack of fodder. Charles VII left the continuing siege to Olivier de Coëtivy and was in Montauban for Christmas. Nevertheless, he had led his army in person and been exposed to danger. His re-established monarchy had been recognized by magnates in the south-west whose support mattered if France were to be united.[47] However, at least for the present, several towns and castles returned to their English allegiance, and Pey Berland did the rounds to present them with Henry VI's pardons.

* * *

In December 1443, Henry VI revived peace overtures to his 'uncle and adversary the king of France.' Approaches were made through François Duke of Brittany to request Charles VII to appoint ambassadors for the purpose. He responded positively by appointing ambassadors who were given safe-conducts to cross territory under English control for negotiations under the auspices of the Duke of Orleans to conclude a peace or at least an extended truce. On 11 February, Henry VI appointed his own representatives, led by Suffolk. At the same time they were to raise the question of marriage between Henry VI and Marguerite of Anjou, then aged sixteen. Charles VII's niece by marriage thus became the centre of Suffolk's diplomatic activity.

Charles VII instructed Juvenal des Ursins, then bishop of Laon, to come to Paris to draw up a dossier of relations between the French and English crowns since Edward III's time, particularly concerning the treaty of Troyes of 1420 which he wanted to nullify.[48] Charles VII decided upon Tours as a meeting place. It was there that the English ambassadors were received in a friendly manner on 17 April 1444 and took part in lavish festivities.[49] Then Marguerite arrived from Angers with her mother and stayed in Beaumont Abbey where the English diplomats went to meet her. Feasting and sport continued with a contest between some of the English archers and their Scottish counterparts for a prize of 1,000 ecus. The Scots won.

The treaty of Tours, signed on 28 May, provided for a general truce in all English and French possessions from 1 June 1445 until 1 April 1446. Suffolk was given a hero's welcome when he arrrived back in England with the betrothal agreed upon, even though it was accompanied only by a twenty-three month truce and René of Anjou could not afford a queenly dowry for his daughter: he was not merely impecunious: he was flat broke. His recent defeats in Lorraine and Italy and his ceaseless obligation to pay his ransom to the Duke of Burgundy for his release twelve years before meant that the titular king of Sicily and Jerusalem had no resources for anything beyond keeping his head above water.[50]

Loans were sought by Henry VI's council to pay for Marguerite to come to be crowned in Westminster Abbey in suitable state. There were hopes that future negotiations for peace would follow.[51] It was doubtful, on the other hand, whether desire for peace would prevail against the

the vested interests of the military gentry in England and Normandy for whom warfare had become 'the prime expression of service to the Crown and the means to favour and reward.'[52] Their rewards took the form of captured estates in Normandy and Maine, where they had settled their families and wanted to stay. Nevertheless, the delighted Henry VI rewarded the Earl of Suffolk with promotion to the rank of marquess and with the profitable wardship of Somerset's orphan daughter, Margaret Beaufort.[53]

Suffolk returned to France to bring the new queen to England and continue negotiations for extending a peace settlement. When he left in October he was accompanied by John Talbot, Earl of Shrewsbury and his countess-to-be with Marguerite (who became known as Margaret) on the way home to England, as well as many other English noblemen and women. Money for the costs of an embassy lasting three months was available but the costs were severely under-estimated since it took much longer.

They had to go all the way to Nancy where Charles VII and René of Anjou were continuing Duke René's struggle against Duke Philip who was backing Metz, the capital of René's duchy of Lorraine, in its bid to be associated with the Empire, and then wait there for two months while Marguerite was fetched from Anjou. Rumours that the French were trying to gain further concessions from the English were spread by gossip-mongers, especially after it was leaked that the county of Maine was to be ceded to Duke René although Suffolk tried to deny it.

The diplomatic wedding, with Suffolk as proxy bridegroom, took place at Nancy. Marguerite came to Rouen, but the countess of Shrewsbury took her place in the procession there because she was indisposed. She crossed from Harfleur to Portsmouth, with sea-sickness added to her other illness. Henry VI disguised himself as an esquire delivering his own letter to her so as to see her for the first time. Margaret did not look at him.

They were married in person at Titchfield Abbey not far from Portsmouth by the king's confessor, William Ayscough, bishop of Salisbury, on 22 April in a low-key solemnization out of respect for Margaret still not being in good health.[54] Then they proceeded to London for the extravagant reception, spectacles and tableaux in the streets which hailed her as the bringer of peace in a corporate fit of wishful thinking on the way to her coronation on 30 May.[55]

There were hopeful signs for the great peace project: Charles VII sent a glittering company of French diplomats across the English Channel 'in order to treat for peace' in July 1445 led by Louis de Bourbon, Count of Vendome and Juvenal des Ursins, now Archbishop of Reims. They were accompanied by ambassadors from Henry IV of Spain, René, Duke of Anjou, and the Duke of Brittany. The Duke of Burgundy was meant to be represented, but pleaded lack of a safe-conduct for not sending an ambassador.

They stayed with Louis de Bourbon in his London lodgings and were brought to Westminster the next day by the Dukes of Buckingham and Suffolk, to be received in state by Henry VI and prominent English councillors. Juvenal des Ursins presented his letters of accreditation and spoke to the king in terms of the good will of Charles VII. They got down to work on 19 July. The English opened with a concession that had aleady been offered at Tours: Henry should retain Normandy and an enlarged Gascony while implicitly abandoning his claim to the crown of France and, along with it, the dual monarchy invented by his father and imposed upon Charles VI at Troyes in 1420. In reply, the French conceded greater Gascony (notwithstanding, as we have seen, the French advances that had already taken place in the valley of the Adour in 1442) but they were intransigent about Normandy which they regarded as occupied territory.

A proposal was made by one of the Frenchmen that all this should be resolved in a personal meeting between the two monarchs. Henry VI agreed to this in principle, but reminded his advisers that the truce agreed at Tours was about to expire. The upshot of all this extravagant diplomacy was no more than the extension of the truce until 1 April 1447. The idea of a personal meeting of the kings was frequently discussed in the following months, but came to nothing eventually, despite the intentions often expressed by both uncle and nephew.[56] The nephew continued in his naïve optimism and the uncle in his cynical singlemindedness. The English peace party did not want to accept the stark fact that Charles VII had favoured Henry VI's marriage to René d'Anjou's daughter solely to prevent him allying with some other French magnate against him.

The personal meeting foundered on the question of the cession of the county of Maine to René of Anjou. René had not raised this issue when the ambassadors were in London but, in November 1445, envoys from Charles VII did. Charles VII had also enlisted his niece Margaret's help; as her letter in reply to his envoys' proposition of 17 December says, she will 'stretch forth the hand' to persuade Henry, and adds that he had already sent his own reply 'at considerable length.'[57] Here she was playing the rôle assigned to medieval queen consorts of an intercessor outlined by Christine de Pisan.[58] Henry agreed to the request on his own responsibility, however unpopular it might be among the occupiers of Le Mans and its castle, together with a truce of twenty years. But Le Mans castle was still in English hands when the accepted date for withdrawal – 30 April 1446 – had passed.[59]

Duke Humphrey remained the principal opponent of this peace policy, and the king's ministers decided to challenge him in the next parliament which was to be held in January 1447 in Cambridge. The venue was changed to Bury St Edmunds in Suffolk's heartland where he could exercise control. The duke was encouraged to go directly to his lodgings and some among the magnates went to put him under house arrest. He had already been unofficially accused of treason because he was opposed to Suffolk's French policy. His supporters were rounded up and imprisoned separately.

All this put him into a depressive state and, on 23 February, he was found dead. He lay in an open coffin in Bury Abbey for a time to show there was no evidence of murder, and then spirited away to St Albans Abbey where he had expressed a wish to be buried.[60] With Gloucester dead, most likely of a severe stroke,[61] opposition to the peace negotiations had been removed. The suspicion grew that the king's servants had had him killed.

Commissioners were appointed to negotiate compensation for dispossessed English residents in Maine. Delaying tactics were adopted by English captains and this made the renewal of war more likely. Henry VI signed a secret engagement with his uncle to hand over Le Mans and all the fortresses in Maine by 30 April 1446 in 'a private letter conceived, written and sent in secret. It was an act of supreme folly which played straight into Charles VII's hands.'[62] By implicitly surrendering his sovereignty over Maine, Henry VI had allowed Charles VII to presume he would eventually surrender it elsewhere in France.

Charles VII's programme was to unite French territory under the house of Valois. All that he was prepared to grant on the day that Maine was handed over to him was to extend the truce once more, this time until 1 April 1450.[63] He had no notion of making peace except as the victor in a decisive conflict. He was never going to bargain anything away, even under cover of a marriage alliance within the family of his staunchest supporters in the house of Anjou.

Chapter Four

The French Monarchy Revived

While he was king of Bourges, Charles VII's horizons were very limited. However, the potential for his project of a France united under a new model of kingship was greatly enhanced when the Duke of Burgundy, Philip the Good, called a peace conference at Arras in 1435. The Duke of Bedford, as regent in France for the fourteen-year-old Henry VI, Charles VII and Burgundy himself sent ambassadors. Representatives from the council of Basle were present on behalf of the Papacy because the civil war in France between Armagnacs and Burgundians, as well as the war against England, had reached European proportions against a background of Ottoman advances into the Balkans.

The English soon withdrew from the discussions because they saw that to negotiate at all would compromise the dual monarchy set up by the treaty of Troyes in 1420. The English had not wanted Charles VII to have any international recognition after his coronation at Reims in 1430, since it would mean that Henry VI would be King of England only. Philip freed himself from the obligations imposed upon him in 1420 by the oath he had taken to maintain the treaty of Troyes after consultation with a papal legate.[1] He then offered a separate peace to Charles VII who accepted it. This put an end to the civil war in France by a reconciliation between the murdered Jean the Fearless's son and the one who was seen as morally responsible for the assassination. The duke recognized Charles VII as his sovereign, and the king pandered to the duke's self interest by handing great tracts of territory over to him: he yielded the Maconnais, the Auxerrois, the county of Boulogne, the castles at Roye, Peronne, Montdidier, and towns on the Somme, Saint-Quentin, Corbie, Amiens, Abbeville, Arleux, and Mortagne. Philip was excused from paying homage for his territories.[2] After the Duke of Bedford died, Paris opened its gates to let Charles VII enter his capital in 1436 although the complete conquest of the île de France was not achieved until 1441.[3]

Even before he opened his campaign to recover Normandy, Charles VII started to prepare for his assault on Gascony.[4] His supporters began to ferment unrest in the south-west, but they reckoned without the resistance of several influential Anglophiles in the region. Among the nobles, there were Gaston de Foix, who held the title of captal de Buch[5] (whose nephew, Gaston IV, count of Foix-Béarn, would be fighting on the French side), Pierre de Montferrand, Gaillard de Durfort, Jean de Lalande, and Jehan d'Anglade. Some exporters of wines and dyestuffs in the urban centres of Bordeaux and Bayonne and their counterparts in smaller towns like Libourne, Bazas, Saint-Sever and Dax would put up a lively opposition. Archbishop Pey Berland of Bordeaux, several canons of cathedrals (at Bordeaux, Bazas and Bayonne) and collegiate churches, like Saint-Seurin in the Bordeaux suburbs, resisted the French approaches with their influential pens and from their persuasive pulpits. Rural populations in the Médoc and the Landes would actively resist the advance of the French commanders. In the recent past, especially when the French were nibbling away at their eastern territories, the Gascons were on the whole content with Lancastrian supremacy.

Charles VII began to ratchet up his tactics for attacking the frontiers of Gascony and occupying *bastides* and small towns of the flat landscape whose life was dominated by the rivers Garonne, Dordogne and, further south, the Adour. The rhythm of his attacks became regular: 1438, 1442, 1451, and the repeat performance at Bordeaux in 1453.[6] Charles VII's aim was to incorporate the whole region as far as the Pyrenees into his re-modelled system of monarchy.[7]

The prelude to his success was his assertion of power over an army loyal only to him, with noble commanders and subordinate captains acting in his name only. Such an objective demanded a certain energy which the king was increasingly able to assert. A gauge of his abilities during the middle years of his reign appeared in his response to the English. In February 1438, the king and the dauphin stopped at Saint-Jean d'Angély on their way to La Rochelle where the provincial estates were called upon to raise funds for war against the enemy (it was not enough). The English then took Saint-Maigrin and Saint-Thomas de Conac, mid-way down the Gironde Estuary.[8] Then, in July 1440, a more effective English campaign in the Saintonge was undertaken by John Holland, Earl of Huntingdon,

Admiral of England, who had been appointed as Henry VI's lieutenant-general and granted his powers as such on 27 March 1439.[9] He arrived in Bordeaux on 2 August[10] causing a great deal of alarm. The *commune* of Saint-Jean d'Angély sent several letters: to La Rochelle, to the seneschal of Saintonge, to the Viscount of Thouars, and to the king himself, to ask for help against the English. They sent sergeants to Taillebourg, Saint-Savinien, Chaniers and Saint-Sauvant to ask whether the English would be able to cross the River Charente.[11] Huntingdon was taking back places that the French had taken from the English the year before. He advanced at least as far as Saujon and burned the abbey at Sablonceaux.

The teenaged Dauphin Louis was appointed as his father's lieutenant in Poitou and Saintonge on 12 December 1439 in order to put a stop to the ravages of independent companies of men-at-arms who were no longer needed in the armies of Burgundy and France after the conclusion of the Treaty of Arras. They had become freebooting adventurers under the command of down-at-heel noblemen, or by their younger or illegitimate sons who could expect no inheritance. Not content with pillaging and robbing people on their farms in the countryside, they tortured them and destroyed their crops and cottages, stripping them of their possessions, thus attracting the name *écorcheurs* (strippers) to themselves. The countryside became depopulated as the country people took refuge in the towns and castles and stayed in them.

In Gascony, the activities of the *écorcheurs* were turned to the profit of Charles VII's government and 'sounded the death-knell of English domination' in the duchy.[12] After devastating great stretches of Burgundy, Auvergne, Rouergue and Languedoc, one of their companies, led by Rodrigue de Villandrando, 'the emperor of the pillagers,' entered Gascony early in 1438 'doubtless at the instigation of Charles VII' rampaging right up to the gates of Bordeaux itself, ransacking Saint-Seurin Abbey which was outside the city walls. Villandrando then joined forces with the king's officers, Poton de Xaintrailles and Charles II d'Albret, who had advanced northwards from the Landes.[13] Because they had no siege equipment, their attack stopped short in the suburbs, but they destroyed the vines.[14] They moved together to the fortress of Blanquefort, near the northern defences of Bordeaux, and then into the Médoc to take Lesparre and Castelnau at either end of it before moving south again into the Landes just before Huntingdon's forces took their place.[15]

Charles VII, under the influence of his Angevin in-laws, found a practical solution to the *écorcheurs* north of the Bordelais by means of taking the French military system out of the hands of feudal lords to make it his own responsibility as the monarch. The Estates-General met at Orleans in October 1439 and he placed a very comprehensive plan before them. A royal ordinance was issued on 2 November containing forty-four clauses.[16] It dealt comprehensively with all abuses that had been features of the military system for years. From now on, captains were to be appointed only by the king, and they were to raise companies consisting of men-at-arms and archers. Detailed instructions for artillery formations were also included. Abuses of the new system were to be punished as treason. The soldiers were to be paid regularly out of monies raised by a new system of taxation. Farmers' work animals, flocks and herds were to be inviolable, as were seeds and standing crops in fields. Foodstuffs could be bought and must be paid for, but not seized from fields or barns. The lords in the vicinity of any infringements were to be responsible for the punishment of those guilty of them.

This ordinance would give the king of France his own army, created to serve the country and not to hold it to ransom. An unforeseen innovation, which caused scandal to some but pleasure to others, was the equal right of everyone to be respected for his life and property, and to have power to defend himself. So, by a single ordinance, the king would place himself above the military aristocracy, give himself an efficient army so as to avoid future disasters like Agincourt or Verneuil, and assure himself of the loyalty and obedience of all the labouring classes against feudal tyranny.[17] This was Magna Carta and the Second Amendment rolled into one. Moreover, it established a further principle: the king could impose taxes without the consent of the Estates-General, and the feudal lords could not raise them at all. The ravages of the freebooters had made any objections to a standing army in royal hands irrelevant. Charles VII of France was not Charles I of England.

However, after his success with the November ordinance, Charles VII suffered a major military setback. Constable Richemont had been besieging an English force at Avranches which was resisted by John Talbot. The king was knocked sideways when he heard of Richemont's failure to take the place. He was at Angers, where his hosts were Charles of Anjou, his brother-in-law, and his mother-in-law, Yolande of Aragon to whom he owed so much in terms of a spirit of determination, both of whom had encouraged him to set his army reforms in motion.[18] These reforms were resisted by certain feudal lords, even princes of the blood royal, who realized that they were a means of transferring power and authority from the aristocracy to the crown.

A revolt began in 1440 which delayed the implementation of the ordinances for five years. The rebels were soon known as *Praguois*[19] because they resembled the military rising of Jan Hus's supporters against the future Emperor Sigismund when he had succeeded as King of Bohemia in 1419.[20]

One of the instigators of the *Praguerie* had his main territorial base in Poitou. Jean II, Duke of Alençon, was a peer of France whose principal domains were in lower Normandy, occupied by the English. In 1423, Charles VII had given him Niort, the second town in Poitou, instead of repaying him the loans he had offered or granting him a pension from the royal treasury. He was godfather to the Dauphin Louis – who was still at Niort as his father's lieutenant-general against the *écorcheurs* – and had been close to Joan of Arc while she was winning battles. He was close to the king too: it was he that had knighted Charles at Reims just before the coronation. He had been a prisoner of the English for three years after his capture at Verneuil in 1424 and financially ruined by his ransom, which did not stop him from trying to involve the Earl of Huntingdon in the *Praguerie*,[21] but the English commander, in return, asked for places in Poitou that France did not possess.[22]

Georges de La Tremouïlle was another leading light in the *Praguerie*. He had been Charles VII's official favourite for six years from 1427 to 1433, the period that included the short ascendancy of Joan of Arc. His rival, Arthur, count of Richemont, supplanted him and was still in office and instrumental in defeating his revolt against the king by force of arms. When the *Praguerie* broke out, La Tremouïlle was still in his golden exile in his castle at Sully enjoying the prospect of gaining vengeance on the king, offering the conspirators considerable financial assistance.[23]

Like Alençon, de La Tremoïlle was well established in Bas-Poitou, with lands at Mareuil-sur-le-Lay and Saint-Hermine, and his second marriage brought him the castle at Gençay which dominated the roads into the Angoumois. Because the king's financial difficulties did not allow the repayment of a large loan to him, he gave him the town of Melle instead, so the road to Saintes was in his power. He had been granted Lusignan Castle in the same way in 1428 but the king had taken it back, in view of its strategic importance, in 1432. The year after, under the 'intelligent inspiration' of Yolande of Aragon and Charles d'Anjou in favour of Richemont, the king deprived La Tremouïlle of his position but he was still a force to be reckoned with in Poitou.

Jean de La Roche was important in Poitou on account of his family's origins there. He was captain of a company of *écorcheurs*, then a servant of the king who pardoned him for his previous activity and appointed him seneschal of the province, where he feathered his own nest as well as asserting the power of the Crown. He was also lord of Barbezieux in the Haute-Saintonge. Still seneschal when the *Praguerie* erupted, he took the side of Alençon and the others until his defeat and death in the same year, 1440.[24]

Charles, Duke of Bourbon, was another prominent *Praguois*, despite not being a Poitevin lord. He was a prince of the blood, and the king's great chamberlain. He joined the plotters despite being involved in the preparation of the November ordinance at Orleans. He went with the court to Tours, and, when the dauphin arrived there, aggravated the tensions that already existed between him and his father. After that, still with the court, he was at Angers where his associates met him and drew up a plan to take the castle, put the king into their safe-keeping and assassinate several of his councillors. Arrangements were all in hand, using the complicity of certain captains who had returned from the failed siege of the English at Avranches, when he changed his plans. Under pretext of going to see his wife in the Bourbonnais, before going on to the Estates-General at Bourges, he took leave of the king. A few days later, he assembled all the malcontents together at Blois and made contact with Jean V of Brittany who had been giving active support to the English when they were besieged at Avranches.[25]

The Bastard of Orleans had heard a rumour that the king, during peace negotiations with the English at Gravelines in 1439, had no intention of pressing for the release of his half-brother Charles, Duke of Orleans, who had been held prisoner in England since Agincourt, twenty-five years before. He took this seriously and joined with the other conspirators in the *Praguerie* until he found that there were no grounds for the rumour. As soon as he learnt that the duke was about to be released by the English, he was reconciled with Charles VII who created him count of Dunois, and actively supported the defeat of the rebellion. Ten years later, we shall see him as commander-in-chief for the king's invasion of Guyenne.

The conspirators succeeded in gaining the support of the precocious Dauphin Louis, the future Louis XI, who was sixteen years old in 1440. For three years now, Charles VII had been taking him on all his journeys in the kingdom like an apprentice, and had been entrusting him with tasks of considerable responsibility, like the collection of taxes in Beaucaire and Carcassonne. Louis had taken part in battles against the English in the Velay and was in command when the town of Château-Landon was taken. Then he was present at the siege of Montereau and was with his father when he made his solemn entry into Paris in 1436. He took part in provincial estates held in Limousin, Auvergne and Languedoc, and was even appointed lieutenant-general in the first of these, entrusted with raising 46,000 livres in taxes from the Estates-General there.

This made him conscious of his own importance and he began to resent the supervision of his father's officials.[26] Nevertheless, the king had sent him into Poitou and Saintonge to overcome the resistance of certain *écorcheur* captains to the 2 November ordinance. Along with three royal councillors, he was arranging the prosecution of those who were opposing the king's orders. Even while he was engaged in this, he threw in his lot with Bourbon and the rest when they exploited his ambition and resentment. He dismissed those of his household officers who did not support him when his godfather Alençon met him at Niort and completely won him over.

Charles VII was on his way from Angers to Niort when he heard about the princes' conspiracy. He realized that they intended to put him under protection, take over the direction of his government, and give royal authority to the dauphin. Once arrived at Amboise, he arranged for a circular letter to be sent to all his *bonnes villes* to put them on their guard against his opponents. This was of immense significance. There was a tradition of alliance between the monarchy and the towns against the feudal lords. The bourgeoisie realized that their trade was at risk if ever the great nobles were able to dominate the monarchy, or if the king were not able to enforce his authority over the great nobles. Even if royal taxation were severe, monarchical order was preferable to feudal anarchy when it came to the protection of their market days and the transport of their goods. Without it the traders would have to submit to the protection payments known as the *patis* exacted by the brigands in return for a measure of security. During the *Praguerie*, the loyalty of the towns to Charles VII turned out to be the deciding factor.[27]

Constable Richemont, Gaucourt and Poton de Xaintrailles were sent to find Bourbon and to explain to him how much harm he was doing to the king and to the poor people of the kingdom. Charles VII moved to the fortress of Loches, made several arrests there, and nearly caught Bourbon himself. Then he moved into Poitou with Richemont, Charles d'Anjou, Marshal Lohéac, Admiral Culant, Xaintrailles and de Brézé. Alençon had established himself in Melle and La Roche and was threatening Saint-Maixent. The king occupied Mirebeau, and Niort welcomed him. It took him less than five days to suppress Alençon, who prevaricated by his overtures to Richemont and Charles d'Anjou – both of whom were his uncles. The king accepted the apparent reality of these discussions which brought about a truce, but Alençon duplicitously appealed to the Earl of Huntingdon for English support.[28]

The king was at Poitiers for Easter, waiting for reinforcements from the Midi. There was to be a great deal of combat involved in the king's suppression of the *Praguerie*, and he conducted a systematic campaign against the conspirators himself. The emblematic encounter was at Saint-Maixent in April 1440. Alençon had been let into the town and castle by treason. From there, the road was open to Poitiers for him to take the king into custody. From there also, he could easily make contact with Charles de Bourbon's forces.

Saint-Maixent was enclosed by walls and contained a castle. There was another, older walled enclosure inside with towers and two gates guarding the ancient Benedictine abbey which gave the town its name. The king had given the revenues of the town to Perette de La Rivière, the Dame de Roche-Guyon, and she lived in the abbey. Her captain, Guyot Le Tirant, commanded the castle, but he was pocketing the revenue meant to pay the garrison while reducing its effective strength. He did not even keep the keys to the town himself. On the morning of 3 April, Guyot took ineffective action, defending a different part of the town while five hundred rebels were let into the castle by one of Dame Rivière's servants whose name was given simply as Jacquet, *comme faux et traitre*.[29] Guyot hid without his armour in the gateway of Saint-Croix and refused to take command of the defenders. He did send a messenger to intercept the king to tell him what was happening, but the man stopped at Lusignan and sold the horse he had borrowed for his journey.

However, the bourgeoisie of Saint-Maixent did not side with the traitors. Their messengers covered the fifty miles to Poitiers in only three hours. The king took to horse immediately sending Admiral Prégent de Coëtivy and Pierre de Brézé, the seneschal of Poitou, on ahead of him with four hundred lances. When they reached Saint-Maixent, they found the bourgeois defenders in possession of the three town gates in the process of lighting fires so that the attackers could not see their way in the smoke. At the same time, the Abbot, Pierre de Clervaux, had sent some of the monks up through the abbey roof to throw tiles down on Alençon's soldiers. At the Saint-Croix Gate, the twenty-four defenders refused to accept defeat when the attackers led out Dame La Rivière' son, the lord of La Roche-Guyon, threatening to execute him there and then. The attackers had pillaged the town and sent their booty to Niort. They destroyed the town's legal archives. The town's losses were later reckoned to be of the value of 40,000 francs.[30]

Charles VII took care to reward the town's residents. Jean Sachier, one of the defenders of the Saint-Croix Gate, was made one of his *valets de chambre*, and then given the profitable post of *aumonier* in the town itself. The abbot de Clervaux was rewarded by being made a member of the king's Great Council and by having all the damage to the fabric of his abbey repaired at the crown's expense. Several additional privileges were granted, like the abbey's monopoly of fishing in the Sèvre Niortaise river, and certain tax exemptions.[31] The king granted the bourgeoisie of Saint-Maixent the privilege of having their own governing body presided over by two elected officials who had the right to have coats of arms.[32]

As soon as Admiral de Coëtivy and Seneschal de Brézé arrived by way of the Saint-Croix Gate in the evening, Alençon shut himself in the castle and then escaped to Niort during the night, leaving his troops to be captured by the king's soldiers. Alençon's men were pardoned because of their previous war record against the English. The king laid siege to Niort and the bourgeoisie there quickly opened the gates to him.[33]

Advancing towards the Bourbonnais, the king received Dunois's submission and was reconciled with him. The payment of Charles d'Orleans' ransom and his release from captivity was imminent. Charles VII issued letters patent from Guéret on 2 May forbidding anyone to obey the princes in revolt on pain of being regarded as traitors and suffering the consequences. All nobles and any others who had the right to bear arms were to rally to him when he required it of them. He then proceeded to dislodge the rebels from Chambord and twenty-five other fortresses.

The outcome was that the princes empowered the Count of Eu, Bourbon's half-brother, and Bertraudon, the Duke of Burgundy's emissary, to offer their submission to the king. The king did not call his campaign off but accepted their surrender on condition that they set Raoul de Gaucourt free, whom they had captured when he surrendered his command of Dauphiné to them. They released him immediately and declared themselves willing to meet the king whenever he proposed. Parleys were held in religious houses in and around Clermont for several days. The princes presented their complaints and the king replied with a long memorandum listing all the *crimes*, *deshonneurs* and *déplaisirs* for which the Duke of Bourbon and his accomplices had been responsible, both before and after they had taken up arms against him.[34]

Apart from La Trémouïlle, who was sent back home to Sully, the leaders were amnestied. The Dauphin was sent away to the Dauphiné with sufficient funds to administer his province, but he was excluded from any participation in government for six years. Nevertheless, hostilities continued until September, especially in the Saintonge where pacification was a long-drawn-out affair. Olivier de Coëtivy, the Admiral's younger brother, took Taillebourg from Maurice and Henri Plusquelec and arrested them for rebellion. The king confiscated their domain and used it to reward Prégent de Coëtivy and Olivier later inherited it (after a dispute with his sister-in-law, a member of the de Raïs family) when Prégent had been taken out by a stray cannonball during the siege of Cherbourg in 1450.

The king relied upon the towns to refuse any overtures made to them by the rebellious princes and free companies of *écorcheurs* in the Midi. There had been a revolt there, associated with the *Praguerie,* led by several independent commanders, and the Viscount of Lomagne, Jean IV of Armagnac's son, was enrolled as captain-general of Languedoc and Guyenne in order to put it down. The seneschal of the Auvergne and the militia of Languedoc, together with the nobles of Velay and the Vivarais, acted together against the rebels. The king was winning public opinion over and learned treatises were written in his support.[35] The Estates of the Auvergne assembled at the same time as the king arrived in Clermont, and spontaneously voted him a supply of 20,000 francs for the conduct of his urgent affairs.

Bourbon and Alençon left Clermont, intending to bring the dauphin to the king, but this headstrong young man could not be persuaded to return with them. Hostilities began again. The king advanced to Roanne. Alençon gave up his struggle soon afterwards, submitted and was reinstated in the king's favour, but Bourbon and the Dauphin, joined by La Tremouïlle and others, moved eastwards to continue with theirs. A message from the king threatened them with reprisals. The Dauphin remained intransigent, but Bourbon persuaded him that further rebellion was impossible. They both came to kneel before the king.

Charles VII told Louis that he was welcome, but when Tremouïlle and some lesser figures were banished to their estates, the Dauphin remonstrated that he had to go to his as well because he had promised his associates that he would. The king's reported reply[36] reveals his own psychology:[37]

Louis, the gates are open, and if they are not large enough for you I will have a long stretch of the wall knocked down for you to go where it seems best to you. You are my son and you cannot engage yourself to serve anyone else without my permission. But if it pleases you to go, God willing, we shall choose someone else of our blood, who will be of more help to us in maintaining our honour and lordship than you have up to this time.

Then he turned to Bourbon, who was rebuked but, nevertheless, reinstated as a prince of the blood – even renaissance kings thought twice before executing their relations. Most of the commoners in the rebellion, not protected by the privileges of noble birth, felt the full force of the royal vengeance.

The king issued *lettres d'abolition* (reinstatement) to Bourbon on 15 July 1440 giving him full amnesty, together with Guy, comte de Montpensier his brother, Jacques and Antoine de Chabannes, as well as other captains and their retinues. Letters were issued confirming these decisions and announcing that military action against the rebels was at an end. The king declared in a letter to the residents of Reims that he was satisfied with the princes' full submission.[38]

Alexandre, bastard of Bourbon, had been pardoned for supporting the duke, his half-brother, who had made him his agent in the armed rising. His actions showed him to be, like the dauphin, a rebel by nature. He had been prominent among the *écorcheur* captains, assisting Rodrigo de Villandrando in 1437, and he was insubordinate towards the king on several occasions. Complaints had been made to the king about his excessive violence and criminality when he was at Bar-sur-Aube. Charles VII was also informed that he and other freebooters were preparing to set out on an unauthorized expedition and he ordered Constable Richemont to arrest him. He was put on trial and condemned to death. On the orders of the Provost of the Merchants, he was sewn into a sack and drowned in the River Aube. Eight of his accomplices were hanged and a further ten or twelve beheaded. This was enough of an example to make the rest of the *écorcheur* captains make their submission. Charles VII enrolled them in his new army, giving them paid responsibility for certain town garrisons, while under threat of severe punishments for infringement of his orders.[39]

It was this energetic suppression of the *Praguerie* and the little revolts in the wake of it that established Charles VII in a position to overcome the English in Normandy and in Gascony and unite France as a single entity. His nineteenth-century biographer expressed this succinctly:

> This audacious feat of arms ended with the complete victory of royalty; and this triumph, it is impossible to deny, was due to the energy and ability of Charles VII. In the midst of the universal disarray occasioned by this revolt he had, with rare promptitude,

taken the measures which the events made necessary; after having suppressed the insurrection in his household at the moment when it was supported by the English, he pursued it wherever it raised its head and it was by imposing [his will] on public opinion that he had imposed his law on the rebels.[40]

The final submission was at Cusset in the middle of July.[41] Resistance to the rebellion by the bourgeoisie of Saint-Maixent was a major factor in the king's triumph over the feudal magnates who had rebelled against his 1439 ordinances. The towns shared his triumph. It was largely the support of the Angevin party led by Yolande of Aragon and Charles of Anjou, together with Constable Richemont and Admiral de Coëtivy, which had brought it about, enhancing a 'patriotic' spirit that was growing in the context of the war with the English, at the same time as the value of endless war with France was beginning to be called in question by members of the household of Henry VI of England and by the king himself when he had assumed authority in 1437.[42]

* * *

Now that Charles VII had established his supremacy over the feudal rebels, he was able to implement what he had intended in the ordinance issued in the Estates-General at Orleans on 2 November 1439. He began with a reform of the national taxation system. From 1443 onwards, he re-ordered the financial organization of France based upon what Charles V had achieved in the fourteenth century. He had separated ordinary receipts of taxation from extraordinary ones. The former were imposed on the domains of the seigneurs, managed by the treasurer of France; the latter were those of the *fisc*, the system of royal taxation, overseen by the finance managers of the five territorial generalities which were Languedoil, Languedoc, Outre-Seine, Yonne and Normandy. The Treasury Court in Paris managed disputes concerning taxes due from the lordships, and the Court of Aids dealt with extraordinary taxation related to the occasional and extra financial needs of the crown at any particular time.[43] Charles VII controlled a similar system more stringently and made possible the essential army reforms that substituted a regular army under the king's direct control for a feudal levy that had recently lapsed into brigandage.

The royal ordinance of 26 May 1445 created a permanent army of fifteen companies of men-at-arms for which the king himself appointed the captains on the basis of their competence, loyalty to the crown and their nobility from among those who had held commands previously. Each of these captains was to be responsible for the recruitment of a company consisting of a hundred 'lances' of six cavalrymen each: a heavy cavalryman (man-at-arms), assisted by an armourer and a page, two archers and a *valet de guerre*. These 'Companies of the Great Ordinance' were to be well and regularly paid. They provided a cavalry stationed in the fortified towns of France. These cavalrymen were to be complemented by a force of nine hundred men for each garrison, men-at-arms and archers, known as 'of the little ordinance', which would be installed in Normandy and Gascony as and when they were taken back from English control. Besides this, the king provided himself with artillery commanded by forty officers organized by Jean and Gaspard Bureau, which would play a decisive role in both conquests. These were lasting improvements, developed still further by Louis XI and Charles VIII.[44]

Thus was created a new kind of military caste, separate from the rest of urban and rural society, always in readiness and at the disposition of the king and those appointed by him. In 1448, the king created a reserve army made up of non-noble archers on foot recruited in each parish on the basis of one archer for each eighty hearths who kept themselves in a state of training for military readiness in return for certain tax exemptions: hence their title of Free Archers. This army of 50,000 was only to be mobilized in case of specific necessity. This gave Charles VII a 'monopoly of warfare'.[45]

The best from among the former *écorcheurs*, like the Bastard of Orleans, now created count of Dunois, were assumed as commanders in the companies of ordinance. This was the instrument with which Charles VII mastered his princes, incorporating them into his new military system, and by which he chased the English out of all French territory except for the pale around Calais. It is worth noting that this military instrument entirely under the king's direction was being perfected at the same time as Le Mans and the other fortresses in Maine were being handed over to Charles VII and that the improbable prospect of a meeting in person between the sovereigns of England and France to conclude a final peace – instead of making temporary truces – was draining into the sand.[46]

*   *   *

The magnates of Poitou and the Duke of Bourbon had been reconciled to the king's design for a renewal of the monarchy, and Charles VII was active on the southern border of his projected kingdom. Feudal magnates there too, Charles II of Albret and Gaston IV of Foix-Béarn assisted the establishment of his authority. The latter was instrumental in the taking of Saint-Sever and Dax and even threatening Bayonne in 1442.[47]

Charles II of Albret threw in his lot with the House of Valois in very special circumstances. Henry VI's lieutenant-general, the Earl of Huntingdon, had laid siege to Tartas at the beginning of August 1440. This was a lordship that belonged to Albret. His men resisted valiantly but were forced to capitulate by a treaty negotiated on the English side by Huntingdon himself, the English seneschal of Gascony, Thomas Rampston, and for the French by Albret's nominees. This treaty contained stipulations tilted very much against the interests of France. A day was fixed between the two sides on which each of them were to appear with an army at Tartas, and if the French army were to prove larger in numbers than that sent by the English, the capitulation would be nullified and Tartas would become French again. This day is usually designated in French as the '*journée de Tartas*'. If the English were to gain in this contest, many lordships would fall into English hands in this most southern part of French-occupied Gascony. Charles VII's reaction was immediate: he wrote to Albret to say that he would be present at Tartas on the appointed day 'at the head of the most numerous army that he would be able to assemble.'[48]

Albret showed signs of sharing the same disloyalty as Armagnac had been showing in his marriage project with Henry VI discussed in the last chapter. But the support offered him at this point by Charles VII was sufficient to remind him that he was still the French king's vassal and was to serve under his banner. The 'Day' had been set for 1 May 1442 and Charles VII began his preparations for assembling a very large army at

Toulouse. When at the request of the English the day was put off until 24 June, Charles did not want to leave this large force together with nothing to do. It was too soon after the *Praguerie* for him to have established his companies of ordinance, and he could not trust the former *écorcheurs* who were his captains, so he dispersed this army with orders to re-assemble when required. The order to reassemble, as it turned out, was soon given. The King came to Toulouse in person, and began his advance to Tartas on 11 June 1442, leaving behind a considerable number of troops because he heard that the English were counting on winning the day with a small contingent. Some towns on the way refused him obedience, but he did not waste time in subduing them so as to be in place on the morning agreed. The army took up its position in battle order before the walls of Tartas and waited for the English to arrive. They waited all day. No English troops appeared. At the end of the afternoon, the keeper of the keys of the town appeared and surrendered to Charles VII. Albret had been given his town back, and he remained on the king's side from then on.[49]

* * *

However, there was one feudal magnate in the south who would demand more time and effort on the king's part, and even then it would be only be his son who gave Charles VII his entire support. We are concerned here with Jean IV, count of Armagnac who emerges as an opportunistic character on the frontiers of France and the Spanish kingdoms. His career illustrates, certainly as much as the story of the *Praguerie*, the nature of resistance to the new monarchical order, maintaining his opposition to the house of Valois for a far longer time by a policy of vacillation.

He inherited his extensive domains at the age of twenty-two from his father, the Constable Bernard VII of Armagnac, who was killed in Paris in June 1418 amid the faction struggle with the Burgundians for control of Paris while the English were making inroads into Normandy subsequent upon Agincourt and before the arrangements for the dual monarchy made at Troyes in 1420. These events would set the scene for the drama of Jean IV of Armagnac's career.[50]

Ambiguous dynastic considerations complicated his situation at the outset. Bernard VII and two of his sisters were married to members of prominent French families. Jean himself had married Blanche, Duke Jean V of Brittany's sister. Her widowed mother had married Henry IV of England in 1401. Jean's second marriage, contracted after he became count, was to the Infante Isabelle, daughter of Charles the Noble, King of Navarre. The couple had been betrothed in 1416 as soon as Blanche had died, and while he was still Viscount of Lomagne.[51] His new marriage would give him five domains and a barony in Navarre and relations with his father-in-law's kingdom that sent messengers criss-crossing the Pyrenees, remained firmly established until Charles the Noble died in 1425. In addition, Jean gave homage through intermediaries to the King of Castille, claiming family ties with that kingdom's royal house in the past. Isabelle's father was Jean's uncle by marriage, and a papal dispensation for the marriage of first cousins was necessary. Jean chose to obtain it from the deposed Spanish anti-pope Benedict XIII, who had retired to his rock of Peñiscola in Valencia, and continued to support him, and his successor, Clement VIII afterwards. His primary liege lord, Charles VI of France, supported Pope Martin V in whose person the Great Schism of the western church was ended at the Council of Constance in 1417. Jean embarrassingly wrote a letter to Joan of Arc while she was in the ascendant to ask her for her inspired opinion on which pope was the authentic one. She replied to him that she was rather busy at the moment preparing her attack on Paris, but that she would give consideration to this important question – twelve years after Martin V's election had ended the schism – once Paris had been taken, which, of course, she was not able to do.[52]

These were the years when Jean IV had to hold off incursions into his territories from independent brigand captains and English contingents alike, which usually meant paying them large sums in what amounted to protection money (known as *patis* or *souffrances*) out of grants-in-aid made by the Three Estates of his Armagnac baronies. An example of this occurred in 1427 when André de Ribes, a notorious *écorcheur*, rampaged in Armagnac territory in service of the English. Jean connived at his activities and gave him privileged protection, being at that moment better disposed towards England than to France. The letters of abolition granted to him later (in 1445) by Charles VII make it clear that he even handed over to Ribes certain baronies in the Agenais and in Quercy to be his legitimately-owned property.[53] In 1431, certain English brigands were destructively active around the town of Condom, and the bourgeois consuls asked for Jean's help against them. Soon afterwards, Rodrigo de Villandrando entered the Rouergue moving around between towns such as Millau and Rodez before Jean paid him to go away. It is unlikely that Jean kept himself aloof from Villandrando's incursions.[54] Thereafter, fresh rampages by Villandrando followed each year, paid off by grants from various meetings of local estates in the county of Armagnac.

These culminated in the great raid of 1438 up to the walls of Bordeaux and then into the Médoc in which Villandrando's brigands received the support of Charles VII's generals, Foix, Albret, and Xaintrailles. The Earl of Huntingdon's arrival meant that the French troops were soon no nearer to Bordeaux than Tartas. In 1439, Jean d'Armagnac's heir, the Viscount of Lomagne, ceased to co-operate in the ambiguous behaviour of his father, and accepted Charles VII's appointment of him as captain-general of Languedoc with a particular mission to disperse the brigands with the aid of the seneschals of Toulouse, Carcassonne and Beaucaire, and paid for by 2,000 livres voted by the Languedoc estates. The Dauphin Louis, before his association with the princes in the *Praguerie*, negotiated with Villandrando, paying him off in June 1439 with 1,000 gold écus to return to his native Castille and to stay there. In all these developments, Jean IV found himself looking both ways towards the kings of France and of England. To understand this ambiguity, we shall have to retrace our steps to his accession twenty years earlier.[55]

As soon as the Constable Bernard d'Armagnac was dead, the new count went to the Dauphin Charles accompanied by several other nobles to ask for justice, says the chronicler Enguerrand de Monstrelet,[56] both for himself and for other lords who had met their end[57] in the riots in the capital. The dauphin replied that those who had thus suffered 'would receive justice in time and place'. This was obviously an empty promise in 1418 in the circumstances of repeated English victories: Henry V was encamped in Normandy and had given orders to the Gascon nobles, Gaillard de Durfort, Lord of Duras, and Bernard de Lesparre together with Jean de Saint-Jean, Mayor of Bordeaux, to receive the homage of Jean d'Armagnac and his brother Bernard. The king/duke also ordered all his Gascon subjects to obey his envoys. Jean IV hedged his bets: he went to Aire-sur-l'Adour on 16 November 1418 to meet Gaston de Foix and Charles d'Albret to make a defensive and offensive alliance against the Burgundians but, even so, signed a truce with the Anglo-Gascons to last until Easter 1419. In February, safe-conducts were issued for a deputation from Armagnac, including the Bishop of Rodez, to travel to Normandy while, at the same time, Jean IV and his brother went to Toulouse to meet the Dauphin who was beginning to assert himself against the English.

The Dauphin effectively prevented Gaston of Foix from allying himself with Henry V, and it was likely that Jean d'Armagnac received similar blandishments. 'The words of the Count of Armagnac were honeyed but his actions were suspect.'[58] His real agenda was to enlarge his own domains as he subsequently showed by encouraging captains in English pay and being indifferent to Joan of Arc's raising of French self-awareness in 1429, despite his letter to her about the authenticity of an anti-pope's dubious but persistent successor.

In 1427, Jean IV had been involved in Jean Duke of Orleans' attempt to make peace with Henry VI's minority government. Orleans had been a prisoner in England since Agincourt, twelve years before, and he wanted to attach a lasting peace to his own release. He was looking for support in France, and Armagnac gave him his, making an engagement with him in a document dated 2 June at his castle at L'Isle Jourdain. 'Such a peace,' he asserted, 'would be profitable and expedient, not only for the public utility of both kingdoms but also for all Christendom which is in trouble as a result of war between them.'[59] Of course, nothing came of all this, but Charles d'Orleans tried again in the same vein in 1433, and Jean IV once more agreed to take part in any negotiation that might be arranged.[60] Once more, Orleans had to stay in England, becoming more of a poet than a diplomat. For Armagnac, there was too much of a Burgundian tendency in these negotiations, and he turned more towards Charles VII for a time. But three years on, and we see him intriguing against the king once more: this time with the Dukes of Bourbon, Alençon and Brittany with support from the inevitable bad penny, Villandrando. Their intention was to remove two of the king's councillors, Christophe Harcourt and Martin

Gouge, Bishop of Clermont, and replace them with d'Albret, who was more likely to further their interests with the king.

All that was needed was for the king to arrive at Rodez as expected. But Charles VII uncovered the intrigue, rapidly left Montpelier, and arrived at Saint-Flour on 14 May 1437 with 4,500 men to surprise the conspirators into abandoning their project. Other plans were soon drawn up by Armagnac for a truce with Henry VI of England, now allegedly in charge of his own government. Charles VII tried to detach him from his double game but had to be content with securing only the support of his son, Lomagne, against him. This latter became a staunch supporter of Charles VII's designs for an authoritarian monarchy which left no place for intransigent feudal magnates. The next five years saw Jean IV becoming more and more eager for an alliance with England, a tendency which resulted in his attempt at a marriage of one of his three daughters to Henry VI, which appeared possible in 1442 when the twenty-one-year-old king took the initiative himself.[61]

Charles VII was too astute at masterminding not to know about Jean IV's secret negotiations with the English ambassadors. He was looking for an opportunity to undercut the independence of the feudal lords on the southern border of France as he had already done in overcoming the open rebellion of the *Praguerie*. His motive was to gain their co-operation as his subordinates for the coming invasion of Gascony. He had gained Charles d'Albret's support by his participation in the 'Day of Tartas', and Gaston IV of Foix-Béarn was already actively on his side. He wanted Armagnac as an ally in this undertaking as well. But he knew that it was going to be difficult to persuade him.

The king saw his chance in the possible resolution of the problem of Marguerite, Countess of Comminges whose story was a long one. In 1419, she had married Mathieu de Foix as her third husband, being twice widowed already. She was twenty-two years older than Mathieu. Her county of Comminges was her dowry, and her new husband had taken over the territory and assumed the title she offered – his only purpose in marrying her. He then proceeded to lock her up, first at Saverdun, and then in his castle at Foix. She was still there twenty years later.

Her first husband had been Jean III of Armagnac, Jean IV's uncle, and her second was another Armagnac, the Viscount of Ferzensaguet. So Jean

IV declared an interest in the lady's lands if not in her plight, which was why, it appeared, the king decided to intervene. In 1439, Charles VII sent commissioners to release her from captivity, ordering them that, should there be resistance from Mathieu de Foix, they were to take her under royal protection and summon her captor to appear before the Dauphin Louis who had just been declared lieutenant-general of Languedoc. The dauphin did not stay in the south very long, on account of moving to Angers when English activity was threatened, and the king sent Poton de Xaintrailles to Languedoc instead. Poton rashly entrusted the elderly countess's protection to Jean IV and, naturally, Jean IV saw his chance of taking over the county and its resources under the pretext of an inheritance from his uncle. He would have succeeded had not Mathieu de Foix called for help from Gaston IV, his brother, and his uncle, the captal de Buch who had five hundred men at their disposal between them.[62]

However, the king was at Toulouse, and received a delegation from the Estates of Comminges seeking his help in the matter. The king intervened again to order Mathieu to set his wife free. He further decreed that the couple should divide the usufruct of the county's revenues between them for their lifetimes, and the survivor should have them all. Mathieu was reconciled to the crown by this means, paying homage to the king and receiving from him letters of abolition for his past cruelty towards the countess. She herself was taken to Toulouse and then to Poitiers for a brief period of liberty. She died before the year was over.[63] The king ordered Jean IV to surrender her lands which he had seized despite the previous decree, but he claimed that she had surrendered them into his keeping by a secret agreement.[64] She was his aunt before she had met Mathieu de Foix, when all was said and done.

Jean IV retained his independent attitude towards the Valois monarchy as seen in this next incident. He had styled himself in his official documents 'by the Grace of God, Count of Armagnac'. The other counts in this story had done the same, and now the king ordered them, under threat of punishment for non-compliance, to abandon the practice. Jean IV did not submit to this, but made an appeal to the *Parlement* of Paris, after the law's delays, on 19 March 1442.[65] The next year, his opposition to the king was even more blatant: he absolutely refused to make his county contribute to the war effort against the English, which Charles VII had been conducting with considerable success after the 'Day of Tartas' had engaged Charles II of Albret and Gaston IV, Count of Foix–Béarn, on his side.

The king had had enough of such pretentiousness on the part of a vassal and sent the Dauphin Louis into the Midi with an army for a punitive expedition. He reached Entraygues at the end of November 1443 and called for help from the seneschal of Toulouse. A well-known *écorcheur* captain with 600 lances, Jean de Salazar, bastard of Armagnac, who had links with Rodrigo de Villandrando and Georges de La Trémouille, enrolled with Jean IV against the dauphin. The dauphin was entirely successful in his military walkabout[66] passing through Toulouse and Albi and retaking the county of Comminges which Jean had not surrendered to the crown as ordered.

Jean IV had taken refuge with his family in his castle at L'Isle Jourdain. When the dauphin arrived there, he came out to meet him but was immediately taken prisoner in the king's name. The countess of Armagnac, Isabelle of Navarre, was also arrested along with the rest of the family. The dauphin handed over L'Isle Jourdain to be pillaged, taking jewels which he later gave as a present to the king's mistress, Agnès Sorel. 'Certain sources' report that a box was found which contained Jean's correspondence with Henry VI's court in England. Not being English, Jean realized that he was beaten and ordered the people of Rodez to take an oath of fidelity to the dauphin, who then returned to the county of Rouergue, captured the bastard of Armagnac at Séverac and put the seneschal of Lyon in charge of the Armagnac lands. Jean IV himself was taken by a circuitous route via Toulouse and Albi to Carcassonne where he was put in prison.

The Viscount of Lomagne, the future Jean V d'Armagnac, had declared himself independent from his father's perpetually autonomous stance and had allied himself with the fortunes of Charles VII. Nevertheless, his filial loyalty caused him to cross the Pyrenees to make contact with his maternal grandfather, John II, King of Castille, to ask him to plead Armagnac's cause with the Valois king. In the winter of 1444–1445, John II sent an envoy, Diego de Valera, to meet Charles VII at Nancy, who took forty days to reflect on the grave wrongs done to him by the Count of Armagnac and accepted that the king of Castille and Leon would act as guarantor for his future good behaviour. Meanwhile Armagnac himself made contact with influential people to plead his cause with the king: the Dukes of Savoy, Orleans, Alençon, and Bourbon, the counts of Foix, Maine, Richemont, and Dunois, and even with the Dauphin. He took the very risky step of writing to the king on his own behalf to plead the deleterious effects of his incarceration, his *douleur et tristesse*.

The king agreed to hold audiences about his case, and the end result was that Armagnac's friends advised him to throw himself upon the king's mercy; and this is what he did. The king issued letters of abolition in August 1445 stipulating his conditions. All the members of Armagnac's family had to take an oath of fidelity to the monarchy, renouncing any alliances made with the King of England, and not to use the formula 'by the grace of God' in their legal acts and deeds. Comminges became a royal domain as did several important Armagnac towns. Jean IV d'Armagnac was pardoned and punished at the same time. He was not actually set free from Carcassonne until February 1446.[67]

He protested against the king's judgement on his treasonable behaviour, but the king kept watch on him, ready to strike if he were to get out of line again. He resigned himself to his son's service in the king's new army and he lived quietly until his final hours in his castle at L'Isle Jourdain where he felt most at home despite its sacking by the king's soldiery. He died there on 5 November 1450.

Jean IV was succeeded by Lomagne, whose loyalty to the king had been long before secured, and so all the southern magnates were in the Valois camp now that the time had come for the final act of the drama of the conquest of Guyenne.

Chapter Five

The First French Conquest of Gascony

harles VII had reformed his army, established a system of national
taxation on a firm footing, and exerted his authority over the
great lords who had defied him. Even the Duke of Burgundy had
decided to co-operate with him. It was an English initiative that gave him
the opportunity to re-open his campaign against Gascony.

The flashpoint for new open warfare to end the extended truce of
Tours was a Breton *bastide* called Fougères in March 1449.[1] A mercenary
force led by a captain from Aragon, François de Souriennes, sponsored
by Somerset and Suffolk, had broken the truce in operation since 1444
by seizing this place situated on the borders of Brittany and Normandy.
However, according to Charles VII, there was a deeper cause for the
resumption of hostilities between France and England in an English
attempt to detach François I, Duke of Brittany, from his allegiance to
the French crown.[2] This led, after a brief time, to the final expulsion
of the English from Normandy which they had conquered and settled
over more than a generation since their victory at Agincourt in 1415.
The decisive battle was at Formigny on 15 April 1450 and Cherbourg
capitulated on 12 August.

The King of France had already made known his intentions about
a complete and permanent conquest of Gascony when he ordered his
generals to invade the duchy westwards from Toulouse in 1442 and had
persuaded the Count of Foix to renounce his allegiance to the king/duke.
He meant to pursue his ambitions in the south-west, confident in the
proved effectiveness of his fiscal and military revolution which had made
the feudal aristocracy of France subordinate to the crown.

The new Count of Armagnac, Jean V, who had supported the king
when he was Viscount of Lomagne, succeeded his rebellious father in
November 1450. He had been brought up at Charles VII's court and had
already fought against Huntingdon in 1439 and against the *Praguerie* in

1440. He was rewarded with the restitution of lands confiscated from his father and – whatever happened in the next reign – was firmly on Charles VII's side when the invasion of Gascony re-opened.[3]

No clear-cut distinction ought to be made between Charles VII's activities for the recovery of Normandy and the conquest of Gascony. From 1450 onwards, he was receiving intelligence reports from his spies in England and his treasurer, Jacques Coeur, was financing their activities.[4] Once in possession of Normandy, he realized his intentions. Ambassadors were sent to Scotland and to the Spanish kingdoms to ask for help.[5]

On 31 March 1450, at Tours, commanders were appointed for the southern campaign,[6] while the war in Normandy still had six months to go. 'And about that time the king of France began to fight in Gascony', was the laconic comment offered by a nearly contemporary English chronicler.[7]

Operations had commenced before that, however. The Count of Foix had taken Mauléon and Guiche, the port that served Bayonne, in 1449, and Albret's son, Amanieu, Count of Orval, was ordered to take Bazas, which he did 'without a blow' on 31 October in that year.[8] The town of Bazas dominated all the territory between the Landes to its south and the Bordelais to the north. It was also a bishopric which included a certain number of towns loyal to Henry VI of England besides others which had already accepted French domination.[9]

Jean, count of Penthièvre was in charge of the siege of Bergerac on the right bank of the river Dordogne. Bazas and Bergerac were the two places from which the 1450 campaign was launched.[10] Penthièvre, accompanied by Marshal de Jallongues, the Gascon Poton de Xaintrailles, the king's master of the horse, Joachim Rouault, and other captains, with 600 lances and additional archers, persevered with the siege until the decisive arrival of Jean Bureau and his artillery pieces. Bergerac capitulated in October 1450. The English garrison and officials were allowed to leave, taking their movable property with them; any who wanted to stay took an oath of fidelity to Charles VII, and carried on with their normal occupations as before.[11] Ribadieu, basing his account on the contemporary official chronicler, a monk of Saint-Denis called Jean Chartier, whose brother was the Bishop of Paris, goes on to say that neighbouring places were taken before Penthièvre withdrew to his winter quarters, and cites Jonzac as one of them, in spite of its being situated a long way north of Bergerac in the Haute-Saintonge. The capitulation of Montferrand, Sainte-Foy and Chalais which he also records, are more probable.[12]

From this point onwards, the interest turns back to Orval in his base at Bazas, from whence he advanced towards Bordeaux with an army of 2,000. He skirted around the city on the left bank to set up camp beside the little river Jalle in front of the castle at Blanquefort. Various independent brigands made cause with him, bringing him hundreds more troops.[13] The Bordelais re-armed their citizens' militia in a hurry. The breaking of the truce on the frontier between Brittany and Normandy had not been known about in Aquitaine and no preparations had been made. The militia was made up of 10,000 men but they were indifferently armed and had minimal military training.

This scratch force of Anglo-Gascons moved towards the count of Orval and took up a position at Castelnau in the south of the Médoc. Orval soon knew about their unconcealed approach and divided his troops, hiding half of them in woodland beside the road along which they were advancing and ordering the others to form up in battle order on the banks of the Jalle near Blanquefort with marshland in front of them. Orval had done his reconnaissance thoroughly beforehand.

The force from Bordeaux was under the command of the mayor of Bordeaux, Gadifer Shorthouse – the same who had been criticized eight years before for his arrogant shortcomings. He had been written off at that time by the English king's lieutenant in Bordeaux, Sir Robert Roos, as being of 'mediocre talent ... and little disposed to recognize any authority superior to hs own'.[14] He had positioned what cavalry he had behind his infantry on the march and they could not avoid pushing the footsloggers on towards the little river which is not at all wide but flowed (as it still does) between high banks at a much lower level than the terrain they were crossing. Shorthouse did not know about Orval's troops concealed among the trees and he advanced towards the enemy troops that he could see, who pretended to turn and run from his advance. As soon as the Bordeaux militia crossed the stream by a bridge, Orval's hidden troops came out of the wood to attack them from behind and on their flank. The other French troops then turned about to drive Shorthouse's cavalry and infantry into the marsh where they could not move. More than 4,000 of them were taken prisoner, wounded or killed where they stood. Orval was too pre-occupied with taking prisoners to follow the others who rushed back to Bordeaux. He returned to Bazas, causing devastation as he went, but did not have the resources or equipment to lay siege to Bordeaux.[15]

All Souls' Day 1450 saw Gadifer Shorthouse sending carts out from Bordeaux to bring back the 1,500 corpses of those cut down in the marshes near where the Pont d'Aquitaine spans the Garonne in our time, on what was to be remembered by the Gascons as the *male journade*.

The enquiry carried out after Archbishop Pey Berland's death to decide upon his saintliness reported that this event had affected him deeply: he felt an 'immeasurable sadness' to the extent that he shut himself up alone in his chapel for forty-eight hours overcome with grief (like all the widows and orphans who did not have chapels of their own). He had the wounded brought to his new St. Peter's Hospital or into his palace. The archiepiscopal see of Bordeaux had inherited from Roman times the idea that whoever held the office was the defender of the people, and he had eventually failed to carry out this function despite all his efforts since his consecration twenty years before.[16]

The Count of Orval sent a report of his success to Charles VII who set about raising a fresh army of 40,000 men in the early months of 1451, dividing it into four corps, each one commanded by a nominee of his own: his cousin Dunois, with his subordinates, Ponthièvre, Charles II d'Albret, and Jean V d'Armagnac. Dunois was to be responsible for the siege and conquest of Blaye. The king also ordered him to take Bourg, Libourne, Saint-Emilion, and the fortress of Fronsac which dominates the Dordogne Valley from its height, regarded by French and English captains alike as the key to the possession of Bordeaux.

All the towns mentioned were the goddaughters (*filleules*) of Bordeaux: an emotional tie as well as a strategic one. Penthièvre was sent to take possession of Castillon and to control the area between the two rivers Garonne and Dordogne known as *Entre Deux Mers* which he had just conquered. Albret was sent to subdue Dax on the Adour River and the strongholds around it. Armagnac was to take Saint-Macaire and Rions, and all the fortresses between Marmande and Cadillac. Since Orval was still occupying Bazas, Bordeaux would be taken in a noose if these plans were to succeed.[17]

The four armies organized on the basis of the king's *compagnies d'ordonnance* began their advance in April 1451. In the same spirit that he had set out to win over several members of the Gascon nobility, Charles VII ordered severe punishments for any of his soldiers who mistreated the people in the territories through which they were advancing, or who took their crops or animals without paying for them. He wanted neither ransoms nor requisitions.[18] Whatever he did subsequently, at present he let it be seen that he was conducting a hearts and minds campaign. Nevertheless, Gascon historians, of whom Henri Ribadieu (1866) and Raymond Corbin (1888) were typical, found it difficult to believe that the king of France was at any point motivated by a benevolent spirit. Corbin's comment was that Charles VII 'doubtless foresaw the soon-to-be-achieved downfall of the liberties and freedoms of Gascony'.[19]

Dunois had taken Montguyon after a siege lasting fourteen days.[20] The captain there, Arnaud de Saint-Jean, a Gascon in the retinue of the captal de Buch, held negotiations with Dunois' captains, the count of Angoulême and Jean Bureau among them, which set the pattern for future capitulations. The Anglo-Gascons were to be free to leave, taking their movable property and their weapons with them, except for any heavy artillery they had in the castle. They were to leave behind any French prisoners they had taken and not to take ransoms or any other payments from them. Any who stayed were to take an oath to remain loyal to the king of France, and any who might come back after having left could equally well take such an oath within fifteen days of their return. Arnaud de Saint-Jean was to have a safe-conduct to go wherever he pleased, and carts and baggage animals to take him as far as Libourne which would be sent back to Montguyon as soon as he left this river port on the Dordogne. The agreement was sealed on 6 May 1451, and the French commander established a garrison at Montguyon.[21]

From there, Dunois opened his campaign against Blaye on the east bank of the Gironde Estuary, one of the many goddaughters of Bordeaux. It was through Blaye that English grain, leather, and wool came into Bordeaux. Gadifer Shorthouse sent five warships there and he and Pierre de Montferrand undertook to prepare the town's defences.

Despite having been deprived of his lordship of Lesparre in the Médoc, when Henry VI gave it to the Earl of Huntingdon to be his headquarters as lieutenant-general, Pierre de Montferrand remained fiercely loyal to the Anglo-Gascon cause. He was married to Mary, the Duke of Bedford's natural daughter, and in exchange for his lost lordship he was given a lesser one in the Landes which gave him the title of Soudic de Trau. His elder brother, Bertrand de Montferrand, arrived to organize the defence of Bourg, a little way to the south and also on the coast of the Gironde. Jacques de Chabannes was sent by Dunois with an advance guard of 2,300 men overland against the brothers.[22]

Huntingdon, meanwhile, transferred his seat of government from the Ombrière Palace in Bordeaux to Lesparre, the better to organize the capital's defence. Archbishop Pey Berland was once more active in stiffening the resistance of the city's council – the *jurade* – and to seek help from England such as he had himself obtained in 1443.[23]

In the middle of May, Dunois left Montguyon to join up with Chabannes before the defences of Blaye, at the same time ordering Penthièvre to abandon the siege of Castillon in order to assist them. A fleet from La Rochelle was summoned to outnumber the little Bordeaux squadron in the Gironde, so it was with a naval engagement that the attack on Blaye began. The Bordeaux ships could not maintain their position, but the town itself held out against Bureau's artillery bombardment until 21 May when Dunois made his advance. Blaye capitulated after three days and Dunois gave favourable terms to its defenders.[24] For Charles VII, this was not conquest so much as recovery of ancient rights, even though it had taken three hundred years to accomplish it. Shorthouse and his deputy mayor and Pierre de Montferrand returned to Bordeaux. The Gascons left Blaye with full war honours.[25]

Bertrand de Montferrand saw that any resistance at Bourg in the face of the French artillery would be disastrous; he surrendered on 29 May. Dunois offered favourable terms once more to the citizens of Bourg, and then called upon those of Bordeaux to recognize the authority of the king of France, who had established himself with a powerful army at Saint-Jean d'Angély, no more than sixty miles to the north. The Three Estates of the Bordelais – that is the clergy, the nobles and the bourgeoisie – refused Dunois's invitation, and he, supported by Bureau and the artillery, moved against Libourne, Saint-Emilion and Fronsac, other goddaughters of the capital of Gascony.

Pey Berland did not let up on his efforts to organize resistance. He had recently completed his building plan designed to prevent the masons of the city from being de-skilled during the financial depression. They built the great bell tower which he commissioned from them outside the east-end of the Cathedral of Saint-André which bears his name (as does the underground car park beneath the square). He now set about the elaborate restoration of the church at Lormont, where he had been *curé* twenty years before, as a gesture of defiance against Charles VII since it was in the path of any military approach from the north – the works would be completed on 5 September. Nevertheless, now that defeat seemed inevitable, even to him, his main contribution to defence took the form of mediation between the divine right claimed by the King of France[26] and the system of government by remote control of the King of England, to whom his loyalty did not waver.

In the documents that concern the successive surrenders of the towns in the Bordelais, meticulously conserved in the remarkable new building of the *Archives Métropole de Bordeaux* into thirty-one printed volumes during the Third Republic and after, a pattern emerges of pragmatic conciliation on the part of the king and his officers, confirming the privileges each town had enjoyed during the long period of English domination and evoking loyalty to the new regime by means of a solemn oath taken by the citizens of influence. The confirmation of privileges by the Count of Angoulême to Saint-Macaire is typical. He informs them that 'of special grace by these presents, they may use and enjoy in peace all the privileges, liberties, usages, customs, establishments and freedoms to which they have been justly and lawfully accustomed to use and enjoy in time past ... the which privileges, etc., we swear to them and promise in good faith to give anew; all and such trust of which they shall inform us'.[27]

The tone of the conquest of Gascony had been set: *suaviter in modo, fortiter in re*, the iron fist in the velvet glove. This was the method adopted by all Charles VII's field commanders in the conquest of Bordeaux and Bayonne and of the smaller towns around them. The success of this policy depended on the nobles and townspeople keeping the oaths they had made to their new sovereign lord. For the most part, the members of the noble and mercantile classes knew when they were beaten. With the example of so many Anglo-Gascon towns and strongholds taken and then reinstated in their new obedience, even the doughty Archbishop Berland, who had led resistance in theory and in practice against Charles VII ever since taking office in 1430, decided it was time for his city to negotiate a peace with this patently invincible system of monarchy that Charles VII had brought into being. After that, the surrender of Bayonne would be quickly accomplished. Since the rulers of Foix-Béarn and Armagnac had been fighting on the king's side, the unified French nation was soon to be extended to the Pyrenees.

* * *

The Valois king's call to the people of Bordeaux to surrender was repeated at the same time as refugees from other places were arriving in the city. Among these was Gaston de Grailly, the captal de Buch (captal was his seigneurial title and Buch was the name of his lordship near Archachon, to the south-west of Bordeaux). Bertrand de Montferrand was one of the last to arrive of those who remained loyal to Henry VI. There were ample precedents now of towns making compromise agreements with Dunois, and Mayor Shorthouse and the *jurade* of Bordeaux requested one for themselves.

What was this *jurade* and who were its members? The *jurade* was a self-perpetuating system of bourgeois government for Bordeaux which had its origins in the early 12th century when the municipality successfully resisted a siege by King Alfonso VIII of Castille.[28] Confirmed in office by successive kings/dukes from John Lackland onwards, it still retained the city in stability and prosperity in the period of domination by the House of Lancaster (1399–1453). Other towns in English Gascony that were also episcopal sees, like Bazas, were also governed by *jurades*.

At the centre of Bordeaux society, traders – for the most part vintners, obviously – were the ruling class. There were great differences between individual traders in respect of their wealth and the volume of their trade. The closest to patricians in the city were the great merchants as opposed to the shopkeepers who were a cut above the labourers. It was only the richest of the elite among the bourgeoisie who were eligible for membership of the *jurade* which governed the city in association with the English-appointed mayor and an assembly of churchmen, nobles and themselves: the Three Estates. They were an oligarchy, with each *jurat* representing a section of the city equivalent to a ward in London. It was hardly a democratic system, but it wasn't feudalism either.

The Bordeaux historian Sandrine Lavaud gives examples of some of the *jurats*. Firstly, Arnaud de Bios, who was elected to the *jurade* in 1406 and was a member of the Council of Thirty during the subsequent year.[29] He was the city treasurer in 1420, then a *jurat* once more in the year after. During the Hundred Years' War, the *jurade* was responsible for the town's defence. Another *jurat*, Benedyct Spina, English by origin but accepted into the town's bourgeoisie, was sent to Henry IV's court in 1407 to report on of the state of the town after it had resisted an attack by the Duke of Orleans, presumably because he spoke better English than the others (though this would not have been the ultimate criterion for choosing him at the time). Many of the bourgeoisie undertook to maintain a man-at-arms out of their own resources or on money borrowed from the town to do so. The *jurats* profited from their duties to the town, for example, by contracts to supply it with goods at their disposal. Arnaud de Bios provided ships for specific voyages on several occasions. Johan de la Geneva supplied the builders with lead for roofing purposes (we could assume that he had bought it from English importers), and gunpowder and saltpetre was provided by Pey de Ferran. The *jurade* also farmed out the collection of taxes to its members for a determined period, or they could benefit from exemption from a particular tax, or be offered a safe-conduct for travel. Benedyct Spina obtained a passport to allow him to go to Spain on business.

In return for these benefits (perhaps liable to be perceived as corrupt practice) the bourgeoisie from whom the *jurats* were selected were intensely loyal to the municipality. In turn, this made them fervent Anglo-Gascons, since it was in their interest to be such. They were called upon to perform military duties in person, like maintaining a guard-post for a time or holding the keys to one of the many city gates. These bourgeois grandees had their domestic premises in the area called La Rouselle, or near the Sainte-Colombe market, or in Les Salinières, Saint-Eloi or

Saint-Michel quarters of the town. They had duties in absence in less salubrious parishes, like La Tropeyte or La Grave, where they had their business premises and warehouses.

There were others, less grand, who shared in the prosperity that the *jurade* maintained, like Guilhem Forton, who lived in a modest house in the rue Bouquinière, by the Sainte-Colombe market. This house had an entry, a living room and two bedrooms on the ground floor, with a cellar for the wine he kept for himself underneath. He had upstairs rooms where he kept tools and disused barrels. All his furniture was functional and none of it had any great value, being similar to what was to be found in workmen's lodgings. The tools he used every day were found ready to hand in his bedroom. Nevertheless, there were eight silver pledges which represented the 805 *livres* owed to him by seventy-eight debtors at his death. His will demonstrates the value of movable capital in this society. This very ordinary house does not announce the fact that Forton had three other houses in the Saint-Michel parish, a vineyard at Graves, and agricultural land at Artigues. Mme Lavaud sardonically remarks that the wealth of Guilhem Forton was certainly real, but he was not ostentatious.[30]

These few examples present the conservative mindset of those who were ready to resist the blandishments of Charles VII and the Count of Dunois and any encouragement to become Frenchmen. If they could not resist their advance by military means, and if there were to be no help from England, they were prepared to stand behind their archbishop and his negotiators, in terms of present-day parlance, for the best deal possible with their new French rulers.

Twenty years after Guilhem Forton made his will, Messire Regnault Girard was required by King Louis XI, in 1465, the fourth year of his reign, to compile a memorandum about how to maintain Bordeaux in a state of security. It starts with an assessment of the town's prosperity after eleven years of incorporation into the kingdom of France: it is 'one of the great and well-populated cities of this kingdom, set on the river (sic) Gironde, and from there to the sea it is about 26 leagues. The river allows sea-going ships to come right into the river called La Lune, which is something very remarkable.'

In a well-worn classical image, Girard compares Bordeaux to a person's stomach, which receives the food given to it and sends it on to the other members.

> The town ... receives ships and merchandise from all parts and all kingdoms and sends them on to various places like the kingdoms of Spain, Navarre and Aragon, and to the lands of Monseigneurs of Armagnac, Foix, Béarn and Albret, and into the lands of Languedoc and other places according to their needs.

Girard then asks what it was that brought such great prosperity to the place. His reply is unequivocal:

> It is the isle of England, a large and rich kingdom with a great merchandise, like fine wool from which they make abundant cloth, lead, tin, metal, coal both from the rock and from the earth, besides other goods, and they have a great number of ships. Twice a year, around All Saints (1 November) and in March, the said English come with their ships laden with the above trade goods, coming down to the said place, Bordeaux.
>
> When the ships have arrived from all the places mentioned above, traders bring money to have their merchandise, and the English bring a great deal of gold and silver too. They all get together and convert their money into Gascon wines and go home, leaving Bordeaux and the country around to prosper. The English leave the merchandise that they cannot sell straight away with their hosts in Bordeaux, still for sale, and the hosts make a great profit out of it when they sell it on to the traders from the other places mentioned above ... if it were not for this trade with England, Bordeaux would not be Bordeaux.[31]

Girard goes on to say that, because there had been such affinity with the English in the past, measures had to be taken (in 1465) to defend the city and the port from their return. That is for us to consider later on. But for the moment, we ought to note that, even in its diminished state even eleven years after the second conquest of 1453 (if Girard is to be believed: he writes in the present tense), Bordeaux had enormous prosperity.

It was certainly prosperous in 1451 on the eve of the first conquest, still profiting from the truce between England and France that lasted from 1445 with Henry VI's marriage to Marguerite of Anjou until 1449 and the Fougères incident. Prosperity and viable government were both realities. Nevertheless, the *jurats* had lived through all the tribulations of the years before the truce and were reading the writing on the wall. Dunois had conquered Normandy after all, and he had taken the great fortress of Fronsac from its English captain, John Strangways, who had been there with a native English garrison since 1438,[32] and he was unable to resist Jean Bureau's advanced weaponry. Unless an English force were to come to their rescue, they had to make provision for themselves in a profitable surrender.

* * *

It was still hoped that Henry VI's government would send armed support against the incursions of Dunois. Rumours of an English fleet on its way to Bordeaux or Bayonne circulated. Sir Richard Woodville, the first Earl Rivers and future father-in-law of King Edward IV, was appointed seneschal of Guyenne on 18 October 1450, and a fleet expedition had been planned before then, but preparations were frustrated by financial incapacity leading to frequent postponements[33] of an army being embarked at the same time as Dunois was making his triumphant inroads. By the time Strangways surrendered Fronsac on 5 June, Rivers had not set sail, and he did not.[34] The nearly contemporary John Benet's *Chronicle* made a bleak announcement in retrospect:

> And the king ordered Lord Rivers with 4,000 men to resist the King of France at Bordeaux. They lay near Plymouth for a year for default of wages, and achieved nothing. And so on 3 July the city of Bordeaux was lost, and then all Gascony ...[35]

It was the captal de Buch who made the first positive response to Dunois's invitation to negotiate a peace settlement. He was 'nearly a king in Aquitaine: his family (the Graillys), his alliances, the timbre of his character and services already rendered made appropriate the trust which the Bordelais had in him.'[36] Henry VI had made him a knight of the Garter. As long ago as 1420, he had been proxy for Henry V's marriage to Charles VI's daughter Catherine of France, the present king's sister. He had his own marriage ties with the French royal family through his wife, Marguerite d'Albret. In the 1420s, he had carried out actions against towns that had rebelled for France against English Gascony: Pyrnormand, Montguyon and Lamothe-Montravel. During the French invasion of 1442, he had fought alongside Sir Edward Hull at Saint-Loube. He was seventy in 1451, and lived in Bordeaux, like his ancestors, on the site of the Roman prefect's palace, Le Puy-Paulin. His disputes with the *jurade* about some grazing land in 1447 had been forgotten by 1451.[37] His older brother's son was Gaston IV of Foix who had professed loyalty to Charles VII and was still besieging Dax for a good while after Fronsac had surrendered to Dunois. Since he was known to leaders on both sides, he was the best man to make approaches to Dunois with proposals drawn up by the *jurade*. He reported back to the Bordeaux leaders, the English officials – Huntingdon and Shorthouse – and the Three Estates of Gascony with Dunois's reactions.

Still hoping against hope that help would come from England, the leaders in Bordeaux drew the negotiations out for as long as they could. When the French negotiators complained, they replied that they had their oath to Henry VI to consider. Charles VII had already nominated his trusty and well-beloved artillery commander, Jean Bureau, to replace Gadifer Shorthouse as Mayor of Bordeaux after it had capitulated, and it was he who acted as Dunois's agent in the negotiations, entering and leaving the town every day with a safe-conduct like a modern commuter to the Gare Saint-Jean. Dunois showed some good will – in his sovereign lord's interest – and accepted some of the proposals.

The Gascon delegation to negotiate with Bureau was made up of Archbishop Berland, Bernard Angevin who was a bourgeois ennobled by Henry VI, Jean de Lalande, lord of La Brède, the captal de Buch's son-in-law, Gaillard du Durfort, lord of Blanquefort who had direct experience of French military efficiency, Guillaume Androu, lord of Lansac, and Bertrand de Montferrand, appointed by the Three Estates of Bordeaux to represent them and make decisions on their authority. They chose the Archbishop as their spokesman.[38]

Dunois appointed Poton de Xaintrailles, a Gascon soldier loyal to Charles VII for thirty years, Jean Bureau, and a judge from Mont de Marsan in the Landes, Ogier Brequit, as the French negotiators. They came to meetings under safe-conduct and were hospitably received by the Bordeaux authorities.[39] They had to refer back to Charles VII himself, who was still seventy miles away at Saint-Jean d'Angély, at every stage, while the Bordeaux plenipotentiaries made their decisions collectively where they were. After two days of exchanges, a draft treaty of twenty-six articles was ready to be placed before the French king for him to ratify. No English troops had appeared. Pey Berland and his team had no choice, encircled as they were by armies ready to move in on them. They were making the best of a bad situation while Charles VII was offering a certain level of magnanimity, at least on the surface. The Gascon Ribadieu makes the comment that the treaty could have been considered a triumph for the Bordelais diplomats.[40]

They were given until 23 June to wait for an English relieving force to arrive at which date they must surrender if it had not. Convention called this 'the day of battle', and it was extended from 15 June for the goddaughter Fronsac as well – although the English garrison there had already surrendered. However, Charles VII maintained the possibility of tightening the noose on Bordeaux's neck by not extending the date for the surrender of Saint-Macaire, Rions or Castillon beyond 13 June. The preamble to the treaty made all that clear.

If no hypothetical English relief force were to appear, the towns of Guyenne agreed that they would take an oath of fidelity to Charles VII in perpetuity. What came next was described by Ribadieu as 'the Gascons' revenge': clauses in which the king was to offer a series of concessions in exchange for submission. He would swear in his turn, to maintain the bourgeois traders and the artisans of Bordeaux in their freedoms, privileges, liberties, statute laws, customs, observances and wages. If the king could not make time to participate in a solemn entrance in person, as he had done at Rouen when Normandy surrendered, Dunois would take the oath on his behalf and ratify the treaty in Bordeaux.

In addition, if residents of Bordeaux or of other towns in Guyenne should decide not to accept French rule, they could leave for wherever they might wish, and take their stock in trade, their capital, their gold, their ships 'and everything whatever'. This concession would apply for six months during which time they would qualify for safe-conducts. If they did decide to go, their lands would be transferred to their close relatives and were not to be confiscated by the French crown. These terms would also apply to ambassadors who had already gone to England if that was their desire.[41] It appeared that a great many would be likely to leave, and not only rich people. Charles VII would give amnesty even to criminals. He seemed to be required to sign everything with his eyes closed, as it were, while the defeated party were meticulous in their demands. They were introducing articles by means of which to recover their fortunes.

However, such an idea ignores the formula adopted by the king and Dunois for the towns already subjugated. Bordeaux did not seem to have qualified for any special treatment when Charles VII ratified the treaty. Even so, nobles and clergy who remained in the conquered territory would retain their lands, houses, lordships and castles: in fact, all they had ever received from the king/duke.[42] The nobles were not to be required to pay any land tax, the only demands on them being the taxes they had always paid in the past. As for the tradesmen, they were still allowed to travel by the rivers or on land with nothing to pay by way of additional charges either to the King of France or to the nobles through whose lordships they passed. All this meant that the Gascons would find the change of regime acceptable. Charles VII had been in no way duped.

The Bordelais already had a university modelled on that of Toulouse – the achievement of Pey Berland just previously – and they now were to have a *Parlement*, a sovereign court of justice, also like Toulouse, which would be a source of profit and prestige. The Gascons were not to be liable for military service according to this treaty. For the moment, the mayor, his deputy and other officials were prisoners, but they were to be released (and in the case of Gadifer Shorthouse, replaced) once the treaty was ratified.[43] The king would entrust the minting of money at Bordeaux to those who had the right to do so beforehand.[44] The king's soldiers, present for the defence of the province, were not to be billeted on the citizens but lodged in hostelries at national expense.[45] All royal officials were bound not to abuse their responsibilities for profit at the expense of the citizens, and to maintain the privileges of Bordeaux.[46] Moreover, the procurator was forbidden to make any exactions without the citizens' consent or giving them previous notice.[47] This was the final clause, but a general amnesty was to be added even for crimes. Refusing to take the oath to the King of France was not to be regarded as a crime during the first six months of the treaty's operation. Ribadieu says that Charles VII was ready in June 1451 to give privileges to Gascony which other provinces in his kingdom did not have.

All these terms received the recorded agreement of the representatives of Bordeaux who had negotiated for them. They promised 'on their bodies and their honour' to keep strictly to the treaty which they had received by letters patent from the king.[48]

* * *

An account of Dunois's entry into Bordeaux is reserved for the next chapter because of its context. With the capitulation of the capital of Aquitaine, there was only one town, Bayonne, left loyal to Henry VI, and armed resistance was organized there against Dunois and Foix, who, after a few days rest and recreation for their troops, went south to complete their task.

An important source for the story of the conquest of Bayonne ought to have been that of Jules Balasque who was writing a very comprehensive narrative of events there from its origins until 1451. He had reached 1356, but his death intervened in 1872, and the archivist of the town, E. Deleurens, was persuaded by friends to conclude the work with a presentation of notes already prepared by M. Balasque, which had no connected sequence. Nevertheless, there were certain important indications given in them about how Bayonne became incorporated into the new France.

Like Bordeaux, Bayonne had particularly close ties with England. From Henry III's time, the residents of the town had the right to take possession of any ships wrecked off their shores, and to the prosperity from the fair held there every year at Michaelmas. Edward II guaranteed their liberties by renewing their reunion with the English crown. Edward III also ratified their liberties and immunities and gave as good prices for their wines as for those from the Garonne Valley, together with favourable tax exemptions. Henry VI's lieutenants had made the ties closer by allowing the municipality to impose charges on trade goods entering and leaving Bayonne. They could even mint their own coinage at the same weight and value as at Bordeaux and other towns in the duchy. It was worth their while to remain in the English orbit and this justified their resistance to the Valois encroachments when they came.[49] The period of Sir Thomas Burton's ten-year mayoral mandate was one of confidence. The profits of wreckage were used on improving the town's fortifications.[50] Like other towns in 1438, they had to cope with the threats and ravages of Rodrigo de Villandrando, known to have French lords encouraging him. Other towns made truces with him, which Henry VI forbade them to do.[51] Another period of calm followed, with Philip Chetwynd as the English mayor, and Thomas Rampston seneschal of Guyenne, until he was discredited by his capture in 1442 that caused such discomfiture in Bordeaux. On 20 October 1442, Archbishop Pey Berland, Rampston, Chetwynd, and the lord of Gramont, were authorized to issue pardons to those who had sided with Charles VII when he took Dax.[52] Repairs to the fortifications of the chateau were authorized, paid for by the salt tax, and Jean de Foix, Earl of Kendal, was granted possession of Mauléon Castle by the Duke of Suffolk, his father-in-law,[53] to strengthen the Anglo-Gascon presence.[54] But at the same time as the Anglo-French truce was broken in March 1449, it was in the hands of Luis de Beaumont, Baron of Guiche, constable of Navarre, and, when it was attacked by Gaston IV, Count of Foix, he handed it over to him.[55] So, when Charles VII ordered his four armies to advance into Guyenne, Foix – together with Albret, Orval and Tartas, and the Scottish captain Robin Petit-Loup – Foix was in a good position to advance towards Dax and lay siege to it.[56]

Guiche, which served as the port for Bayonne twelve miles away from it, was also attacked on Gaston de Foix's orders, and Luis de Beaumont, John Astley – the English mayor of Bayonne – and George Swyllington went to relieve the place with 4,000 men; 1,200 of the men were killed or taken prisoner, including Swyllington himself and 'almost all of his company of sixty lances.' Guiche was taken, but Foix did not advance any further. In January 1450 he went home.[57]

Before Beaumont's party had set out for Guiche, 'the horizon became darker and darker.' A party was formed in December 1449 to resist the invaders, and the residents of Bayonne took an oath of fidelity to Henry

VI on the sacred host and Saint-Léon's body.[58] Seven months later, on 8 July 1450, Foix was back in Dax, and the town and all the Landes area capitulated to him in exchange for the maintenance of their ancient freedoms. This was soon confirmed by letters patent from the king, signed at Taillebourg.[59]

When he left Bordeaux, Dunois made his way towards the River Adour with his artillery to take possession of the last Anglo-Gascon bastion at Bayonne. His letters of conciliation, carried by the Berry herald, were rejected by the Bayonnais, who, as the Bordelais had done, were hoping against hope for help from England. Jean de Beaumont, Prior of St. John of Jerusalem, the constable of Navarre's brother, brought men at arms into Bayonne to defend it and waited for Dunois to arrive.[60]

Dunois ordered an attack on the suburbs of Bayonne on 7 August 1451.[61] Foix, Chabannes, Xaintrailles, and Gaspard Bureau, *maître d'artillerie*, had joined him. Foix had command of the advance guard. The English troops went out to meet the attackers but soon withdrew again behind their boulevard when the *culeuvrines*, the *serpentines* and the *ribeaudequins* opened fire.[62] The French took the boulevard and laid siege to the fort in the Saint-Léon suburb to the south. There were serious mining undertakings by the sappers and accompanying salvoes from the mortars and cannon. Seeing they could not keep the fort, the English set fire to it, but sixty of them lost their lives during the retreat. Foix established himself in the Augustinian Abbey, saved from the flames, while Albret, Tartas, and Penthièvre took the Saint-Esprit bridge on the north side of the town. The French troops were engaged for fifteen days in this operation against strong English resistance. In the end the deciding factor was the arrival in the Adour of a squadron of twelve Biscayan warships,[63] carrying men and provisions, ordered by Foix to sustain the attackers.[64]

Then came supernatural aid in natural form. Let Guillaume Leseur, the count of Foix's enthusiastic contemporary, tell what was seen, based on recollections of people who were there:

> On a Friday morning [20 August], by the will and pleasure of our Lord, in their view [i.e., of the besieged] and of the French, there appeared in the sky, in full daylight, the form of a great white cross

right over the middle of the town. Moved by this great sign, they recognized their inadequacy and, seeing their ruin and imminent peril and the danger they were in, besought and humbly begged Monsieur the Count of Foix and Monsieur the Count of Dunois … for negotiations so as to come to an arrangement.[65]

Dunois offered the churchmen, nobles and people of Bayonne a similar treaty to the one that Bordeaux had received in June, but Jean de Beaumont, with his company, was to be held prisoner 'at the will and mercy of King Charles'.[66] The triumphal entries followed, and Dunois left to report what had happened to the king at Taillebourg, while Foix went to Orthez and Mont de Marsan to get his breath back before he made his own way there.[67]

So all Gascony was incorporated into Charles VII's kingdom. He was not only 'Charles the Victorious;' he was 'Charles the well-served.'

*   *   *

Albeit with certain significant exceptions on a global scale, we are all secularists now; but for Frenchmen living in the middle of the fifteenth century, a sign in the sky in the form of the white cross of St. Michael the Archangel that had been adopted as Charles VII's emblem was unquestionably an indication of the favour of Almighty God toward his victory as far as the Pyrenees. Helen Castor in her wonderful appraisal of Joan of Arc has drawn attention to what Henry Beaufort, bishop of Winchester, who was also Chancellor of England, said in his address at the opening of the parliament that assembled in March 1416, not quite six months after Agincourt. God had 'spoken' in favour of the English cause in the war with France three times already: in the naval battle at Sluys in 1340, at Poitiers in 1356 when even the French king was taken prisoner, and then, finally, at Agincourt.[68] Like the Bellman in Lewis Carroll's ballad 'The Hunting of the Snark', God could have said, 'What I tell you three times is true!'

Dunois understood that God had spoken again in the sign in the sky over Bayonne in 1451. There were some Englishmen – and some of their Gascon associates – who didn't know when they were beaten, as we shall

The Duchy of Guyenne

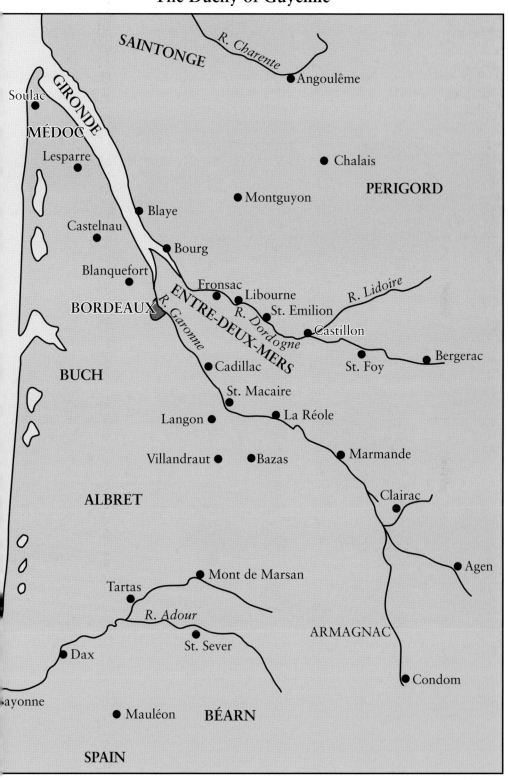

1. Principal towns, localities and rivers in Gascony in 1399. The low-lying landscape is dominated by the river system.

2. The coronation of Henry V from the king's chantry chapel in Westminster Abbey representing the mystical nature of kingship.

3. The Founder's Statue © the Provost and Fellows of Eton College portraying Henry VI at his most royal.

4. The Adoration of the Magi showing a kindly Charles VII offering his triumphs to the Christ-Child.

5. Pey Berland's Tower and St Andrew's Cathedral in Bordeaux.

6. The castle of Quatre-Sols at La Reole besieged by by Charles VII in 1442.

7. The castle of Blanquefort, property of Gaillard de Dufort, defended against the count of Clermont and focus of the Bordeaux militia's defeat in 1450.

Calais to Picquigny 1475

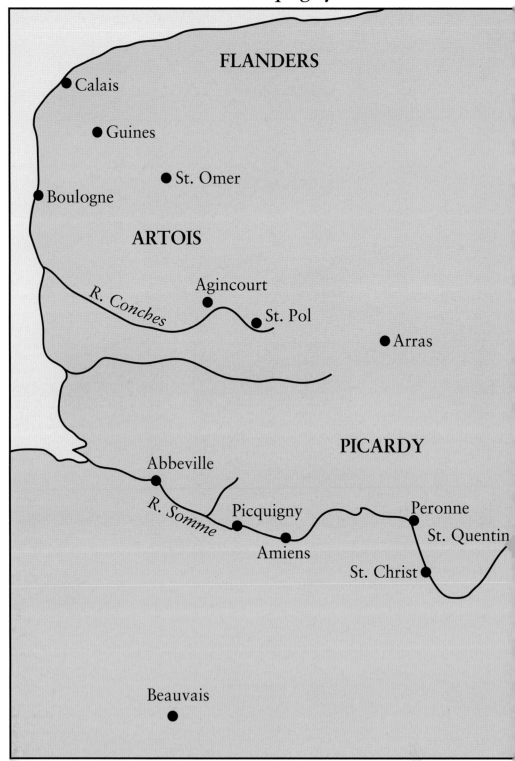

8. Edward IV's invasion route to Reims for his intended French coronation.

see in the next chapter, but it is always the really last word that counts. It had to be said louder after the siege of Bordeaux in October 1453; but, at the moment when the French generals toasted each other and their victorious king at Taillebourg in Bordeaux 1450 vintage, there was no doubt about the justice of the French victory. Nowadays aircrafts' contrails are seen criss-crossing the sky over south-west France. There were no explanations of this kind possible for Dunois and his staff.

Chapter Six

The Anglo-Gascons Take Back Control

Charles VII's government assumed power in Bordeaux in a carefully prepared piece of political theatre beginning in the early morning of 23 June as agreed. The Herald of Bordeaux stood on the ramparts to call for help from the English, greeted, as expected, by thunderclaps of silence. The ceremonial could have begun then, but the entry of Dunois's forces (with some uncontrollable elements deliberately kept back at a safe distance) did not take place until a week later. The cathedral chapter's registers record that *Civitas Burdegale est regni Franciae* on 29 June. The day after, Dunois in his white armour assembled the procession at the Chartrons Gate where he received the keys presented to him by the *jurats*, and the parade filed into the city led by the archers. After the captains and their troops came a white palfrey led without a rider carrying the royal seal to represent the king's presence. Archbishop Juvenal des Ursins of Reims, the Chancellor of France, followed immediately behind. Then came Dunois and his subordinate generals. They all made their way to Saint-Andrew's Cathedral to be met by Archbishop Pey Berland in the splendour of his cope and mitre and with his archiepiscopal cross carried before him.[1] The fact of his wearing a penitent's hair shirt next to his skin was his own secret until his final days. He washed it himself in private.[2]

Olivier de Coëtivy, Seigneur of Taillebourg, the newly appointed seneschal of Guyenne, drew attention to himself with a scene of his own in this spectacle. All the French dignitaries who processed into the cathedral nave followed the example of Dunois in swearing a solemn oath on the Gospels held out for them by Pey Berland to uphold the particular customs of Guyenne even though it had become a province of France. Not so the new seneschal: he refused to speak in the *occitan* language of Bordeaux and took his oath in French with no mention of the freedoms, privileges and customs at all. Moreover, the Chancellor of France (the other archbishop present) ordered all who were present to obey the seneschal as they would the king in person.[3]

Since the previous invasion inland by way of the River Adour had stopped short of Bayonne, and its inhabitants remained loyal to the King of England, Dunois left the Château d'Ombrière within a few days to conduct a campaign against them. The military governor of Guyenne, the Count of Clermont, and the new mayor, Jean Bureau, also left for royal service elsewhere. Coëtivy was left in complete charge with only a small garrison to support him.[4]

It is worth our while to pause for a moment to take note of Olivier de Coëtivy since he has a considerable part to play in the story of the consolidation of French royal power in Guyenne. The Coëtivy family originated in Brittany. During the first part of the fifteenth century, there were four brothers, three of whom became prominent in the entourage of Charles VII, introduced into his court by their uncle, Tanguy du Châtel, whose association with Charles when he was the rejected Dauphin we have already seen. The oldest was Prégent de Coëtivy, Admiral of France, who had been instrumental in the suppression of the rebellion against Charles VII by feudal magnates known as the *Praguerie* in 1440 and rewarded with the great castle and lordship of Taillebourg in the Saintonge, which dominated a major stretch of the River Charente, for ousting Maurice Plusquelec and his brother who had sided with the rebels. He was also given the wardship of the three young daughters born to the king by his mistress Agnès Sorel, dame de Beauté. Prégent was killed by a stray cannon ball during the siege of Cherbourg in 1450, and his younger brother Olivier, after a dispute with Prégent's widow, inherited the castle and the wardships. The third brother, Alain, became a cardinal and papal legate whom we shall meet in Bordeaux later on, and the fourth, Christophe, was a military man who did not share the prominence of his brothers. Olivier had fought under the command of Charles d'Albret at Saint-Sever and Dax in 1442 and was knighted for his bravery on the battlefield of Formigny in 1450.

Being himself at Taillebourg to direct the initial stages of Dunois's campaign, Charles VII had appointed Olivier as seneschal of Guyenne, ready to take office after the expected victory. Olivier responded to the trust placed in him by unwavering loyalty to the Valois king. Once in command of Bordeaux, he alienated the commercial classes there and the nobles who held lands round about. He had not taken any oath to maintain their liberties and set about ignoring them. With the support of Jean de Fou, Bureau's assistant mayor, and the lord of Messignac, the seneschal began to impose a French monarchical style of government and taxation, regardless of the treaty ratified by the king.[5] This was abhorrent to the members of the *jurade*, since it flew in the face of the oaths that his superiors had made in the Cathedral. They realized what they had lost in the system accepted by the English kings/dukes who appointed seneschals, constables and mayors but left them as autonomous administrators while contributing to their prosperity by buying their wines.

The citizens were disgruntled. After a year, in July 1452, a delegation was sent to Charles VII, finding his itinerant court once more at Bourges. They approached him direct for a redress of their grievances, taking with them the letters with the great seal attached in which he had undertaken to maintain their privileges only a year before. They protested that when they were under English domination they were exempt from land tax, and they never had soldiers billeted on them. They would know how to defend themselves if they were to be attacked in future. After consulting his council, the king replied that the defence of Guyenne required sacrifices and he was not able to exempt them from payment of taxes. Troops were necessary – he meant French troops, not Gascon ones – to assure the defence of the province and the taxes imposed by the seneschal were meant to pay their wages in the spirit of the ordinance of 1445. The Estates-General ought to be called to regularize the situation. According to the chronicler Thomas Basin, cited by Ribadieu, the king had good reason to fear the 'frauds and machinations of the English in Aquitaine', who were deprived of the wines and were not able to sell their cloth on to the Spaniards as they had been accustomed to do.[6]

Indeed, as the Gascon Rolls clearly indicate, Henry VI's government gave the appearance of being in a state of denial about the defeat and carried on making grants and appointments in Gascony as if nothing had happened.[7] On 20 October, the captal de Buch was made captain of the town and castle of Bazas and in January 1452 he was given other lordships. On 18 February, Robert of Rokeley was confirmed as castellan of Lesparre, despite the desire of Pierre de Montferrand to have his fortress back now that the Earl of Huntingdon no longer needed it.

When their deputation returned from Bourges, they expressed more vociferous indignation. The situation was made worse when Clermont, the military governor, ordered – from his absence – the Three Estates to put all the Guyenne fortresses on a war footing at the first signal he might give, as was required of any province of the kingdom.[8]

What happened next is not entirely clear. Jean Chartier, monk of Saint Denis, Charles VII's official chronicler, claimed that, at the beginning of September 1452, certain Gascon nobles, following the initiative of Pierre de Montferrand, 'who could be compared to Judas' for breaking their oath to Charles VII along with some of the *jurats*, had found a way of sailing to England under false colours, and, once there, had 'arranged and plotted great treason' in re-affirming their allegiance to the English 'should they desire to return'.[9] Henry VI and his council had agreed to send John Talbot, Earl of Shrewsbury, to the Bordelais country with a relief expedition in October.[10]

There was another chronicler, writing twenty years after the events in question, Thomas Basin who, as Bishop of Lisieux, had been very supportive towards Charles VII but was exiled from court when Louis XI reversed his father's policies at his accession in 1461. Basin presents a slightly different account of what happened, asserting that the Gascons and people of Bordeaux sent a delegation – the members of which are not named – to tell the English that, were they to return, they would be admitted and welcomed back.[11]

The present-day English historian Malcolm Vale has claimed that Basin's assertion 'may well be fictitious',[12] pointing out that his French counterparts in the nineteenth century onwards, like Henri Ribadieu,[13] Gaston du Fresne de Beaucourt,[14] Robert Boutruche,[15] and Yves Renouard[16] have specified the personnel of the delegation as Jean Chartier had: Pierre de Montferrand, soudic de La Trau, Gaston de Grailly, captal de Buch, and his son Jean, who was married to Margaret de la Pole, and had been the Earl of Kendal (*Candale* in Gascon) since 1446. These accounts assert that this delegation urged Henry VI's council to send John Talbot's expedition off to take back control of Gascony.

Pierre de Montferrand was certainly an Anglophile, married to Mary, the Duke of Bedford's natural daughter. As such, he had led the naval battle in the Gironde before Blaye the year before against the French and Breton fleet from La Rochelle and, defeated, had been treated graciously when he took his oath to Charles VII. He had gone to Bordeaux after that and was still there when Talbot reached the city.[17] Furthermore, Gaston and Jean de Grailly were not present when Dunois made his triumphant entry into Bordeaux. Since they were both Knights of the Garter they were not able to swear the oath to Charles VII and went instead to the Kingdom of Aragon. They kept faith with Henry VI but took no part in any delegation to him in 1452. Kendal did go and live in England, but not until after 1453.[18]

There was, however, a Gascon from Bordeaux who had had access to the English court since 1449. This was Pey de Tasta (Pierre de Tastar), Dean of the Collegiate Church of Saint-Seurin (Severin), situated outside the city walls. He had been granted the revenues of several English parishes and cathedral prebends to support his status as a diplomat, and he was in a position to influence discussion in the royal council of which he was a member and frequently present at its meetings.[19] He was still active in this capacity even after the Yorkists had ousted the Lancastrian party – until his death in 1467.[20]

How, then, did Talbot's expedition to recover Gascony come about?

In the opening months of 1452, Richard, Duke of York was beginning to assert himself against the Lancastrian government. He had already accused the Duke of Somerset of treason for not having defended Rouen vigorously enough in 1450. John Talbot had been held hostage there by the French conqueror, and Charles VII kept him prisoner until mid-1450, by which time the conquest of Normandy was complete. Then he released him to make a pilgrimage to Rome as he had told him that was his only wish.

Upon his return to England afterwards, Talbot may have looked forward to a measure of retirement, being over sixty, but he was required to deal with a dispute that had arisen between him and Lord Berkeley over an inheritance, and to defend his position at the king's court at a time when the dispute between York and Somerset was becoming more and more intense. He maintained his connection with Somerset, and received from him, along with his son Lord de Lisle, the governorship of Portsmouth. He was also associated with York, but, when York tried to replace Somerset as the king's chief adviser in February 1452,[21] Talbot stood by the king and Somerset and was required to arbitrate between the two factions.[22]

Charles VII, meanwhile, was making plans to unify his kingdom further by taking Calais.[23] In March 1452, Talbot was appointed to command a fleet for use against a French attack there and fend off possible raids on English coastal towns. Recruiting measures were well in hand when Charles VII was known to have decided not to go for Calais after all. Talbot was then appointed to punish rebels who were still active in the wake of Jack Cade,[24] maintaining the unrest expressed in his rebellion in south-eastern England after the loss of Normandy.

Then, suddenly, preparations against France were restarted for reasons that are not clear. An aggressive action being planned can be seen in Talbot's commission issued on 6 July for command of 'an army for the keeping of the sea in which journey he must achieve much good'.[25]

It could be speculated that Dean Pierre de Tastar's lobbying in the English king's council had influenced the decision to give Talbot full administrative and military power and authority as Henry VI's lieutenant in Gascony on 2 September 1452.[26] The details of conditions and personnel in the Bordelais shown in the sixteen clauses of the long document suggests that someone who knew the territory well had been consulted, but, of course, although it would be simple to suggest that it had been Tastar, there were many ways besides for the council to have gathered such information.

The French commanders expected Talbot to disembark in Normandy, which explains their lack of preparation when he landed his troops unopposed near Soulac on the northern tip of the Médoc peninsula on 17 October. His march from the Atlantic coast to Bordeaux took only six days and met with no resistance. The late eighteenth century Bordelais antiquarian, Abbé Jacques Baurein, found an oral tradition still current in the Médoc that held Talbot's troops accountable for the widespread destruction of farmsteads and religious buildings there, when in reality the damage was done a year later by French soldiers led by Clermont, Foix and Albret in reprisal for the rebellion in the Bordelais. Elsewhere,

Baurein reports that, even after 300 years, '*le roi Talbot*' was still invoked as a bogeyman figure with whom mothers threatened their badly-behaved children.[27]

How was it possible for John Talbot, Earl of Shrewsbury, to re-establish English domination in Bordeaux and the areas surrounding it so easily? His rapid passage across the Médoc can be explained by the fact that the lordships inland from Soulac had, before the French conquest, been held by those most sympathetic to an English return. Pierre de Montferrand had not long ago been lord of Lesparre, just south of Soulac. Even with only his poor lordship in the Landes called La Trau, he still felt part of the Bordelais Anglo-Gascon establishment, despite the oath to Charles VII that he had been compelled to take after his defeat at Blaye. Similarly, Gaillard de Durfort lord of Blanquefort, just north of Bordeaux, remained loyal to his Anglo-Gascon past. Both of these nobles would be included in the list of twenty names certified by Clermont, the lieutenant-governor of Guyenne issued in October 1453, after the second conquest, as 'the most blameworthy of rebellion' in Bordeaux whom the king of France had banished.[28] Perhaps Talbot's easy passage through these territories can be explained by local constant loyalty to their recently dispossessed *seigneurs*. The people between the Atlantic and Bordeaux were used to English domination and did not hinder its re-establishment.

Resentment among the residents of Bordeaux against Seneschal Olivier de Coêtivy's ignoring of their customs and privileges need not have produced a general uprising against French rule, but there was a conspiracy instigated by Pierre de Montferrand centred on a religious fraternity in the parish of Saint-Michel near the Garonne waterfront to admit Talbot when he should arrive. This was confirmed by information gained afterwards under torture by French judges from one of Mayor Shorthouse's former sergeants,[29] and an account provided by someone, probably a priest, implicating Pey de Tasta, about the breaking down of the Beyssac Gate to let Talbot's troops in.

They overpowered the limited French garrison quickly in a surprise attack on the night of 22–23 October 1452.[30] By the morning, Talbot had established his command post, there had been minimal resistance, and in the following days he imposed his rule in the suburbs of Bordeaux, the Médoc and the Entre-Deux-Mers. By Christmas, he had taken the towns in these areas. The conspiracy had allowed a comparatively simple takeover, but those who had planned it very soon faced a new problem.

Talbot's regime was harsher than Coëtivy's had promised to be. He imposed new taxes to pay his troops who behaved like an occupying force rather than as the liberators it was hoped they would be. Then, despite the great financial slump which was gaining in intensity,[31] the spring of 1453 saw the arrival of substantial reinforcements under the command of Talbot's son by his second marriage, recently created Viscount Lisle. The Duke of Somerset had consolidated his power somewhat in Henry VI's court and in the royal council, after the news of Talbot's success had reached Westminster.

The mandate for the payment of Lisle's troops was issued as early as 30 January. By this, Lisle's salary was fixed at six shillings a day, while bannerets were to receive four shillings, knights two shillings, and they were themselves responsible for providing their own horses, weaponry and armour. Spearmen were to receive twelve pence, and archers six, 'with rewards accustomed'. A commission for taking ships under the king's orders was issued on 19 July and mandates followed for the requisitioning of ships to transport these reinforcements to the mayors of Plymouth and Dartmouth, to the bailliff of Fowey, and to the mayor and sheriff of Bristol on 17 August. There had already been a mandate issued for the shipping of 1,000 quarters of wheat for the provisioning of Bordeaux issued to Sir Thomas Browne on 1 August, and it is interesting to note that one of the signatures on it was that of the Bordelais Pey Tasta, dean of of Saint-Seurin, alongside that of the treasurer and Speaker Thorpe of the House of Commons.[32]

'The shame of 1450 had been effaced.'[33] The 1453 Parliament[34] produced more than 22,450 pounds in a grant to pay for Lisle's troops and transport.[35] Twenty-six ships from England arrived in Bordeaux with provisions for them.[36] This force re-took the fortress of Fronsac, still regarded as the key to the security of the Bordelais.

This was, for the moment a success story, dependent upon Somerset's political re-establishment within the king's council, but there lurked behind it a dire need for promised loans to be translated into hard cash. On 3 August 1453, a letter sent in the king's name to the abbot of Bermondsey, reminding him that at the time when Lisle, Moleyns,

Camoys and others were sent 'for the succour and relief of our duchy,' he had promised to make a loan of forty pounds, but it had not yet been paid into the treasury, 'whereof we marvel'. He is asked to pay it in immediately against an undertaking to repay it once the tax guaranteed by parliament had been received 'at midsummer next coming'. A threat follows that if he does not cough up immediately, the abbot will have to come to Westminster to explain himself and face 'our great displeasure'. The day after, requests for new loans were dispatched to nine other individuals, including a canon of St.Paul's Cathedral, William Brewster, the dean of the Chapel Royal, William Say, the abbot of Christchurch in London, Sir Thomas Tyrelle, and an alderman of the city of London, Nicholas Wyfold, expressng 'great necessity' and the need for urgency, and adding the same threat that had been offered to the abbot of Bermondsey. So there was need for the council to extract what can only be seen as forced loans in the present circumstances. Three weeks later, letters went to the abbot of 'Saint Osyes in Essex' and to the prior of St. Botolph in Colchester demanding pettifogging sums of twenty pounds from each that had been promised but not yet paid, once more threatening royal displeasure if the money was not provided against an assurance that it would be repaid out of an expected grant by the clergy in the next Canterbury convocation. The same assurance of repayment out of future tithe receipts from the same convocation was offered to the mayor and fellowship of the Calais Staple for a loan of seven thousand pounds that that they had already paid was made on 11 July 1454, that is, a good while after Bordeaux had been lost.[37]

*　*　*

From May 1453 onwards, Charles VII's plans for a second conquest of Guyenne began to take effect. The expense of providing for the occupation of the newly re-acquired Normandy coupled with the necessary re-conquest of Guyenne was going to be enormous. The *compagnies d'ordonnance* had to be paid for out of funds in the royal treasury. There was no time for the necessary delays to allow the normal processes of taxation. Liquid capital was needed yesterday. Charles VII had recourse to his money-bags, his *argentier*, Jacques Coeur.

It is worth pausing to examine this man's career. He was the son of a furrier (*pelletier marchand*) in Bourges and he stood out from his contemporaries which allowed him a reputation for financial and commercial acumen during his lifetime. The chronicler Thomas Basin praised him effusively. Coeur equipped fleets for trade in cloth between Alexandria, Africa and the Orient, using the river Rhone to bring expensive silk cloth and perfumes into France. He grew up among furriers at the court of Jean de Berry, then of the Dauphin Charles at Bourges, setting up a money workshop (*atelier monetaire*) in the town in 1427. He took part in financing Joan of Arc's army. His next move was to become *maître des monnaies* in Paris in 1436. Three years later, he was *Grand Argentier* to Charles VII, which means that he was responsible for the purchase by the king's account of all provisions needed for the court, the kind of career that had been open to talent since the time of Philippe le Bel in the early fourteenth century.

The task of a royal moneyer involved being a purveyor of luxury goods on very favourable terms. He bought in the king's name and sold in his own or by using 'straw men'. In Jacques Coeur's case, because of his close association with the king, and the king's need for finance for his actions in Normandy and Aquitaine, the moneyer acquired a political rôle as well. He was put in charge of raising taxes in Languedoc, before the invasion of Guyenne began, as well as being supervisor of the salt tax there. He was ambassador to Genoa in 1446 and involved in the various meetings taking place to resolve the remaining issues left by the ending of the Great Schism in the western Church thirty years before.[38] Politics gave an extra dimension to what he did as a financier, which means that he was able to circumvent the usual Italian intermediaries when he made his contacts in the Orient.

He owned a fleet of four galleys which plied Mediterranean routes to provide the royal court with spices. Because he had become essential to the consolidation of the king's position at the head of French society, Charles VII ennobled him in 1441 after the defeat of the *Praguerie* with lordships confiscated from disgraced nobles like Georges de La Tremouille or the Duke of Bourbon in his native Berry, Poitou, the Bourbonnais and the Nivernais. By virtue of this he became a courtier and set up a sort of pawnbroker's shop to supply the nobility and their ladies with fine clothes and expensive plate armour as well as ready cash. He set up a business at Tours, but he always accompanied the king on his progresses. One of his sons became archbishop of Bourges at the age of twenty-six, and another married Isabelle Bureau, whose father had also been ennobled for his services as an essential artilleryman.[39] He also set up offices in Italian cities and he profited from mineral deposits in the Lyonnais and the Beaujolais. His success as a *parvenu* naturally incited jealousy at court and he was accused of corruption. In early 1452 this goose was a convenient provider of all the golden eggs that the king needed. The king had already taken a great deal of finance from him for the maintenance of ships and galleys and it was Coeur's money that had paid for the first invasion of Guyenne, intended to be re-paid in due course from the treasury of Poitou.

In July 1452, while Charles VII was Olivier de Coëtivy's guest at Taillebourg, Coeur was arrested, ostensibly on suspicion of having poisoned Agnès Sorel who had died in February 1450 (the real cause of her death was the mercury used to treat her illness). After his trial and exile, Coeur's fortune was put up for auction and the king's procurator-general was to conduct an enquiry in the Paris *Parlement* which would keep him occupied until 1457. Charges of minting false money, having commercial relations with the Saracens (which was forbidden by law), forging the king's seal for his own use, and misappropriating the Languedoc revenues were brought against him. He was found guilty of all this on 23 February 1453, but not of having poisoned the king's *maîtresse en titre*. He was to do penance, to buy back a Christian slave from the Saracens whom he was alleged to have sold to them, to repay 10,000 écus to the treasury and to be exiled from France.[40] The palace that he built for himself at Bourges, after the sale of all his movable goods, was left to his birthplace and remains as a monument to his prosperity, suitably adorned with a statue of him in front of it.[41]

So there was to be adequate financial backing for the four army corps that would be ready to invade the Bordelais for a second time. The count of Clermont was appointed as the king's lieutenant-general as well as military governor of Guyenne as he was already. He took up his position on the southern frontier of France. The count of Foix assembled his army in the Béarn to operate alongside Clermont. Marshals of France

Jallongues and Lohéac, Admiral Bueil, Chabannes, Rouault, Penthièvre, and Beaumont, the Seneschal of Poitou, were to recover the length of the Dordogne. The fourth army commanded by the king in person, was held in reserve. Clermont's staff included Charles II of Albret, his son Orval, who had brought terror to the Bordelais in 1450, Poton de Xaintrailles and, among others, Foix's brother Lautrec.[42]

Foix advanced northwards to take Saint-Sever and the Bazadais, and then moved into the Médoc. Clermont began to move towards Bordeaux and received a dispatch from Talbot, dated 21 June 1453, brought by two heralds, to say that he was looking forward to an honourable encounter with the French commanders but one that would not harm the poor people of the province.[43] Clermont and Foix joined forces while Talbot moved to Martignas and hesitated. When he saw the size of his opponents' contingents, he forgot his promise to the *jurade* that he would bring Clermont back as his prisoner and hastily withdrew to Bordeaux.[44] Unable to find provisions all at once for so large a force, Clermont and Foix separated to see what would happen.

Meanwhile, the third army corps took Chalais in the Angoumois which had re-admitted the English. A force under the lord of Anglade went out from Bordeaux to its aid, but soon returned with Rouault's troops in pursuit as far as Gensac, where the chase was called off. From Gensac, on the advice of Jean Bureau, French divisions surrounded Castillon and delegated the conduct of the siege to him and Rouault who took the town and reinforced it with an artillery park nearby where the little river Lidoire joins the Dordogne.[45]

Talbot, well-experienced from nearly thirty years of combat in Normandy, would have preferred not to have marched out of Bordeaux to fight at Castillon. He did not understand the system whereby the towns around were considered as god-daughters (*filleules*) by the *jurade* of Bordeaux and entitled to its help in times of danger. The chronicler Mathieu d'Escouchy asserted that Talbot planned to remain within the walls of Bordeaux, resist attack and then retaliate. But Talbot's chivalric principles were touched by the charge of cowardice made against him and he went out to Castillon against his better judgement.[46] Admiral de Bueil made the reasonable suggestion, however, that Talbot had decided to take on Bureau before he went against larger armies of Clermont and Foix.[47]

Talbot reached Castillon after a day's and a night's march from Bordeaux on 17 July at dawn. He led his vanguard cavalry to take the Saint-Laurence Priory on the northern edge of the town, where he intended to wait for his infantry and artillery to catch up with him. French troops that he had pushed out of the priory rushed to take shelter among Bureau's artillerymen who were only two kilometres away. Talbot let his troops broach the barrels of wine they had found in the priory cellar, and told his chaplain to get things ready for Mass.

At that moment, he was told that the French seemed to be abandoning their artillery emplacement because a cloud of dust was seen rising above it. Talbot accepted the proposition that this signalled withdrawal from conflict on the part of the enemy and gave the order to go off in pursuit without waiting for the main body of his army to arrive.

It was a dry July morning in south-west France and dust was unavoidable as horses were moved away from the guns in anticipation of an engagement. Sir Thomas Everingham, Talbot's standard bearer, returning from reconnaissance, said that there was no sign of withdrawal on the part of Bureau's artillery: on the contrary, 'everything was calm over there; they were behind their palisades, not at all troubled, and very prepared to all appearances to sell their lives dearly.'[48] Everingham advised Talbot to wait until the rest of the Anglo-Gascon army had arrived but Talbot did not accept his observations. He had already been accused of delaying by the citizens of Bordeaux and decided upon precipitate action. He ordered such cavalry as he had with him, as was usual, to dismount and advance towards the French defences. The loyal Everingham was in front with Talbot's banner.

Henri Ribadieu,[49] followed recently by George Minois,[50] relied for their information on the Memoirs of Jacques du Clercq, a contemporary chronicler,[51] to provide accounts of Talbot's comportment on the battlefield. It is helpful to look at that source scrupulously. Talbot was mounted on a 'little palfrey' (de Clercq says *haquenée*) and did not dismount like the others because he was an old man (he seems to have been little more than sixty, though some accounts have him as nearly eighty); he had twenty-four banners unfurled, including Henry VI's standard of St. George, that of the Trinity, and his own. His attack began with great valour. The palfrey was soon a victim to the artillery and fell on top of Talbot, who was wearing no armour apart from his *brigandine*,[52] which was 'a sleeveless jacket' to which 'small, rectangular plates of iron were rivetted' for 'flexible protection'.[53] He was not wearing full plate armour because, when he was held as a hostage at Rouen three years earlier, Charles VII did not hold him to ransom, and even gave him money, in return for which, he promised 'of his own will' never to wear armour against the French king or his people again, and that he would go to Rome as a penitent. As we have seen, once he had returned to England, he was not able to leave his old life behind him and began warfare again.

Talbot was held to have been one of the most valiant among English knights and commanders. His career stretched from the battle of Shrewsbury in 1403, where he fought for Henry IV against the House of Lancaster's opponents, through active service in Ireland and France until this time.[54] He was created a Knight of the Garter in 1424.[55]

As an independent commander, he became conspicuous for his personal valour, but there were also instances of a cruel, even murderous, tendency in him. He ostensibly maintained the ideals of chivalry, one of the main characteristics of which was the faithful keeping of oaths once made: his 'small palfrey', for example, could not have borne his weight if he had been wearing plate armour. When his tomb was opened in 1884, he was found to have a fractured skull.[56] His body was identified by means of a known dental peculiarity and the severity and nature of his wounds testify to his body being unprotected. His brigandine (Beaucourt calls it a *gorgerette*) was brought to Charles VII at La Rochefoucauld by Jacques de Chabannes and the king said, 'God have mercy on this good knight.'[57]

The lords of Montaubau and Hinnaudière with the Duke of Brittany's troops over whom they had command, came down from the heights above the Dordogne to support the French forces. The English survivors of the cannonades turned their backs and were chased away by them, leaving their banners on the ground.[58] Even so, several Englishmen and Gascons escaped to find refuge in the town and castle of Castillon. These included the captal de Buch's son Kendal, Bertrand de Montferrand and the lord of Anglade. Pierre de Montferrand escaped. The next day, the French brought their cannon before the town and more prisoners were taken, including Kendal. In the end, the Anglo-Gascons no longer had an army of any mobility and, since their most daring commander was dead, they could do nothing more than withstand three months of siege in Bordeaux itself.[59]

In his recently published biography of Charles VII, Philippe Contamine based his account of the battle on three immediately contemporary letters. The first is by an unknown person who quotes from another letter from Guy de La Roche, the seneschal of Angoulême which relates how Jacques de Chabannes and Joachim Rouault were assailed near the artillery park by Talbot's impetuous advance to place his banners in front of the cannon. Gerard de Samain, an experienced gunner, gave the order to fire and at each shot five or six of the English fell and the rest drew back. The French troops rushed out of the gun emplacement on foot and on horseback to make straight for Talbot himself. He was thrown to the ground, one of the archers slashed at his throat and *lui bailla une epée parmi le fondement*. Some of the English turned and were chased as far as Saint-Emilion. Others took refuge in Castillon.[60]

The second letter, written a mere five days after the battle, was from Charles VII in person to correspondents in Lyon. He insists that there were Gascons in Talbot's force at Castillon at nine in the morning. The Anglo-Gascon attack on the French camp lasted an hour and they fought resolutely. Talbot died along with many others. The survivors took to boats on the Dordogne to get away, or ran off aimlessly, or took refuge in Castillon. The king does not name any of his field commanders, nor does he mention his artillery. However, what he does say is that Clermont and Foix went immediately to the Médoc after the battle. French ships were moored in the Gironde and Bordeaux found itself directly threatened.

And the third letter in Contamine's presentation was written by the Count of Maine's herald, sent to Poitiers reporting in the broadest terms that Talbot had been defeated, an indication that the news spread to the great towns of the kingdom very quickly.[61]

It is likely that the news of Talbot's defeat and death reached Henry VI's court at Clarendon in the first week of August. The king was subsequently taken ill, and his lapse into a cataleptic stupor was sudden. Royal writs that were as a rule regularly issued suddenly stopped after 11 August, and members of the council at Westminster attempted to fill the void by taking over routine administrative duties.[62] The king was taken to Windsor and remained in seclusion throughout the winter of

1453–1454.[63] In contrast, Charles VII ordered *Te Deum* to be sung at the news of Castillon.

* * *

What sort of man was John Talbot, created Earl of Shrewsbury in 1442? We can see that he was pious in a conventional fashion, and fervent for chivalric ideals. When Margaret of Anjou had arrived in England as Henry VI's Queen in 1445, Talbot and his countess, Margaret Beauchamp, who had accompanied her from France, presented her with an illuminated book containing fourteen essays about the way knights were supposed to conduct themselves. After more than twenty years as a Knight of the Garter, he certainly respected the order's values.[64] This chivalric spirit remains full of contradictions for us as we try to understand it in the context of late medieval warfare. A great deal had changed in society since the days of William the Marshal. The Black Death had so diminished the population of Europe that a stratified order in society was giving (or even had given) way to relations governed by patronage and the cash nexus, conditions known to English historians at least since 1945 as 'bastard feudalism',where a market set by labourers or tenants was more important than one set by landowners:[65] the world represented in the *Paston Letters*.[66]

This was reflected in the organization of European armies, especially such as fought each other in the stages of the Hundred Years War conducted between the houses of Lancaster and Valois. 'Old Talbot,' 'England's Achilles,' could be seen as a survivor from two centuries before. As Malcolm Vale has said, '… if the knight really passed away in the fifteenth century, he spent a long time a-dying.'[67] The world of late medieval chivalry as it was evolving is not our world and cannot be. Malcolm Vale again: '… despite changes in technique and strategy the single combat – and, above all, the associated notion of individual honour – retained its importance.'[68] This was Talbot's world and we have to take it seriously if we are to be able to assess his impact on events. This was the man who told his chaplain on the morning that would see his death, 'I will never hear Mass unless I have this day spilt the blood of the company of Frenchmen which is over there in the field before me.'[69]

Talbot, says his biographer, was by nature irascible, often brutal, cruel, even vicious.

> During the summer of 1451, Talbot ruthlessly and shamelessly exploited his own high renown and position of favour at court, as well as the general powerlessness of the crown in the face of popular unrest and baronial feuding [Cade's rebellion and the return of Richard, Duke of York from Ireland] to further his own private ambitions. Behind the public image of England's champion, lay a grasping and self-seeking baron, whose propensity for creating domestic disturbance was undiminished by decades of fighting against the French. At the same time, Talbot was not prepared to throw himself into the principal feud undermining the Lancastrian monarchy – that between York and Somerset. There was nothing altruistic or statesmanlike in this – merely another calculation of self-interest. Talbot was placed in a potential dilemma by the conflict between York and Somerset, for he was closely attached to both.[70]

Jean Chartier said of him after his death:

> This famous and renowned English commander spent a long time as the most redoubtable flail and the most determined enemy of France, of whom he appeared to be the dread and terror. [71]

Concrete examples of his cruelty are documented. At Laval in 1428, he had sixty-five men, including priests, executed as traitors, presumably without due process of law. Similarly, in the garrisons at Jouy and Crépy in 1434, and at Gisors two years later, he hanged citizens for surrendering to the French and, after his raid into Santerre in 1440, he burned over three hundred men, women and children at Lihors in their village church, a horror comparable to the action of the Nazis at Oradour-sur-Glâne in 1944. The examples multiply, but according to the rules of war at the time, none of this would have appeared excessive – at least to the perpetrator.[72] Chivalry was on its way out in mid-fifteenth century warfare, but its code was still binding upon Talbot as he single-mindedly applied his devotion to the Lancastrian cause.

Yet the rise of self-conscious support for a particular monarch as such, and the development of stable gunpowder that did not ignite when jolted in carts – both phenomena of Talbot's lifetime – were calling all in doubt. The last word on Talbot could well be:

> ... it is possible that acting upon incorrect information, Talbot unfurled his banner [at Castillon] and opened the battle before he discovered that he was launching his men against an impenetrable position: to have retreated then would have brought lasting dishonour ... A deep and genuine commitment to the code of chivalry *as he understood it* offers the most convincing key to Talbot's character and career.[73]

This uncompromisingly military figure had been granted total administrative and judicial authority over the lands in Gascony that he was to re-take, and once he had assumed them the Bordelais had no difficulty in seeing him as a conqueror, rather than the liberator for whom they had hoped. They had never expected anything like this from an English lieutenant-governor, even from the Black Prince or from John of Gaunt. From December 1452, all ships arriving in the Gironde Estuary had to put in at La Marque and at Lussac in the Médoc to pay charges before they were permitted to enter the Garonne and the port of Bordeaux, which 'suggests a harshness which was uncharacteristic of the English administration of the Duchy'.[74] The inhabitants of Libourne remained loyal to France and 'implored the French garrison not to desert them'.[75] From the moment they arrived, the English troops ransacked houses and churches, stealing jewelled reliquaries and anything valuable they could lay their hands or their sword points on. New taxes were imposed and harshly collected, and it seemed as though this situation could have been permanent when, from March 1453, Talbot's staff was enlarged by the arrival of his son, Viscount Lisle (who would also die on the field of Castillon), Roger, Baron Camoys (who would be appointed as English seneschal to replace Coëtivy on 4 July[76]), John Lisle, Robert Hungerford, Lord Moleyns and John, Bastard of Somerset. So nearly 5,000 troops were stationed in revived English Gascony until October 1453 whereas, previously, troops were usually and for the most part raised at need within the duchy itself. This was not the kind of English return that any of the Gascons had hoped for.

One of those moments that bring a note of levity to such a study as this comes from a document that an erudite eighteenth-century antiquarian in Bordeaux, the Abbé Jacques Baurein, found in the administrative archives of the Ombrière Palace. It is a solicitor's minute (*procès-verbal*) which relates the circumstances of Olivier de Coëtivy's capture. It underlines Talbot's triumphalist and self-interested attitude to his task.[77]

Coëtivy, once Talbot's troops were in charge of Bordeaux, tried to escape from Bordeaux and make his way back, in armour, to Taillebourg – emphasizing the fact that no French force of any size had been left at his disposal.[78] Talbot had issued orders that morning that no resident of Bordeaux would be allowed by the English to take any Frenchman prisoner.

The document was written and reproduced in Gascon, but Baurein obligingly gave a French version for the benefit of his contemporaries and any other parties who would be interested later on. The document was registered on 4 February 1453 (*notaires* are in no hurry, then as now) by a notary at the Ombrière called Jean Bodeti on Talbot's own orders. Talbot was himself present at the meeting which the document records, together with other witnesses, when a statement was made by an esquire (*écuyer*) whose name was Bertholet de Rivière. This man and another esquire, Louis de Berthais, had left Bordeaux under the terms of the 1451 peace treaty (de Rivière was from Bayonne and Berthais from Dax[79]), made their way to England, and returned as members of Talbot's expeditionary force.

On the morning after the English had been let into the city these two Gascon second-lieutenants passed one Arnaud Bec, a trader (*negoçiant*) of English origin, who recognized them. Apparently in some excitement, he invited them to come with him to see something that might interest them. He knew where one, or even two, Frenchmen were hiding, and proposed that it would be easy to take them prisoner. If they helped him to do so, he would give them half of what he would receive for their ransom. They agreed, taking an oath on the Four Gospels. They went with him to a garden outside the Cor Gate[80] under the ramparts where they found Olivier de Coëtivy and, with him, the Lord of Messignac.

They arrested them and led them back into the city to hide them in Arnaud Bec's house.

All this was taken down by the notary, who went on to record how Talbot reacted to this information. He told them that the half-ransom they were expecting would belong to him, seeing that Arnaud Bec, as a resident of Bordeaux, had no right to take Coëtivy and Messignac prisoners, or anyone else for that matter, since he had, that very morning, specifically forbidden any such action by residents. Besides, Bec was guilty of concealing the prisoners in his house. The other half of the ransom belonged to Talbot as well, seeing that Rivière and Berthais had made themselves accessories to Bec's crime of acting against his decree – his English origins evidently making no difference to the decision from Talbot's point of view.

Rivière and Berthais did not accept the injustice of their predicament, and there exists a petition bearing the date of 23 July 1454 which they presented to 'the right high and mighty prince and our undoubted lord, the Duke of York, protector of England, and to our sovereign lord's full noble and solemn council,' claiming restitution of the ransoms which the late and, in their case unlamented, Talbot had taken from them.

They pleaded that they had come to Bordeaux in Talbot's army at their own expense and with twenty men in their own service and, each in his own way, had survived the carnage and aftermath of Castillon. Berthelot de Rivière was taken prisoner at Castillon 'in the field', but was released at the end of the siege of Bordeaux and, remaining loyal to the king of England as a faithful Gascon, migrated to England again as he had previously done in 1451. He had nothing to live on now beyond his trust in his sovereign lord. Louis de Berthais had been captured among the English defending Chalais and was still being held prisoner in France, not being able to afford his ransom because he, like Rivière, had lost his lands and buildings in 1451. They hoped still to be of military use to the English cause. They asked for Olivier de Coëtivy to be restored to de Rivière's custody and that his ransom should be paid to him and his brother in arms as would have happened if Talbot had not confiscated it. They note that it is evident that Talbot had felt the need to justify himself by having a document drawn up by the notary in the Ombrière.

Receipt of this document by the king's council is signed by William Wayneflete, bishop of Winchester, by Pey Tasta, dean of Saint-Seurin (not surprisingly), by the Duke of York himself, by the Earl of Salisbury, by Bourgchier (probably the archbishop of Canterbury or, if not, by his brother), by one of the Beaumont family and by the prior of St John of Jerusalem. Added to the parchment is a note that says, 'The king by the advice of the council [a phrase which conveniently conceals the fact that the king was in a comatose state at the time], wills that letters be sent under the privy seal to the new Earl of Shrewsbury to have the said prisoner brought before the king and his council in the month of Michaelmas next [i.e., September 1454] and that in the meantime he is in no wise to enlarge [set free] the prisoner. And this upon the penalty of six thousand pounds.' Evidently no notice was taken of this decision because, as we shall see, Olivier de Coëtivy was a prominent figure in subsequent events in Bordeaux, and he regulated his account with the Shrewsbury family from there. We have not heard the last of Berthais ...

The fact that he was improperly arrested did not make Coëtivy any the less a valuable prize. Old Talbot shipped him and Messignac off to England along with the deputy mayor, Jean de Fou. He would be a guest of the countess of Shrewsbury and of Talbot's son by his first marriage (himself a prominent figure in the forthcoming Wars of the Roses) until January 1455, when he was released to go home to raise his ransom.

Chapter Seven

Charles VII Reconquers Bordeaux

After Castillon, reprisals and royal revenge set in. In Charles VII's eyes, the Bordelais had broken the solemn oath they had taken in June 1451 to be his loyal subjects. They deserved to be punished, either for having welcomed Talbot and his expeditionary force, or having acquiesced in his assumption of power. Whatever their attitude had been, they were traitors to their king, and the generous terms of the 1451 treaty were null and void. It was in this spirit that French military action was undertaken for the second time.

Gaillard de Durfort managed to escape from his pursuers after the battle of Castillon and made his way around Bordeaux to his substantial fortress at Blanquefort to prepare to resist a siege. The fortress is still to be seen among fields outside the suburban town behind the bends of the little River Jalle which serves it as a moat. He provided himself with adequate manpower, artillery pieces and provisions in this secure position. Clermont arrived soon after him, intending to reduce the place as quickly as possible, but found himself thwarted. He laid his siege straight away, and remained in person to supervise the action, sending his subordinates, Foix, Lautrec, Xaintrailles and Albret off towards the Dordogne to attack other castles. Xaintrailles took Saint-Macaire. Villandraut and Langon soon fell to Albret's siege. Cadillac, Benauge and Rions held out against Foix and Lautrec for a good while.[1]

Charles VII reserved his personal anger against traitors for Bordeaux itself. Under his own command, the reserve army began to move only a few days after Castillon. He reached Libourne, which had not been enthusiastic for Talbot on 8 August 1453, and besieged the great fortress of Fronsac once again which offered little resistance. He went into the Entre-Deux-Mers country, to establish himself and his council in Montferrand Castle, property of Bernard de Montferrand, on 13 August. He directed the siege of Bordeaux from there for upwards of eight weeks.

The capital of his province of Guyenne had the appearance of impregnability: there were three fortified enclosures within a circumference of close on six kilometres with ramparts recently strengthened on the initiative of Pey Berland.[2] Its walls were protected by twenty towers, and the River Garonne is 600 metres wide along the city's waterfront. A substantial fleet had been assembled beforehand to prevent direct approach to the port.[3]

Charles VII had been assembling his own fleet too over recent weeks with ships brought from Brittany, La Rochelle and Spain, anchoring them at the mouth of the Gironde Estuary ready to be moved south against the city. On the right bank of the Garonne, he set about constructing his *bastille* at Lormont to serve as a platform for Jean Bureau's artillery pieces under the overall command of Admiral de Bueil, count of Sancerre.[4] The defenders matched this with a huge *bastille* of their own to protect their fleet anchored behind it.[5]

The defence of the city was directed by Roger, Baron Camoys. His earlier career was not distinguished in any conventional sense but he had gained prominence of a certain kind in Normandy. He had been captured by the French at Le Mans in 1438, and had been in captivity for nine years because he did not have the resources, as a banneret or a younger son, to pay his ransom. Once he was released, the truce was in operation so he lived off the land with other unwaged soldiers gathered round him. He turned the fortified Abbey of Savigny into his stronghold from which he attacked French and English villages alike. English commanders defended themselves against Camoys and his men. At the end of summer in 1447, he was ordered to leave the Exmes region and his people were threatened by the commander there with hanging. He moved then to another ruined fortress which he repaired to be his base. Thomas Hoo was then chancellor of Normandy and he paid other unemployed troops to act against him. He seems to have crossed to England after the final defeat in Normandy at Formigny on 15 April 1450.[6] Then he reappears in regular service as part of Talbot's reinforcements. He fought in Talbot's army at Castillon as a captain in Viscount Lisle's company, and his appointment as the last English seneschal was dated 4 July 1453.[7] His subordinate commanders included several Gascon nobles, the new English mayor, Henry Retford, at his post since 4 December 1452, and members of the *jurade*.[8]

Camoys was styled as Governor of Bordeaux for the King of England in a 'Treaty' between himself and the Three Estates of the town on the subject of the expenses necessary for defence measures against the besiegers.[9] Those who promised to reimburse him for his expenses are named in a roll-call of Bordeaux society: Archbishop Pey Berland, Pierre de Montferrand, Gaillard de Durfort, François de Montferrand, Bernard Angevin, the Dean of St. Andrew's Cathedral, the Canon Treasurer of Saint-Seurin (Pey de Tasta, the Dean, was a permanent member of the English royal council now), and several lawyers and individual *jurats*. The Three Estates met in the cathedral and Camoys declared to them

> the inconveniences which could arise, as much in the town as in all Guyenne... and that they were in danger of becoming under the subjection of the king of France, at which they all responded in loud voices, crying piteously that they regarded death as dearer than coming under the said subjection to the king.

The document records the decision to renew the town's defences, and the English captains and their troops took on the work 'for otherwise it was not possible to offer any resistance'. The Estates agreed to raise a tax to pay for these works. The king's procurator of Bordeaux was to be sent to England to seek financial aid from the government, and Gervase Clifton was to detach two of the ships he had at his disposal to take him there. Details are given of the pay for Camoys's own lances and archers, and for those of other named commanders, and of moneys sent to help maintain Gaillardet at Cadillac. Sums were set aside for the construction of the bastille in the river which would protect the ships in the port and provide a useful springboard for attacks on the similar French construction at Lormont, and for all the required war materiel. Specific locations, like the archbishop's palace and the Sainte-Croix mill were to be defended with detachments of troops (though the French soon set fire to the mill with cannon to prevent its use). The total sum agreed for all this was 17,600 francs in money of Bordeaux, and Lady Camoys claimed it from the Bordelais in April 1455.[10]

The French troops occupied the right bank of the Garonne, and from the Lormont bastille they had a clear view of everything within the range of their cannon. Clermont's tactic was to ravage the countryside at the same time as maintaining his siege against Blanquefort, preventing supplies of foodstuffs reaching Bordeaux from the suburbs, from the territory of Buch or from the Landes. He knew that starvation was his most powerful weapon. Disease would be added later but, of course, that would affect attackers and defenders alike. The blockade of the estuary facilitated his policy since ships carrying the usual supplies of wheat from England could not approach.[11] Up to 1,600 lances were positioned in and around the bastille at Lormont, with six fighting men in each lance.[12] But their bastille was a mixed blessing to the king's army because the archers were exposed to attack in their turn. Such a fortification was never as strong as a walled town, as the English had found to their cost in their constructions around Orleans in 1429, or at Mont Saint-Michel.

There were several indecisive skirmishes. The Lormont fort had to fend off many a spirited attack by hit-and-run Gascon soldiers and sailors from behind their own bastille in the river, and they understood the tricky tides on the Garonne. So 'the besieged became the besiegers and showed more than once that they counted for something.'[13] Perhaps they were motivated by the hope of ransoms that conspicuous captives might eventually bring them, or by having hostages as bargaining counters if they were defeated in the end. They certainly took as many French prisoners as they could during these forays across the river.

Charles VII himself was enormously active: visiting operations at Saint-Macaire, Cadillac and elsewhere in Entre-Deux-Mers. He was often at Lormont and sent Bureau and his artillerymen all over the place. At the end of September, he was at Cadillac when the English defenders offered him 10,000 silver écus to be let free, but the king replied that he did not need the money and had them all arrested. The garrison captain, the Gascon Gaillardet, had held out for six weeks. He was beheaded as a traitor.[14]

What happened at Cadillac caused despair in besieged Bordeaux, especially when it was known that Rions and Benauge were surrendering as well. Only Blanquefort was holding out. There would be no help for Bordeaux from higher up the Garonne. Scottish allies of Charles VII, under Robin Petit-Loup would see to that. Scarcity began to take hold. Several of the English in the city thought seriously of leaving and finding a way of returning home if possible. Camoys needed all the manpower he could keep, so he had all the sails and rigging taken off the ships in which they had arrived in April 1452, then moored them behind the bastille. There was tension between the English who wanted to leave and the Gascons who feared the worst if they were to surrender. Morale deteriorated until the Gascons came to agree with the Englishmen.[15]

At the same time, Gaillard de Durfort made overtures for the surrender of Blanquefort to Clermont, asking for a safe-conduct from Charles VII. When it was refused, Durfort escaped across the marshes to Bordeaux so as to avoid Gaillardet's fate and to offer his services to Camoys.[16] It was this, together with increasing artillery bombardment from Lormont, that persuaded Camoys to look for an opportunity to negotiate with the king and his council at Montferrand. Safe-conducts were issued, and, in early October, a hundred representatives from Bordeaux churchmen, nobles and 'others of the community' were 'before the king's presence' offering surrender in return for their property and their lives.

The chronicler d'Éscouchy gave the king's reply in full. He pointed out 'the great faults' that he found in them, and said that 'with the aid of our Creator' he was determined to take Bordeaux, 'all who are in it, and their property at our will and pleasure; that their bodies shall be punished according to their offences for having gone against their oath and disregarded our deeds before this time in such a way as to be an example to others and a memorial in times to come'.

The effect of this cold shower was increased by Bureau's arrival in the council chamber to tell the king – while the Bordeaux deputation was still there – that his reconnaissance had shown that, in a short time, he could make life impossible in the city by precisely targetted artillery and offer the king whatever might be left. The king replied that his intention was not to leave Guyenne without having united the province with France under his power.[17] Bordeaux's recovered autonomy under its English king/duke was to be at an end.

The representatives returned. The hostilities continued. Ships attacked each other in front of Lormont where the Garonne was wide enough for manoeuvres. The Gascons' bastille changed hands from one day to the next. The king's intentions were still seen as unacceptable to the townspeople but, realizing that a solution had to be found, they prevailed upon Camoys to make approaches to Joachim Rouault who had been the constable after the conquest of 1451 and whose moderation had been compared at the time with Coëtivy's intransigence. Camoys agreed, and Rouault obtained permission from the king to come into the city under safe-conduct to discuss what might eventually be decided.

The outcome was that thirty prominent citizens would go to Lormont to meet for talks with Charles VII's delegates. The principal negotiators for the king were to be Louis de Beaumont, seneschal of Poitou, and a diplomat who had served in Venice called Jean de Jambes. Camoys, as Henry VI's lieutenant-general, made a plea for clemency, realizing that Charles VII was overhearing everything that was said. The king's response was as uncompromisingly harsh as last time: the citizens were guilty of great faults and offences against him: punishment was unavoidable. Wrangling went on all day, and the delegates went back home with nothing agreed except that their safe-conducts were extended until the next day.

In the morning, surrender terms crystallized after several false starts. The king would be ready to grant '*abolition*' (amnesty) to the citizens in return for their renunciation of all their long-established privileges, a one-off payment of 100,000 silver marks and the handing over to him of twenty named leaders of the 1452 conspiracy to re-admit the English (including Pey de Tasta who was safe in London and Pierre de Montferrand who wasn't). Even if the money payment were to be acceptable to them, the Bordeaux negotiators realized that the twenty men would face certain execution. They refused. They left.[18]

The decisive day was 9 October, when a third meeting took place. Roger de Camoys and ten others went to the lion's den in Montferrand to speak to the king in person. Surrounded by his nobles, princes and counsellors, Charles VII received them in a theatrical display of pomp in contrast to their own bedraggled appearance out from under the bombardment. Camoys again asked for amnesty of persons and property, while agreeing to the 100,000 écus and any other financial exactions the king might see fit to make, and to the renunciation of the former privileges.[19] The king responded by dismissing the Englishmen and Gascons in order to consult his council.

The background to these discussions was the outbreak of a fever epidemic in the French army.[20] This naturally became a prior consideration for the king's council, and their advice was to confirm what Camoys had accepted so long as justice was seen to be done to the leading traitors. The Bordeaux delegation was called in again. They resisted any agreement that would result in the execution of such men as Pierre de Montferrand or Gaillard de Durfort among the twenty hostages to be handed over. Agreement was reached in the end and the king gave his word: they would be banished from the kingdom in perpetuity instead.[21]

The treaty was signed immediately: Bordeaux was obliged to find the 100,000 écus, and French prisoners taken during the siege had to be released without paying ransoms despite any agreement that had been made with them previously.[22] The treaty of 9 October took away all Bordeaux's particular privileges: the right to mint its own currency, to vote its own taxes, to have a sovereign court of justice (*Parlement*) according to the 1451 treaty, freedom from billeting of soldiers and from military service outside the Bordelais. The number of citizens who would be allowed to leave Bordeaux and live elsewhere (that meant in England) and retain their moveable possessions or bequeath them to their kinsfolk was now limited to forty.[23]

All this was drawn up into letters patent issued from Montferrand – only ninety-nine lines in length as opposed to the 321 in the letter of June 1451 dated from Saint-Jean d'Angély. It is made clear that military action had been carried out

for the aid of our good and loyal vassals and subjects, having reduced by force the places which our enemies had taken, and brought them back into our obedience; and we have sent and placed our said army in great power as much by water as by land close to our city of Bordeaux in which the churchmen, the nobles, the bourgeois traders and the inhabitants have knowingly wrongly acted towards us. Since 'the greater part of the inhabitants of our town are not the principal cause of the said rebellion and disobedience', and they have asked to be pardoned, they are received back into the king's good grace and mercy. They have now acknowledged the king as their sovereign and natural lord.

All the terms for the punishment of the rebels follow in the document.[24]

Three days later, six Englishman and six Gascons were given as hostages and, two days after that, the city's bastille (in the area nowadays called the Bastide, where the Archives Métropole building is located) was demolished.[25] The actual opening of the gates to the French – the *Reddition* – was delayed until 19 October. Rions and Benauge had not surrendered at the same time as Cadillac as expected, and French forces soon made short work of taking them.[26]

Just before the capitulation of Bordeaux became effective, a convention was agreed between 'Jean de Bueil, Count of Sancerre, Admiral of France in the king's name, and Roger de Camoys, Knight, having charge over other people of the English nation at Bordeaux'. The document is dated 5 October 1453 at Lormont. It allowed all ships to sail freely from the port during the course of the following day. They were permitted to take all their large and small cannon, gunpowder and 'all other war material of whatever kind and all things necessary for the navigation of each vessel'. A general safe-conduct was issued to the fleet under the royal seal and one each for the named captains of particular ships in case they should become separated from the convoy by bad weather or any other cause. The safe-conducts were valid for three months and the ships could be laden with wine or any other merchandise that it seemed appropriate to take to England or anywhere else during the three months allowed. Other safe-conducts were issued for those going home by the land route, that is, by way of Calais. The English did not have to pay the usual charge for these sealed documents, except reasonable fees for the clerks and secretaries who drew them up. It was emphatically repeated that the people leaving with Camoys could take away all their movable property and that Camoys could take away all his artillery pieces. All French prisoners were to be set free that same day.[27] The implication of all this was that the English were not to be held to blame for having been invited in by the treason of the conspirators in Bordeaux. The English soldiers embarked, each one receiving an écu from King Charles and with the honours of war. Presumably, their transport ships had been re-rigged in the ten days between the signing of the treaty and the raising of the fleurs de lys to replace the leopards on the public buildings.

In the royal mausoleum in the Abbey of Saint-Denis, Charles VII is called 'The Victorious'. There were celebrations all over France. Charles, Duke of Orleans, wrote a celebratory ballad to glorify the king who had recovered Normandy and Guyenne. Gold, silver and bronze medals were struck in the Paris mint. There were morality plays on the theme of victory in Troyes to efface the memory of the perfidious treaty of 1420 that gave away the crown. In Compiègne there was a spectacle entitled '*The Discomfiture of Talbot*'.[28]

From the English point of view the events of 1453 were once more bleakly summarized in John Benet's Chronicle:

> Immediately after Easter the king sent 1,000 men to Gascony, with three barons, namely Lord Moleyns, Lord [Roger] Camoys and Lord Lisle, who besieged the town of Fronsac, and took it. And about the feast of St. Laurence there were killed in Gascony the Earl of Shrewsbury and his son, Lord Lisle, and Sir Edward Hull, and Lord Moleyns was captured by the French. And about Michaelmas the city of Bordeaux was lost again.[29]

*   *   *

What was the effect of the second French conquest on the inhabitants of Bordeaux? The fine to be exacted was severe, but the new taxes to be imposed upon the production and export of wine was to be a worse blow to a region where everyone, from the labourer to the bourgeois trader and the noble landowner, gained his livelihood from the vines.[30] Those who had taken advantage of the conqueror's permission to leave for England with their families and domestic support continued to regard the French monarchy as foreign. They met together in London and formed a colony that followed with great interest what was going on back home. They were desperate enough to see their exile as rectifiable – sooner or later – by their return. Letters in Henry VI's name to several of these refugees set a limit to the time that pensions offered to them would continue to be paid.

An entry in the Gascon Rolls for 21 April 1454 is one of many that illustrates what was done by the king's council in respect of economic migrants who were also refugees after the second conquest. It concerns a grant to Gaillard IV of Durfort, knight, lord of Duras and Blanquefort, for his good services, by the advice and with the consent of the king's council, of a hundred pounds a year to be taken at the receipt of the Exchequer, from the treasurer or the chamberlains of England, at Easter and Michaelmas by equal portions until Durfort is restored to his lordships in the duchy of Aquitaine or receives some other compensation.

A term is set to the council's willingness (or ability) to help Durfort, but the entry records the conditions in which the grant was made as follows:

Durfort has expounded lamentingly to the king and his council that in the present year, when the French adversary occupied the duchy of Aquitaine against God and justice, he wished to remain loyal to the king, and stocked his castles and fortalices with men and victuals, and was besieged in Blanquefort by the counts of Clermont and Foix, the lords of Albret, of Orval, Poton de Xaintrailles, and many other captains and a great army, but was able to make such resistance as that they were unable to take the places. Durfort was able to hold both places (*sic*) and his other lands and lordships until Bordeaux was captured by the enemy, and compelled Durfort by force to hand the same over in return for a safe-conduct whereby he is destroyed and totally disinherited and has come to England to seek remedy.[31]

This entry gives, at least, a version of events, and there has been special pleading to make Durfort appear more successful than we have seen him to be. There are other entries, also from the 32nd regnal year of Henry VI that deal with poor Durfort's troubles, but the king's government's supportive, even if limited, attitude towards him is clearly stated in this one. He did settle for an English career and is later seen as active in Calais.

However, men-at-arms even if they were born English, left unemployed at the end of 1453, looked towards Gascony for a recovery of their livelihood. All exiles received letters from friends and family still in Bordeaux and many looked forward to a moment that would enable them to return. They even developed plans for further military action and presented it for the English government's approval.

Pierre de Morlanes had been the captain of a company raised in Gascony (Morlanes is in the Béarn) in Talbot's army. In exile, he offered his services to the English crown for the recovery of Aquitaine a second time.[32] His proposal was acknowledged but he had no part in the expedition that actually did take place, commanded by another, more conspicuous Gascon, Pierre de Montferrand, who, as we have seen, was active in the defence of Blaye in 1451 and, once defeated, took the oath to Charles VII. He is regarded as having taken part in the conspiracy the parish of Saint-Michel that admitted Talbot into Bordeaux in October 1452.[33]

On 24 July 1453, a week after Castillon, Montferrand was pardoned by Henry VI for having taken that oath.[34] The wording in the document which pardons him is precise. He is given a pardon

by the king's special grace … notwithstanding whatever oath or oaths he has sworn to the king's adversary of France, provided that he had dispensation from those in authority over him and imposing silence in these matters on the king's proctor, provided that he swore an oath of fealty to the king's lieutenant-general or the seneschal of Aquitaine, or to the lieutenant of either of them.

It is impossible to establish which one of these he chose to receive his oath in the turmoil after Castillon, but it is evident that he was in England after Roger de Camoys and his troops left the Gironde. In any case, he had been exiled from France.

The document recounts Montferrand's activity during the last two years. It identifies Montferrand as one who had 'strived with all his might to preserve the king's domains and remain loyal to him'. As we have seen, he went to the defence of Blaye, the taking of which Charles VII recognized as essential for the safety of Bordeaux. Montferrand, personally targetted for revenge after Bordeaux had been retaken and fearing for his life while 'searching for a way to save his lands and lordships, made an agreement with the king's adversary … was compelled to remain obedient to him against his intention up until the previous October, when the Earl of Shrewsbury … came, and he hastened to join him, and advised his friends and neighbours to follow him. Nonetheless,

Montferrand fears that ... as long as the king's adversaries are strong in the duchy, his interests are at risk without support from the king.'[35]

He kept faith with Henry VI but broke his oath to Charles VII for a second time by returning to Guyenne in June 1454. His landing party was deliberately kept small to avoid arousing suspicion when he arrived, presumably in the Médoc since he had been lord of Lesparre.[36] Hatred for the oppressive French regime, says the Gascon Ribadieu during the Second Empire, guaranteed him a welcome from the locals. He claimed to have a safe-conduct from the French king and had arrived under the pretext of completing certain unfinished business. He had hopes of overcoming the mistrust of the French, but he trusted, says Ribadieu who relies for his information upon Jean Chartier, too much to his good fortune. He could not avoid being discovered in breach of his banishment order, nor the punishment that followed. He and two companions were arrested.

To avoid a popular rising in his support in Bordeaux, the three men were taken to Poitiers and handed over to a special commission, the members of which were notorious for their severity and self-interest. Luis de Beaumont was known as avaricious in amassing more than a fair share of the booty after Castillon, being required to give the excess back to the common purse and Robin Petit-Loup, the Scottish captain who had been active in the Landes during the siege of Bordeaux and was now seneschal there, administering his territory with extremes of brutality. Montferrand's sentence was a foregone conclusion, very likely after torture, despite his noble status. The commission condemned him to death 'lawfully and in good right' says the official historian Jean Chartier, cited by Ribadieu who quotes also from another chronicler to add that Montferrand's body was hacked into six pieces which were hung up over the different gates of Poitiers.[37]

Marie, natural daughter of the Duke of Bedford, Pierre Montferrand's widow, remained in England, living on a meagre royal pension of twenty pounds a year from Edward IV, although she was Henry IV's granddaughter. Her children were kept as hostages in France.

All this was in contrast to what happened in the case of Bertrand de Montferrand, who was Pierre's elder brother. He had inherited the lordship of Montferrand from their father and this made him a leading member of the Bordelais nobility, while Pierre, eventually, after losing his claim to the barony of Lesparre by the decision of Henry VI in council, had to be content with the undistinguished lordship of Trau in the Landes, inherited from their mother.

Bertrand had been the defender of Bourg during the 1451 invasion. He was discouraged by the defeat of his brother at Blaye and did not push for a spirited resistance. He negotiated a surrender after only six days of siege and was given a safe-conduct to go to Bordeaux with a company of men-at-arms. His letters of abolition – the form of words of his pardon, restitution in the French king's favour and restoration of his property – were dated 7 July 1451 from Queen Marie's residence at Montils-lès-Tours.[38]

*   *   *

There was an extra sting in the already poisonous tail of the settlement imposed upon Bordeaux after the 1453 conquest in the form of Charles VII's order that two entirely new fortresses were to be constructed within the perimeter of the existing ramparts. One was called the Hâ – so-called from the quarter it dominated at the north-west, with five towers, the largest of which defended the eastern approach to the town, and the other the Tropeyte facing towards the north – named after a stream no longer visible and soon corrupted to Trompette – at the north end on the Garonne waterfront, defended by three towers and a barbican.[39]

These forts were to be erected at the expense of the inhabitants, including those of the god-daughter towns, with the people themselves providing finance or labour according to social status and involving the destruction of houses and business premises to make room for the enormous structures. They were intended to be constant reminders of the recent defeat and loss of the autonomy that they used to have under the English king/dukes. It would be well into Louis XI's reign before they were completed (Louis XIV added a state of the military art *glacis* on the typical Vaubanesque star pattern, completed in 1691, and the fortress remained in place until demolished by the intendant Tournon in 1818 to make way for the spacious *allées* of our time).[40]

The old palace of the Ombrière was no longer suitable for the purposes of a citadel in the paranoid political climate of Charles VII's last years and the greater part of Louis XI's reign, being surrounded by other buildings and without a platform for the now essential artillery pieces. A return by the English was greatly feared, so these new structures faced both the Gironde and the hinterland, so that from whichever direction 'the former enemy' might return, they could be repulsed.[41]

The same fear of an English renewal of the war that would never be officially over can be seen in the elevation of the new *châtelet* on the highest point above the town of Jonzac in around 1470, which replaced an older fortress (held on and off by the English) demolished in conflict further down the slope on the escarpment above the river Seugne.[42] Louis XI granted permission to Olivier de Coëtivy to repair his bastion beside the Gironde at Didonne, near Royan, that had been damaged by the Black Prince in a fourteenth century *chevauchée*.[43] Coëtivy also issued an order to Jean Isle, lord of Matassière, in 1475, to have his castle at Saint-Savinien sur Charente repaired to be ready to resist the English should they invade.[44]

With the defence organized in terms of military installations, Charles VII also asserted himself in terms of the appointment of personnel to control his newly-acquired province of Guyenne. Those who had supported him throughout the conquest needed to have grounds for continued loyalty. As for the conquered, there were no mass dispossessions and the lordships of indigenous nobles were confirmed by the victorious king. This was his basic policy. He regarded as traitors those who had broken their oath of fidelity to him made after the 1451 submission. In April 1454, even those who had been in England at the time of the second submission were to be allowed to return if they took the oath.[45]

Monarchy depended upon personal rule little short of divine right absolutism. And this kind of rule depended upon personal favours. The obvious choice of administrators and other officials was from among people who depended on the king for what they possessed. It was feudalism, but not as the great lords had known it before the ordinances for taxation and the organization of the army, which were the preludes to the unification of France from the English Channel to the Pyrenees. Former free-booting captains with military experience had carried out the conquest, so they were the most likely candidates to be trusted with maintaining the monarchy where it had not existed before.

Poton de Xaintrailles (Saint-Trails) himself a Gascon, was regarded by the king as greatly deserving of reward. He had been a freebooting captain (*écorcheur*) after the signing of peace between the Duke of Burgundy and Charles VII in 1435, and had then been a subordinate commander under Dunois and Clermont. He now received the rank of marshal, and command of the new Tropeyte fortress in the initial stages of its being built. Antoine de Chabannes had acted against the king in the *Praguerie* rebellion of 1440 but, like his fellow rebels, had been reconciled to the king. He had taken Blanquefort from Gaillard de Durfort in 1453, and then received a lordship of his own, being ennobled as Count of Dammartin. He had also taken part in the king's resumption of Jean IV of Armagnac's lands and received a part of them for himself.

However, Charles VII was not prepared – Olivier de Coëtivy, as we shall see, was an exception – to allow the men he appointed to office to put down roots in the places which they had received from him. This aspect of royal control was not something they resented because, if they were deprived eventually of lands or administrations in Guyenne, they were as like as not compensated with lordships in other French provinces, particularly under Louis XI. An example is one of Charles d'Albret's officers, Estévot de Taluresse, who was deprived of his offices when he took part in the War of the Public Weal but was later appointed as seneschal of Carcassonne.[46]

Charles VII's generals imitated the king in making appointments from among their trusted subordinates. Estévot de Taluresse was closely associated with Charles II d'Albret who put him in charge of Montferrand castle and then made him mayor and captain-general of Bayonne, Saint-Jean de Luz, and Capbreton, while his uncle governed the now famous Tartas.

Because of the rebellion against him, the king withdrew his offer of a *Parlement* in Bordeaux that he had promised in the 1451 treaty for the purpose of regulating judicial appeals without them having to be heard in Paris or Toulouse. Certainly, for a time, there remained a punitive aspect to the king's personal control of Guyenne. For instance, in his commissioners' ordinances concerning the reform of justice in the province issued on 28

January 1455, there is talk of 'frivolous appeals' being made, for which
fines were to be imposed. Correctives against deliberately caused delays
and fines not being paid were also issued. Specific reference was made
to the registers kept in the Chateau de l'Ombrière 'during the time that
the said duchy was under jurisdiction of the kings of England', when
there had been 'frauds and malpractices'. In 192 separate clauses, the
commissioners' report gives details about officials to be appointed, from
judges to clerks, porters and ushers, the terms of their holding office, the
fines to be paid for malpractice, the frequency of assizes, how prisoners
in the cells were to be treated severely. The signatories to this report are
national office holders, not regional ones.[47]

Nowhere was this spirit of punitive regulation more visible after the
conquest than in the wine trade with England. Wine was the staple of
Bordeaux's commerce left, before the great humiliation of 1453, to the
fluctuations of productivity of the Gascon vineyards and the availability
of transport ships in English ports all the way round the coast from
Hull to Fowey, but with emphasis on those from London, Southampton
and Bristol. The king/duke of Aquitaine was the principal buyer of
the product, that in the Middle Ages did not keep, but was sold and
consumed in the same year before the next vintage. New supplies were
always needed and were usually provided on the quaysides of the Gascon
ports by established traders.

*   *   *

An essential element in opinion forming in any medieval European city
was always the higher clergy. The stance taken by the influential canons
of Saint Andrew's Cathedral and of the Collegiate church of Saint-
Seurin was crucial during and after the second conquest. They expressed
solidarity with their revered Archbishop Pey Berland and they knew what
he thought of the incorporation of Gascony into the French kingdom.
He had been a signatory to the 'treaty' made with Lord Camoys in his
cathedral church at the beginning of the siege.

Since his election in 1430, Pey Berland had shown himself opposed
to the policies of the Valois king and his encroachments into Gascon

territory. The members of the two Bordeaux chapters willingly accepted his leadership while he remained in office and continued to be loyal to him when he had withdrawn from it, replaced by a despised royal toady whom they considered – in ecclesiastical terms – to be a jumped-up *parvenu* and unacceptable to them since he was a Frenchman.

By the time of Berland's forced resignation, the seneschal of Guyenne was once more Olivier de Coëtivy, the king's right-hand man, whom we last saw being packed off to England as a prisoner of war before the battle of Castillon. We see him back in power, the king's agent and instrument, whose entire loyalty to the monarch – this time backed up by sufficient police powers – turned the screw on any Gascon resistance that remained.

Archbishop Berland, born into a family of free graziers in the Médoc in about 1375, whose career we have followed in earlier chapters, entered his office in 1430, the year after Charles VII's coronation at Reims by the good offices of Joan of Arc. Berland resisted Charles VII's claim to authority over the church in the duchy of Aquitaine because of the homage he expected – but never received – from the King of England. In the early years of divisive nationalism in Europe, Pey Berland was an Anglo-Gascon. Another disaffected Gascon, four hundred years later, said of him:

> He was not only a powerful personality, he was also a great patriot and a holy bishop. He consecrated himself to the defence of his country ... he had the envied privilege of heroic souls to represent the national cause after the conquest, and to be persecuted for it. He had lasting popularity because of his virtue and his ordeals.[48]

The Pragmatic Sanction of Bourges, decreed by Charles VII in 1438 to give himself power over the appointment of French bishops in disregard of papal authority, making use of the tendancy of some churchmen to favour conciliar government in the Church, was abhorrent to Berland. As his predecessor's secretary, Berland had become known – and even liked – in Rome and was loyal to successive popes as well as to Henry VI and his council. As the Gascon archbishop and not a French functionary, Berland did not consider himself bound by Charles VII's pragmatic

sanction. However, once Gascony had become part of France, the king
intended sooner or later to appoint his own archbishop.

So we find Pey Berland on 7 July 1452 on his knees before the high altar
in his cathedral of Saint-André, witnessed by Dean Johan de Lostade,
the Archdeacons of Médoc and Cernes and the eight canons, taking an
oath on holy relics never on any pretext to give up his archbishopric
of Bordeaux but, on the contrary, to live and die in office. A deed was
drawn up by a notary to make this oath public and it was inscribed in the
cathedral registers.[49]

The Dean of the Collegiate Church of Saint-Seurin, Pey de Tasta, as
we have seen, was able to live in England in a style appropriate for a
member of Henry VI's royal council by being granted the revenues of
rich church benefices there in plurality. He continued to represent the
interests of Bordeaux at the English court in his quality as the Dean of
Saint-Seurin, and his canons accepted that he would remain an absentee
without any need to replace him.

Henry VI gave members of Tasta's household what would have been
lucrative concessions in Bordeaux had the city not been in French hands,
as rewards for his loyal service. Guilhem Pineau, a Gascon, referred to in
the Gascon Rolls as the dean's servant as well as a faithful subject, received
a grant for his lifetime of houses, lands and property in certain named
villages such as Brissac, with all their rents, dues and appurtenances,
which had been forfeited to the king/duke. Everything depended upon
a successful English re-conquest, but it was the thought that counted.
He was also given an official post which gave him a wage out of the
profits from affixing seals on the houses of people under arrest and of
the guardianship of all rivers and fisheries in the Bordelais that were in
the king's gift. Furthermore, he was given the right to collect the tax on
new cooking pots formerly gathered by the king's messengers. This, if
the duchy were still in English hands, would have given him an income
of fifty pounds.[50] The main point of all that was to maintain Pey Tasta in
a position to keep the English government informed about conditions in
Bordeaux with a view an eventual re-conquest.

Tasta had some part in Talbot's expedition, more likely in its
preparation beforehand than in actually taking part in it as is asserted in
the anonymous *récit* in the Gironde Historical Archives where it is said

that he came with the English army (and presumably went back again afterwards!).[51] He never took up the exercise of his deanery again. After Castillon, he signed 'tragic' letters asking the mayors of southern English ports to provide a fleet to re-take Bordeaux and, among other actions, to sell all the tin that had been seized in Southampton to help equip this phantom fleet.[52]

Apart from these meagre and mistaken assertions, there are no further references extant of the two ecclesiastical chapters' attitudes during Talbot's occupation of the Bordelais, nor during the first full year of Valois domination.[53] However, on 31 January 1456, the town's complaint to the king that the men of the Church were not paying tax on the sale of their wines as everyone else did, resulted in Seneschal Coëtivy being instructed by the king to draw up a dossier to be used against them. The king was aware of the exemption maintained for the chapters by the king/duke Edward I's successors, and the fact that he took the town's complaint seriously, suggests that he was turning a hostile eye on the canons of Saint-André and Saint-Seurin.[54]

Meanwhile, there had been constant pressure on Pey Berland to resign and it had its outcome on 24 September 1456 when he accepted his nomination by Pope Callixtus III (who was hand in glove with Charles VII) to the Archbishopric of Madia (no one seems to have known where it was, but it had revenues attached to it) despite the solemn oath he had taken four years before. The pope advised him personally to hand over the administration of the archdiocese to his legate, who just happened to be the seneschal's brother, Cardinal Alain de Coëtivy. Pey Berland complied in obedience to the pope, and retired, hermit-like, to Saint-Raphaël's College, his own foundation situated where the Hôtel de Ville now is, named after his birthplace in the Médoc.[55]

Blaise de Gréele was nominated by the king under the terms of his own pragmatic sanction as the next archbishop. At the time he was no more than a sub-deacon in the diocese of Clermont but, politically, he was a counsellor to the king and trusted by him. From the first day he set foot in the Gascon archdiocese, he was automatically disliked as the foreign king's creature, representing Bordeaux's recent humiliation. He had been ordained priest in haste, and then consecrated bishop by Juvenal des Ursins, Archbishop of Reims and Chancellor of France, Jean de Mailly,

Bishop of Noyon in Picardy, and Guillaume Chartier, bishop of Paris, in the basilica of Saint-Denis.[56]

Despite his apparent generosity towards Pey Berland, represented by the revenues of Madia, the pope agreed to Charles VII's request that he should instruct Blaise, in a letter dated 15 February 1457, to threaten any churchman of Bordeaux with excommunication and imprisonment if he had taken part in any conspiracy in favour of the English enemy at any time since June 1451. After the Fall of Constantinople to the Ottomans, Callixtus was trying to rally the crowned heads of Europe for another crusade. The chapters did all they could to frustrate Blaise as he tried to embark upon his new primacy in the province of Guyenne.

Pey Berland's death on 17 January 1458, changed the character of the conflict between the chapters and the king. They were in no mood to accept the authority of Blaise de Gréele any more than to acquiesce in the new regime. On 5 November 1456, the canons of Saint-Seurin, in order to maintain Pey de Tasta in office as their dean despite his continued absence in England, revived a statute of 1324 which permitted such absence in time of war, or if the dean were to be chosen as an ambassador as, indeed, he had been. He was not named in the document they issued but they accepted that their canon treasurer had the right to issue it.[57] They must have found it difficult not to show their satisfaction when Coëtivy announced that they did not have to pay tax on the sale of their wines at present, merely to provide caution money until such time as their case should be decided, as it was on 8 May 1458.[58] The profits from the sales were the patrimony of the poor in Bordeaux, and Berland's charitable instincts were still active. They eventually won their case before the same seneschal.[59]

After that, the chapters' conflicts became more ecclesiastical than political because their intransigent opponent was Blaise de Gréele rather then Olivier de Coëtivy. There was a new pope, Aeneas Sylvius Piccolomini, Pius II, who deplored Charles VII's Pragmatic Sanction and wanted to be able to direct the rulers of Christendom towards unified action against the Ottomans and stem their advance westwards. The canons of the two Bordelais chapters looked to him for support in their opposition to Archbishop Blaise, who was launching new offensives against them.[60] He was soon behaving like the wolverine in a Canadian forest who is not satisfied until he has killed and eaten all the other animals in his territory, using all the facilities for litigation that the tribunals in Bordeaux, particularly the *Grands Jours* of 1459, could provide.

But if, like the head teacher after a playground fight, we ask who started this rumpus, we shall have to admit that it was the Chapter of Saint-André. On 7 June 1458, according to their registers, they appealed against abuses perpetrated by Gréele before seneschal Coëtivy who set a date for a hearing a week later. The archbishop's lawyer lost the case over the possession of rights which remained to the Dean and Chapter, even though the judge ordered the whole dossier to be handed over to the *Parlement* of Paris for scrutiny. The archbishop persisted in demanding the rights that he had claimed before the judge of appeal in Guyenne. The judgement went against him in October.[61] The archbishop then began a series of interrogations about the way the canons carried out their ecclesiastical duties. In his visitations, he raised all sorts of footling questions about, for example, the seals they used on their documents, the vestments the canons wore for the offices, the arrangement of their stalls in the quire and then about the money that Pey Berland had left them in his will.

Faced with these irritations, the canons went for a definitive solution in the form of a directive from Pope Pius II. He replied with his papal bull of 25 February 1459, by which he freed both chapters from the archbishop's control. Saint-Raphaël's College, where priests in the archdiocese received their training, was included in this exemption. The pope took the three institutions under his immediate protection, forbidding the archbishop to act against this judgement.

The chapters had power over their own internal jurisdiction with the possibility of appeal only to the pope himself. Moreover, the Archbishop of Toulouse, and the Bishops of Aire and Bazas were ordered to ensure that these rules were properly obeyed. The chapters and the college had to pay for their new privileges to the papal treasury, but the charge was to be no more than six gold florins in any one year. This rosy situation for the chapters did not last. Archbishop Blaise, still confident in having been chosen by the king, denounced the papal interference to the seneschal (not that he was competent to do anything against it) and by issuing a wholesale excommunication against the Chapters and the Dean of Saint-

André. Charles VII stuck his oar in now, issuing a simple order that the pope was not to be obeyed.[62]

The autumn of 1459 saw the second of the series of *Grands Jours* offered by Charles VII after he had withdrawn the prospect of a *Parlement* in Bordeaux. Blaise de Gréele made an appeal on 8 October against the decision of the judge who maintained the chapters' rights, but the judgement once more went against him. On 24 October, the Archbishop of Toulouse officially published the pope's bull of exemption which the court discussed in full. The king intervened once more to maintain the suspension of the chapters' privileges. On 3 November, the case was referred to the Paris *Parlement* for a hearing to be held three months in the future, and meanwhile the chapters were to retain their privileges and enjoy their liberty.[63] The affair would drag on for another two years: an ecclesiastical football.[64]

Archbishop Blaise now resorted to the tactic of inserting his own nominee whenever a vacancy in one of the chapters occurred. His candidate for a stall in the cathedral was Guillaume Dornac. The chapter refused to accept him and maintained in the *Grands Jours* that the archbishop had no power to nominate without violating the terms of Charles VII's pragmatic sanctions. We even see the judge threatening the archbishop and his nominee themselves with excommunication![65]

Yet Dornac was successful at Saint-Seurin. Despite Pey de Tasta still being alive in England, Dornac was elected dean on 28 November. The administrator (*syndic*) of the chapter forbade him nevertheless to seek confirmation from the archbishop or to take an oath to him, since he would contravene the pragmatic sanction if he did. The deeds issued by the chapter of Saint-Seurin continued to bear de Tasta's name. The canons did not dare to say that he was in England, but simply said that he was 'away from Bordeaux'. The last such document was issued on 6 April 1461 after eighteen months. On 27 April, Guillaume Dornac acted officially as dean. Pey de Tasta was now fully integrated into the English diplomatic service: he was put in charge of negotiations with Burgundy in 1461 and in 1466 and, in 1467 between Edward IV, Yorkist king of England, and Louis XI. His will was dated 1468, but it is not known precisely when he died.[66]

The affair of Pius II's papal bull finally came before the Paris *Parlement* in January 1462 – after Charles VII's death. Blaise de Gréele made a plea that the bull made it impossible for him to function as archbishop and deprived him of necessary revenue. He could not supervise the worship carried on in the churches if he could not make visitations, and standards in the archdiocese were slipping. He claimed that the bull was issued by a pope who was ill-informed of the situation in Bordeaux.[67] He also maintained that to pay fees to the pope, as the chapters had done, was in contravention of the pragmatic sanction. Ever since it had been in operation, this pragmatic sanction had been a stick with which to beat both sides in church disputes. No wonder that Louis XI, in accordance with his general policy of overturning his father's decisions, would soon revoke it.

The canons responded in a spirited manner by saying little more than that the archbishop had acted 'with intolerable crudity and with an undisciplined purpose of avenging himself on the chapters'. The *Parlement* judged in favour of the chapters on 20 March. Blaise raised further objections in May when the seneschal's lieutenant issued the letters patent that made the judgement against him binding in Bordeaux. It was only then that he gave in.

Blaise de Gréele's megalomania as Primate of Bordeaux extended outside his archdiocese into the ecclesiastical province, where at least one of his tentatives, his claim to have power to confirm or reject elections to the bishopric of Saintes, was opposed by the Dean and Chapter there, and by the Archbishop of Bourges who claimed the primacy of Aquitaine for himself.[68] At the time of his death in 1463, Blaise was known to have been fighting twenty-six cases in court concerning his judicial rights.[69]

* * *

The integration of Bordeaux and the towns around, the 'god-daughters,' was a lengthy process in all its commercial, judicial and ecclesiastical aspects. The Valois king was now in possession of all his national territory except for Calais and its pale. The preoccupations and uncertainties caused by the Wars of the Roses in England prevented any serious initiatives for a return to Gascony, though, as we have noticed in passing, the

Gascon Rolls contain plenty of parchment transactions that anticipated eventual re-conquest. In the end, both crowned heads, the Valois and the triumphant Yorkist produced the common-sense expedient of the French paying the English not to invade France (or at least to go away again, having done so). Edward IV accepted the principle involved, calling the pensions he received 'tribute,' and used some of the profit to embellish St George's Chapel at Windsor for the Knights of the Garter to celebrate their occasions. Neither side took much notice of the fleurs-de-lys on the English royal coat of arms until the peace of Amiens in 1802, when rulers of France had abandoned them for a while and they no longer meant anything in England.

*   *   *

There was a postscript to Charles VII's victorious extension of Valois rule over all the territory of France except Calais and its pale which took the form of the reinstatement of Joan of Arc, and the discrediting, after a meticulous re-examination, of the 1431 trial presided over by Bishop Cauchon of Beauvais in Rouen, as well as the examination of the memories of those who were still alive at the time of Joan's claim to bring God's message to Dauphin Charles, her liberation of Orleans, her victories at Patay and Jargeau, the coronation she made possible at Reims, the subsequent failure to take Paris, her capture by the Burgundians, her transfer to the English, her trial and execution at Rouen.[70]

As soon as Rouen had been taken from the English in 1450, there was a serious attempt to re-examine all the documentation but it was not brought to a conclusion. Then there was the visit to France and England in 1452 by Pope Nicolas V's legate, himself a Frenchman, Cardinal d'Estouteville, to try and reconcile the two countries in order to send an expedition to try and recover Constantinople from the Ottomans, which also examined some of the material of the trial. D'Estouteville became Archbishop of Rouen himself, but the *procès* did not make any further progress for another four years.

Then in 1456, with Charles VII's consent, in response to a petition from Joan's mother Isabelle and other surviving members of the family from Domrémy, the major re-examination of the whole phenomenon of

Joan was opened at Notre Dame de Paris with them present. The event attracted such crowds that the hearings had to be transferred to the cathedral sacristy to allow them to be carried on with any semblance of order. Evidence was taken from survivors everywhere that Joan had been active, and nothing was left unexamined about the trial and execution. It was a kind of retrial for Joan, and the final decision was that the Rouen trial under the aegis of the English had set out to declare her a heretic and therefore to discredit her, which included many legal irregularities and downright prejudicial conclusions which made Joan's execution unavoidable. The fact the the theologians of the University of Paris had accepted the decision was the cause of Charles VII's non-intervention, since their advice to him was that he should not be associated with her heretical opinions which orthodox belief could not have accepted. That 'she was all innocence' – words from one of the witness of this new examination – was accepted, and the judgement made twenty-five years before was reversed.[71]

As in the months of Joan's successful activity, the outcome of Charles VII's campaigns had justified her claims for the legitimacy of his kingship: a pragmatic rejection of all that had been involved in the 1420 treaty of Troyes. The military victories of 1450 to 1453 which booted out the English were justified in this moral victory of 1456.

Chapter Eight

Consolidation in Guyenne

As early as 1419, while he was Dauphin and before his attempted exclusion from the throne, Charles VII was making use of contacts with Scotland to reinforce his military capability. An army of 6,000 Scots came to France then, and another contingent early in 1421, along with troops from Lombardy to aid him against the Anglo-Burgundian alliance. Scottish archers had been formed, even before that, into an elite bodyguard for the Dauphin as regent for the ailing Charles VI.[1] John Stuart of Darnley had been involved in this from the first and, in 1427, he was created Count of Evreux as a reward for conquering the town from the English. The following year, he was back in Scotland on a diplomatic mission in company with the Archbishop of Reims and Alain Chartier to renew the Franco-Scottish alliance in the form of a marriage treaty for the Dauphin Louis and Margaret of Scotland linked to further military assistance. Despite his recently improved relations with the English, James I gave authority to his ambassadors to arrange the marriage. He renewed the *antiques alliances* at Perth on 17 July 1428, and two days later he announced the betrothal of Margaret and Louis, the wedding to be solemnized at Candlemas (2 February 1429), along with the proposed arrival of another army of 6,000 men.[2]

Over twenty years later, Charles VII was still relying on his Scottish companies. They participated in both conquests of Bordeaux and in the taking of Bayonne, as we have seen. They were now deployed to enforce control in the Landes and the valley of the Adour because they could be relied on more than the indigenous Gascon nobles. Scottish garrisons were established in Bayonne, Dax, Saint-Sever and Grenade-sur-Adour, where they held the ring between conquered lordships. The leading figure among their commanders was Robin Petit-Loup, a native of Dundee (where his name was Petit-Loch), who would soon establish his position by his marriage with the seigneur de Gramont's daughter which turned him into a *grand seigneur*. He was granted a substantial royal pension in 1451, and then reimbursed for his losses during his campaigns. The king appointed him Seneschal of the Landes, Captain of Dax and Saint-Sever, and gave him charge over Manciet and Lectoure in Armagnac territory. He also received the lordship of Sauveterre.[3] All this did not represent any real integration into the Gascon nobility, however: he was solely to be the instrument of royal control, which was extended beyond Guyenne into the county of Comminges. He left no male heir for Sauveterre.[4]

The consolidation of French power in the Landes was carried out by Petit-Loup's Scottish troops who acquired a reputation for brutal violence which complemented royal policy. Charles VII publicly reasserted that he would maintain the ancient customs of the places he had conquered, but his officials asserted his power in a very uncompromising manner. Petit-Loup's recorded actions against opponents labelled 'brigands' were carried out to restrain the many Gascons in the Landes who maintained their loyalty to the English king/duke. They were rebels in the sense that the Bordelais had been rebels in 1452, but for Petit-Loup they were also common criminals for whom he provided public gallows. The evidence for the success of this policy lies in the increasing tendency of the French authorities to issue pardons for the rebels between 1451 and 1463.[5]

That the Scottish companies were an indispensable element in the campaigns undertaken by Charles VII is perfectly illustrated by Jean Fouquet's painting of the Adoration of the Magi done in about 1452.[6] The king offering gold to the infant Jesus is recognizably portrayed as Charles VII, and the gold represents his triumph in Gascony. Behind him stand his bodyguards who had accompanied him on his progress, and they are dressed in the red, white and green uniforms that they wore when the king entered Rouen having conquered Normandy in 1450. Pierre Prétou suggests that the fleur-de-lys banner being carried towards a town represents the conquest of Bayonne, and he takes Herod's massacre of the innocents also shown in the picture, to be 'an impertinent analogy' for English domination. In all this, 'the Scottish soldiers, separating a country at war from the king's household, hold a key position.'[7]

This may well be a representation of the taking of Bayonne, but Petit-Loup's company played a significant part in the subjection of Bordeaux as well. During the rebellion of 1452, Talbot had no help from anywhere to the south of the Garonne because the Scots were already stationed in the Landes and, while avoiding pitched battles, intervened to prevent any musters of pro-English troops there, based on the reports of his efficient spy network. As Charles VII's seneschal, his determined activity outside the city walls prevented the effectiveness of Roger de Camoys's defence of Bordeaux during the siege. By the time the second conquest of the capital of Guyenne was complete, Petit-Loup was well on the way to consolidating his position in the Landes, based on his captaincies of the fortified towns there: Dax and Saint-Sever.[8]

In 1457, Charles VII had a long letter sent to James II of Scotland, reviewing his policy under several headings, one of which was his border security in south-western France. He mentions the provinces of Poitou and Saintonge as being 'continually in a state of fear in respect to the enemy because they lie upon the sea-coast where the enemy can make a descent any day'.[9] The seneschal he appointed for the Saintonge was a Scot, Patrick Folcart, who profited from a pension of 1,000 *livres tournois*.[10] However, the situation in Gascony required not so much defence as policing. Since the duchy had been English for 'three hundred years or more and the inhabitants of the land are all in favour of the English party,' the measures needed to be taken there by the king in 'his lands' had to be more severe than elsewhere, implying the need for special measures to win over the nobility of the region.[11] By the time of Petit-Loup's death, it seems that the Gascons had accepted the conquest, and Louis XI's royal progress in the Landes in 1462–1463 bore this out – especially as he had removed the 'malicious' Scots.[12]

*   *   *

How did Charles VII control Guyenne now that it was part of France? The answer boils down to whom he chose as its governors. Those who had taken the oath to him needed to have grounds for their sustained loyalty. There were no mass dispossessions and the lordships of indigenous nobles were confirmed by the victorious king. This was his basic policy. Those whom he regarded as having committed treason were the ones who had broken their oath to him made after the first submission in 1451.

The king's rule was personal, only one step short of the kind of absolutism that caused Louis XIV to build the Palace of Versailles to deprive the great lords of their autonomy 200 years later. This kind of rule depended upon mutual favours. The obvious choice of administrators was from among people who depended upon the king for what they held. It was feudalism, but not as the great lords had known it before the ordinances that were the preludes to the unification of France. Former freebooting captains with military experience had carried out the conquest of Guyenne, so they were the most likely candidates to be trusted with maintaining the monarchy where it had not existed before.

The Scottish captains were of vital importance to the king, but they were not the only ones suitable to rule the new territories. While Olivier de Coëtivy was held as the guest of the Talbot family in the Welsh marches, he was replaced in his absence by Théude de Valpergue, who, with his brother Boniface, had fought for the king against the freebooters of the *Praguerie* and then in the conquest. They were Italians. Boniface was appointed captain of Bayonne, and Théude took over from him in 1459, holding the captaincy of Lectoure as well.[13]

It is worth concentrating on the career of Olivier de Coëtivy after he was released from captivity in January 1455. He had a safe-conduct to return to France granted at the request of the second Earl of Shrewsbury[14] so that he could raise the ransom required of 12,000 écus, a dozen pieces of silver plate worth 100 marks and a racehorse (*coursier*). Charles VII wanted Coëtivy back in the Ombrière Palace to enforce the settlement being imposed on the new French province. He arranged for a portion of the total sum of 44,000 écus required for the release of the Earl of Kendal, captured at Castillon, to be put towards Coëtivy's ransom.[15] Even so, Coëtivy took more than a year to raise the whole sum and send it to the Countess of Shrewsbury from Bordeaux after a year's delay.

He resumed his responsibilities as seneschal of Guyenne immediately after his return to Taillebourg.[16] Jehan Augier, treasurer of France in Guyenne and accountant in Bordeaux, was instructed by the king to make Olivier's expenses of office available to him in letters dated between January and May 1455. There was, however, a delay of nearly a year before Coëtivy issued confirmation of the king's letters patent which reduced the penalties to which the citizens of Bordeaux were collectively liable because of their rebellion (later registered by the *Parlement* of Paris on 24 January 1457) together with the king's order to his deputy in his absence for their reinstatement as Frenchmen (the process known as *abolition*) and the re-granting of their privileges. From then on, he was fully active in his office of Grand Seneschal. On 14 July 1456, he issued an order for all those interested in the refusal of the clergy to pay certain local taxes on wines known as *yssac* and *cartonnage* to appear before the sub-mayor and the jurats in accordance with the king's edict published in April.[17] Twelve days later, he issued other instructions about the trade in wines with the *Haut-Pays* and about other commercial transactions,[18] so he was exercising the full extent of his powers from the Ombrière Palace.

Coëtivy was not best pleased with Robin Petit-Loup's activity as seneschal of the Landes. During the first *Grands Jours* held in Bordeaux in October 1456, when judges were sent from Paris to hear pleas brought in the absence of the *Parlement* promised in 1451 but denied after the rebellion, Coëtivy, in his capacity of Grand Seneschal, brought an action against Petit-Loup 'for excess and abuse of his powers'. A judge of appeal named Vidal du Palais, Jean Baudry, the king's procurator-general in Guyenne and a junior, Pierre Brager, represented Coëtivy before Judge Torbetas, who presided, against Jehan Lefilz, assistant seneschal of the Landes, and Arnault-Guillaume de Lacoste 'so-called' king's procurator of the Landes.

Maître Brager opened with an appeal to precedent: there had always been a grand seneschal of Guyenne, from whom resort was had to the *Parlement* of Paris since appeals could legally have been made to the *Parlement* of Paris even in the times of English domination. This grand seneschal could appoint deputies for the Landes and beyond. All who appealed against these deputy-seneschals did so to the judge of Gascony at Bordeaux. This was not simply a matter of usage, but of law. For the last two years, it had pleased the king to empower officials, one of whom was Jean Bureau, treasurer of France, to decide in cases of abuse, put matters back in good order and to do justice. These officials had ordered the grand seneschal of Guyenne to hold his assizes in the Landes and beyond, and that cases be judged by him. This order was made public. The deputy seneschal before Petit-Loup, Messire Richart, was nominated by the grand seneschal. The excesses of which Petit-Loup was charged included the imprisonment of certain persons who were under the protection of the grand seneschal and keeping them under guard for a long time. The Dame of Urtebize, for example, and several others who were entitled to be released according to the ordinance were treated in this way. Their appeals had been quashed. They had been kept in prison without even a candle. It was also claimed that Petit-Loup had obstructed the election of a mayor for Dax, whose appointment was also the responsibility of the grand seneschal, for an entire year. He should be required to make amends for all this.

Lefilz, for the defence, claimed that Petit-Loup was seneschal-in-chief of the Landes by order of the king himself. Enquiry would be made to the king's procurator as to the rights and prerogatives of this *sénéchaussée*. Lefilz himself had administered justice as Petit-Loup's deputy. A year and a half before, people could not travel safely in the Landes, and the plaintiffs themselves well knew that, at the present time, by means of the diligent care taken by the defendants to restore justice, travellers could go in complete safety.

In the end, it was ruled that no decision could be made in this court, and that the matter had to be referred to the king's procurator and the *Parlement*, either of Paris or Toulouse, for a definitive judgement. Meanwhile, neither party was to be allowed to act further in the matter.[19]

* * *

Charles VII had three natural daughters from his long association with Agnès Sorel, La Dame de Beauté. Prégent de Coëtivy had been appointed their guardian after he had received the lordship and castle of Taillebourg on the Charente as his reward for helping to overcome the *Praguerie*. Prégent's death during the siege of Cherbourg in 1450 meant that Olivier, his younger brother, after a dispute with Prégent's mother-in-law, the widow of Gilles de Raïs, inherited the lordship and castle. The king had already declared the trust he had in Olivier when he had left him in charge of the royal garrison at La Réole. When the king came to Taillebourg to supervise the advance into Gascony he put Olivier in charge of the three young girls' upbringing as well, apportioning large sums of money to be spent on them. When Olivier returned from captivity in early 1455, he and the second daughter, Marie, found themselves attracted to each other, and eventually Olivier wrote from Bordeaux to ask the king for her hand in marriage.

The king's reply dated 28 May 1458 was as warm as any official document was capable of being: it encouraged Olivier to arrange for the wedding to take place at Taillebourg in August if not sooner. It took until 28 October, nevertheless, for these arrangements to be finalized in another letter which said: 'Having in consideration the great, praiseworthy and continual services rendered by the late Tanguy du Châtel, Olivier's uncle, and by the Admiral of France, his brother; having also regard to what the late Prégent de Coëtivy ... had done for him in taking Marie as a child to his castle at Taillebourg, where, as much during the admiral's life as since, she has been fed and nourished', the king declared his consent to the marriage and gave Marie a dowry of twelve thousand gold écus, payable over six years, as well as endowing Olivier, Marie and their heirs with the lordships of Royan and Mornac in the Saintonge, both in the crown's possession since Jacques de Pons had been banished for his part in the *Praguerie* and further rebellion afterwards. Then, while at Vendôme in November he legitimized Marie, giving her the right to call herself 'de Valois' and have her own coat of arms based on his own. He added another gift of 1,450 livres tournois 'for dresses and other clothing as she pleases for her wedding day'. That day at last arrived on 25 November 1458, and they were married in the presence of Pierre Doriole, a royal counsellor who represented the king. 'La dame de Taillebourg' showed herself to be an exemplary fifteenth-century wife in her letters to Olivier, to which, sadly, his replies have not survived to be included in the collection published by the Vendéan archivist, Paul Marchegay.[20]

It seems that the couple were content together, in spite of (or because of) Olivier's necessary and frequent absences. The same could not be said of her sister Charlotte, who married Jacques de Brézé in 1462 and gave him five children. One day after the hunt, her husband discovered her *in flagrante dilectu* with his huntsman, and ran them both through with his dagger, giving rise to a long lawsuit. The other sister, Jeanne, married Antoine de Bueil, the admiral's son, and their life and death was to all appearances uneventful.[21]

All was well for Olivier and Marie for as long as Charles VII lived. When Marie's half-brother Louis XI came to the throne in 1461, he reversed pretty well all their father's policies. Olivier was no longer seneschal of Guyenne, and Royan and Mornac were taken away from him to give them back to Jacques de Pons the new king's fellow *Praguois* from 1440. Olivier de Coëtivy was perhaps the most important contributor in the growing stability of Guyenne as war with England (but not the fear of it) receded in people's memories. Louis XI realized this for himself and, after a while, offered the Coëtivys compensation for the lordships of which he had deprived them with that of Rochefort.

Further down the pecking order of administrators, it was rare that officials from before the conquest remained in their posts, and there was a tendency for these appointments to be seen as property to be inherited. This led to a certain stagnation in public affairs because the conquest provided the only real opportunity for a widespread replacement of personnel. Once it had happened, there was no real need to repeat it.

The punitive aspect of administration is more fully expressed in a document printed in Barkhausen's collection, which is to do with taxation. In the time of English domination, the regulation of the Bordeaux trade and export of wines was certainly strict, and, on the whole, efficient.[22] But now, the vintners of Bordeaux no longer had the right to sell their wines for immediate export immediately after the grape-harvest before those of the hinterland (*Haut-Pays*) who, beforehand, could only sell theirs after Martinmas (11 November).[23] (The wine that was sold was always from the new vintage, intended to be consumed in the same year, so there was a constant need for fresh supplies, year after year.) The receiver-general was to be responsible for the collection of the tax of 25 *sols tournois* on each barrel, paid either by the seller or the buyer. The sellers were to pay an additional 4 *deniers* for each barrel. The receiver or his agents were to keep a register of all payments, under pain of having to pay quadruple for all entries which they left out or of being dismissed. The receiver and the controllers oversaw all transactions and lived 'where they exercise their offices'. There was also a visitor of ships who went on board, either when they arrived or when they left. Agents were to be established at Blaye, Bourg and Libourne to provide reports to the receiver-general of cargoes leaving those ports. If duties had not been paid, the cargoes were to be confiscated for the king's profit. More reasonable were the charges to be levied for the maintenance of the Cordouan lighthouse at the mouth of the Gironde Estuary. People who denounced fraudsters would have the right to receive a quarter of the sums recovered. The taxation of twenty-five *sous* a barrel would be farmed out by auction every year with a starting price of 20,000 *livres*; each auctioneer would receive twelve *deniers* for each *livre* paid, and there would be an adjudicator who would regulate the payment of these sums into the king's treasury.to be offered for sale:

Other taxes were to be paid on produce and merchandise entering Bordeaux to be offered for sale: poultry, birds, fruit, fresh herbs, eggs, cheese, lettuce, 'and all other small things to be eaten ... and which do not keep for very long.' 'And if it happened that anyone, of whatever estate he may be, caused produce from the *Haut-Pays*, outside the region of conquest, to be brought into the town of Bordeaux or elsewhere in the *pays de conquête*, he would pay twelve *deniers* in the *livre* on the said produce and merchandise on entering and leaving. Each barrel of wine sold in this manner would attract a tax of twenty-five *sols* tournois. To avoid fraud, the receiver had to give receipts for all this, signed by controllers in designated places and fines would be paid for not having or not issuing these receipts or, in the case of officials, for not keeping proper registers of them. The officials concerned were to live at these collection points on pain of dismissal.[24]

So nothing is overlooked, no breach of the ordinances is possible, and all this under the menacing shadow of the Tropeyte fortress being built beside the quay on the site of destroyed warehouses and dwellings by what amounted to forced labour from the whole of the Bordelais coming in daily to carry out the construction work. Even when the price to be paid by the town for rebellion had been reduced from 100,000 to 30,000 gold écus, it was still a deliberately oppressive sum. Furthermore, Bordeaux's right to mint its own coinage had been suppressed. It could have been said that Seneschal Coëtivy before his capture or *le roi Talbot* before his defeat had shown the same inclinations before the re-conquest. Nevertheless, these tight controls were now being used in the interest of the conquerors and nobody else.

Charles VII's hostile and punitive reaction to the members of the Bordeaux *jurade* who had welcomed Talbot within their walls in October 1452 invites comparison with the rewards he gave to the ecclesiastics and bourgeoisie of Saint-Maixent who had resisted the military onslaughts of his opponents of the *Praguerie* revolt twelve years before. This upfront style of kingship was nothing if not personal rule, represented by these rewards and punishments. The Abbot of Saint-Maixent and his successors became members in perpetuity of the king's Great Council, whereas Pey Berland was soon replaced with papal connivance by Blaise de Gréele, a creature from the royal *coterie.* Bordeaux and its *jurade* were fined a huge sum – huge even after it was reduced – and the townsmen had to build and maintain the two new royal-strongholds within their walls. Another obvious comparison is with contemporary events in England, where personal kingship was in abeyance in the person of Henry VI while potentates like Suffolk made 'a determined attempt to find a substitute for a non-operational king'.[25]

* * *

From the point of view of all the inhabitants of the Bordelais, the importance of the consolidation of French power over them was its effect upon the wine trade with England. English wine imports, mostly from Gascony, have been estimated at towards 12,000 barrels in the single year 1447–1478, and 13,000 in the year after. These were the last two years of the truce that began in 1445 at the time of Henry VI's marriage to Margaret of Anjou. Good seasons had followed the end of the destruction of vines in time of open warfare, the truce had reduced the danger from privateers at sea and ships were not then being commandeered by the English crown for military purposes. When fighting began again, the taking of Guiche (the port next in importance in Gascony to Bordeaux) near Bayonne, together with fifteen other towns, caused exports to England to plummet. Less than 6,000 barrels were exported in 1449–1450. In autumn 1450, when Charles VII's armies were approaching Bordeaux, English ships were collected for a relieving force and kept idle off-shore for months. French ships from Brittany and La Rochelle blockaded the Gironde in the spring of 1451. 'War was more catastrophic for the wine trade than actual surrender.'[26]

Even so, the surrender of Bordeaux in June did not put a stop to the wine trade with England. Its continuance was written into the peace treaty. Ten English ships received safe-conducts at Saint-Jean d'Angély – the port on the River Boutonne, a tributary of the Charente near its estuary, inland from Rochefort – for passage to Bordeaux on the day the treaty was signed. Twenty more ships were licensed in England, with the traders still confident of a good reception. They received safe-conducts when they arrived and unloaded their wheat cargoes. At least twenty-six English ships were in port at Bordeaux in January 1452, with over 1,000 men on board, forty of whom were traders. The names of the ships, their masters and their home ports are given in a document drawn up to record their presence by Guillaume de Rouille, the visitor acting on the orders of the seneschal of Guyenne (whose name is not given in the document, but who must have been de Coëtivy at that time).[27] Moreover, English traders were still loading wine they bought on foreign ships at Bayonne. 7,000 barrels left Gascony for English ports in 1451–1452. During Talbot's occupation, neither licences nor safe-conducts were needed and nearly 10,000 barrels were imported.[28] Even after the second conquest of October 1453, trade was not too much disrupted from an English point of view at first. The terms of trade were 'much less favourable' and 'some dislocation of trade was inevitable', but imports of wines from Gascony in 1453–1454 was again estimated at 6,000 barrels. The next year, there was a recovery to 9,500 barrels, and the bulk of this was still carried in English ships as a detailed account from Southampton confirms. There were no convoys as in the past, and arrivals in English ports were 'scattered,' but the four ships that put into Southampton during that season had nothing but wine in their holds, confirmed by their bills of lading. Fifty-eight licences to trade were issued in 1454 and thirty-two in 1455, some to English denizen traders, but also to Gascons who had decided to settle in London, Bristol or Southampton.[29]

This did not stop the regulations issued by Charles VII's commissioners in January 1455 being punitive for the exporters, and in the next season – 1455–1456 – they began to bite 'and the whole direct trade was threatened with extinction'. Charles VII had taken additional action to forbid his officials to grant safe-conducts to 'the former enemy'. Again, a punitive intention; but the outcry against it was so great that he relented to allow the issue of eighty passes a year. These were to be granted directly by the king in person or by his admiral, not as a matter of bureaucratic routine. The amount of wine transported fell to less than 5,000 barrels, and in the following year to 3,000. General uncertainty and the difficulty of securing licences or safe-conducts, the predations of Breton ships and French attacks on English ports were all inhibiting factors for English traders and mariners.[30] Even if they reached the Gironde, they had to put in at Soulac to collect a permit and pay the fee, then again at Blaye to unload their armament, with payment of another fee, and, on arrival at Bordeaux, they had to have a permit from the mayor to stay at designated lodgings and submit to what amounted to a curfew between 5 pm and 7 am.[31]

When Louis XI succeeded his father as King of France in 1461, the situation did not immediately improve for the English. The new king had a pact with Queen Margaret, his cousin, and forbade wine exports to Edward IV's now Yorkist England. This only lasted for one season, however. Under Louis XI, the punitive action was against English traders, not the Gascons. He made a royal progress among them in 1462[32] and was mending fences there following the sensible advice he had received from his counsellor, Regnault Girard. 'The English should therefore be allowed to trade once again as freely as they would.'[33]

But this is to anticipate the outcome. At the same conference under the auspices of the *Comité Internationale des Sciences Historiques* in Paris in 1946 as Professor Carus-Wilson of the London School of Economics gave her paper, Dr. Yves Renouard, Head of the Faculty of Letters at the University of Bordeaux and later a Professor at the Sorbonne, presented another in parallel, covering similar ground, but different enough to provide a complementary point of view.[34]

The political union between England and Aquitaine had seemed before the French conquest to be intertwined with the prosperity of economic relations. The new conditions after the surrender of 1451 were briskly established. English traders and mariners were from now on the enemies of the dominant power in Bordeaux. Charles VII established this clearly in a series of ordinances and in the preamble to the treaty.[35] The English traders and Gascon proprietors could still have active commercial relations so as to export the wine harvest of 1451, provided it was completed before the expiry of the date fixed for it: 20 December. The document affirms that the wine exported to England in 1451 exceeded by a third the quantity taken the year before. After the cut-off date, it seemed that this commerce, traditional since the establishment of the English mercantile marine, seemed interrupted for as long as French occupation would last. In addition, the treaty offered safety and fiscal advantages to any traders from any nation who came to Bordeaux down rivers or by land routes ('*par eau douce ou par terre*').[36] Charles VII intended to turn the export of wine towards his own country in order, more or less, to break all ties between England and Aquitaine.

There had been no notices telling the English traders and shipowners not to come, which accounts for there being twenty-six English ships on the Garonne in January 1452 already referred to. They had obtained their safe-conducts from the Admiral of France and the seneschal of Guyenne had ordered an exceptional inspection at that time. The 'brutal interruption of trade' which could have been expected did not happen after the expiry of the delay of six months fixed by the treaty of capitulation.[37]

After Talbot's reception into the town, the situation returned to what it had been before June 1451. The English ships were unhindered while loading and exporting the wines from the 1452 harvest. In spite of the precarious state of affairs, the amount of wine carried to England in 1452–1453 returned to five-sixths of what it had been in 1446–1448.[38]

After the second capitulation the new taxes already noted were imposed for the French crown's benefit as a punishment for the city's treason, but there was nothing to say that Charles VII had forbidden trade with the English in any formal way. Yet commerce in wine was open to all nations' traders. A state of war with England continued, and English traders had to leave Bordeaux under safe-conduct.

The convention agreed between Admiral Jean de Bueil and Roger de Camoys dated 5 October 1453 allowed all English ships to sail freely from the port during the next day, laden with wine or any other merchandise that seemed appropriate, to be taken to England or anywhere else during the time allowed by the safe-conducts that were issued. This has the appearance of a desire on the part of Charles VII to rid himself of the English as soon as possible. Even so, John d'Ormont sent wine to England in April 1454 under a safe-conduct issued by Bueil and Dunois.

Then, suddenly, on 27 October 1455, Charles VII utterly forbade his lieutenants-general, military governors, constables, the Admiral of France and all other officials to provide English traders or ships' captains with safe-conducts in order to prevent any trade at all between them and the producers of Bordeaux. The king's intention to put an end to all English influence in his new province of Guyenne was made plain. Nevertheless, the king's Great Council intervened on Christmas Eve 1455 to permit the Duke of Bourbon, recently appointed governor of Guyenne, to grant licences and securities for Englishmen to come to Bordeaux to take on cargoes of wine.[39]

The minutes of the *Grands Jours* of 1456 and 1459 present disputes about the trade, giving the names of the ships involved: the *Ghost* of London, the *Warry* of Sandwich, the *Anne* of Southampton, the *Marguerite* of Orwell, and the *Antoine* of Hull.[40] In 1458, some English sailors escaped from imprisonment in the Ombrière and caused disturbances in the city: a decree issued during the *Grands Jours* on 3 November 1459 shows that such disturbances were frequent.[41]

The text Renouard refers to is especially interesting for what it suggests about conditions towards the end of Charles VII's reign, and a section of it is worth quoting in full:

> *Item*, and because it is said that Englishmen are allowed to come into this town without guides or guards at night without lanterns, and go about as well in the *Médoc* and *Entre-Deux-Mers* buying wines from house to house, communicating with and talking to people in town and country in secret, and hearing what the military are doing, which is too dangerous a thing, and to which another remedy needs to be found because, whenever such a great number of Englishmen are present – and still more could arrive – who are not controlled, irreparable damage could result; the Court enjoins on the mayor and jurats that they must diligently take steps to police the town of Bordeaux in respect of the matters mentioned above.

Renouard concludes simply that there was no interruption in the export of Gascon wines after the conquest of Guyenne in 1453, but that the amount carried was much less than in the preceding decade.[42] Because of the difficulty in obtaining safe-conducts and the harassment of English traders and mariners once arrived in Bordeaux, it took a great deal of determination for anyone to fit out a ship for the enterprise. It is 'very

likely' (*vraiment semblable*), says Renouard, that wines were exported in
ships from Brittany and Flanders since their mariners did not face the
same inconveniences, but they had not replaced the English entirely, as
Girard's memorandum to Louis XI bore out. Charles VII's regulations
and the lessening of production made the prices for Gascon wines higher,
and this in turn diminished the number of Englishmen prepared to face
the risks involved. Then, from 1459 onwards, the Wars of the Roses
reached an active phase. Hostilities on land and sea made economic life
increasingly difficult. Between 1456 and 1462 the average annual wine
imports to England from Gascony was reduced to 'about a third' of the
1449 figure.[43]

There was something else that contributed to the material decline of
trade in Bordeaux from the norm of 1449, and that was the desire of a
good number of Gascon nobles and traders to live elsewhere. Some went
to live in Brittany, others in English ports like Bristol, while those who
stayed in Bordeaux suffered under conditions of diminished trade and
from the heavy charges imposed by the new regime.[44] Their discontent
was expressed in the preambles to royal ordinances in the next reign,
such as this from a letter patent issued at Amboise on 12 July 1462:[45]
'merchandise had no movement in our town of Bordeaux or in its
suburbs', quoted by Renouard. But it is worth quoting more from the
document to enable us to see more through the eyes of people who were
there and had expressed their grievances to be reported to the new king.

> The *jurats* and councillors of our said town of Bordeaux have
> demonstrated to us the great harm that they have to put up with
> because the aforementioned English merchants no longer come and
> trade in the said town nor in the region, under safe-conduct. [They
> have also told us] what great profit could return there and in the
> surrounding countryside if we were pleased to consent to the return
> of the said English merchants ...[46]

Renouard draws our attention to historians active before the publication of
the customs accounts who went beyond the complaints of the mayor and
the jurats to affirm directly (and erroneously) that the port of Bordeaux
was closed for trade with England and that the vines were abandoned.[47]

Louis XI inherited the throne of France on 22 July 1461 but was not particularly concerned with the province of Guyenne for the first six months of his reign. However, when he made a progress there in the following year, he saw the reality of things for himself. His attitude was complicated by the civil war in England at the same time. He was hoping to support a king of England who would abandon the claim to territories in France and to the French throne itself in return for his own support. The measures he took corresponded to the way the internecine conflict in England was going. He envisaged at first the prospect of Bordeaux without the English, issuing ordinances in March 1462 to welcome traders from the Hanseatic League, the Spanish kingdoms, Flanders, and the Low Countries, creating two open markets every year at Bordeaux, one at the beginning of Lent and the other in August, each to last eight days, with considerably reduced tariffs.[48] He forbade access to the English who were still 'his enemies', even if they had managed to obtain safe-conducts. Renouard points out that this was the only actual interdiction of their docking in the port since Charles VII's angry spat seven years earlier.[49]

This situation too was short-lived because three months later, on 28 June, Louis signed a truce for a hundred years with Queen Margaret who was then a refugee at Tours, allowing Lancastrian supporters to live in Bordeaux in consideration of special licences issued from his court.[50] Edward IV forbade the export of Gascon wines in the holds of English ships at the same time as a political riposte. A few Lancastrian supporters did profit from this, but Breton shipmasters were quick to make up some of the deficiency in supplies to England.

Louis XI, in spite of his support in principle of the Lancastrian queen, sensed that the Yorkists would be the winners and signed the truce of Hesdin with Edward IV which, on the pretext of stopping piracy, forbade the issue of safe-conducts to any Englishmen. But then, on 12 July 1463, he issued the ordinance of Amboise which did allow safe-conducts to be issued again. If the English were to arrive once more to pay for their purchases in gold, this would save the Gascon monoculture of wine. But there was to be even stricter control of English shipping arriving at the port, to which Edward IV replied by similar restrictions upon French traders arriving in English ports. Nevertheless, with increased stability once Yorkist rule had been established, the wine trade grew again. In the five years between 1463 and 1468, the amount of wine exported to England reached half the amount of what it had been before 1449.[51]

All this happened despite there being no safe-conducts granted by Edward IV recorded in the final Gascon Roll, which covers the first two and the seventh years of his reign, after the two granted in sequence to Thomas de Contis of Bayonne. As the roll's editor, Stuart J. Harris, points out, there were only three safe-conducts altogether recorded in this roll dated 1461 – all five recipients were from Bordeaux (smaller traders attached themselves to larger ones for safe-conducts to save expense) and they were allowed to use them only to come to England, not to go home again afterwards. The other entries in this short roll are about rewards given for loyal service to the English crown by other Gascons, who could not hope to profit from the offices to which they were appointed, such as responsibility for the writing office in the Chateau d'Ombrière granted to Phélipe de Laplace.[52]

The ordinance of July 1463 continued in operation until war broke out again between France and England in March 1468 and lasted until the restoration of Henry VI in October 1470. Then it was restored and remained in force while Charles de Bourbon was governor of Guyenne from 1470 to 1472 and until the truce of Brussels expired and Edward IV landed his army in Picardy hoping for Burgundian support. Nevertheless, while the Yorkist regime lasted in England, the import of Gascon wine never exceeded two-thirds of the pre-1449 figure.[53]

The commerce in Gascon wines and English trade goods had become an English monopoly in the past because the English were mariners, and the Gascons had a tendency to be what used to be called landlubbers. If Gascon ships were involved at all, it was from Bayonne that they came – until the estuary of the Adour silted up. The fear on the part of the French government that the English would return in force one day was not entirely groundless. While Louis XI was making his progress in Gascony in 1462, English privateers in the Gironde nearly captured the ship he happened to be on.[54] In 1467, the king convinced himself that the unusually large fleet of English ships that came into Bordeaux for the wines must be the advance guard for an invasion.[55] But in May 1469, at the same time as Edward IV was making his appeal for help to Jean V d'Armagnac and Charles d'Albret via a secret agent called John Boon[56] to assist him in re-conquering Gascony, thirty English ships arrived in Bordeaux and Bayonne; several hundred men had been brought over masquerading as traders. The suspicions of the Admiral of Guyenne were aroused and, when he had impounded the ships, the men on board confessed that they were an invasion force.[57]

Louis XI, like his father (for once!) feared that this English trade with Gascony would turn into a Trojan horse. Charles VII had had the experience of Pierre de Montferrand's return in 1454, and there had been a conspiracy of certain nobles and churchmen in favour of expelling the French from Bordeaux in 1456, but both of these occurred at a time when the English were incapable of giving them support, and Charles VII had had no difficulty in suppressing them by means of the garrison he maintained in the town.

There was 'a rapid and astonishing rallying'[58] to the King of France at the time of the treaty of Picquigny by those who had been Anglophiles twenty years previously. At first, so many Gascons chose to transfer their businesses to England in the years 1451–1453 that they caused a certain de-population of Bordeaux and the area around it by all the elements most loyal to the English king/duke.[59] There were many empty houses. These emigrants were replaced by newcomers from the Midi, tradespeople who had followed the French armies as they had invaded. They are listed in the king's instructions to Seneschal Coëtivy on 25 July 1457 as 'drapers, tailors, cutters, shoemakers, barbers and other mechanical people'. They had the idea that, since they had provided services to military personnel on the march, they would be exempt from taxation if they set up shop in Bordeaux when the conquest was complete. The seneschal was ordered to inform them that they must pay the same as everyone else.[60] These people were French nationals (as we would say, and they were beginning to) and they had no regard for Bordeaux's former status as an English duchy. By their presence in considerable numbers, they gradually changed the sentiments of the townspeople.

Furthermore, Charles VII's brutal repression of the Bordelais in 1453, with military occupation, the clearances for the Hâ and Tropeyte fortresses and the forced labour to construct them, together with the control exercised by his officials, particularly of his son-in-law Coëtivy, prevented any chance of a popular rising in support of an English return being successful. Louis XI carried on with this policy, at least for the first years of his reign, with guard posts at Soulac on the northern point of the Médoc, where Talbot had landed his force in 1452, and at Royan with a courier service ready to give early warning of any English presence off the coast. Each and every English ship arriving in the Gironde still had to unload its guns and other armament at Blaye and submit to an inspection by a crown official. Tickets were issued to the traders for their lodgings ashore by the Mayor of Bordeaux, and they were required to wear a cross of St. George on their clothing and to remain indoors from five in the evening till seven in the morning. They were not supposed to leave the town to taste or buy wines in other places without an escort of archers. Although this regulation was not always maintained, as we have seen, the measures were effective in restricting the influence of such Englishmen who did come to Bordeaux and, in spite of them, there was a general return to prosperity among the Gascon winegrowers and traders.

Moreover, in order to attract more foreign settlers, Louis XI suppressed a law which said that the property of foreigners who died on French soil should be appropriated by the state. The Guyennais of 1475, when the Hundred Years' War (though nobody at the time called it that) was halted by the truce made at Picquigny, were part of a new generation who had no direct memory of the years before the invasions. They accepted French rule because they had not known anything different.

* * *

Another prominent English economic historian, M.K. James, gave further information about the stabilization of Bordeaux under Charles VII and Louis XI. The Gascon migration to England of the 1450s was composed of men from Bordeaux with their families and a number of people from Bayonne 'whose proved loyalty to the English no longer stood them in good stead' at home.[61] The nobles among them were welcomed by the King of England and his government, and we have already noted some of their names, but the bulk of them were traders looking for privileges comparable to the ones they had lost in Gascony. This had happened already in 1451 after the first French conquest, and immigrants obtained licences to bring their wine and other trade goods to England. Members of the Makanam family were English by origin and they rediscovered their roots at that time. During 1452–1453, the migrants were less numerous, but more came in the wake of the final capitulation of Bordeaux in October 1453 and this tendency continued for the next two years.[62] Licences were granted only to the more prominent among them such as were recorded in the Gascon rolls of those years,[63] but the lesser traders were allowed to add their goods to those of the licence-holders in the same ships. Some had licences for more than one ship, as in the case of Richard Lancastel who brought eight ships to England in 1451. Gascons became an important presence in English ports.[64] As they settled for trade, they also sought participation in the civic life of the towns where they settled.

> Many of them settled in London where opportunities for trading were good, but considerable settlement certainly took place also in Bristol and other great cities and may well have spread all over England. Most of them continued in the wine trade, where their specialized knowledge and their contacts with Bordeaux stood them in good stead but whether they dealt in wine or not, they almost certainly engaged in trade of some kind. Amaneu Gallet, John Dorta, John Fawne, Arnold Makanam, Philip de la Place, and John Gaucem all became very prominent vintners of London; Amaneu Bertet became a draper of London ... Elias Hugon was sometimes called a merchant and sometimes a hosier in Exeter, a vintner in Coventry or a taverner or vintner in Westminster, etc., etc.

The important thing was that these Gascon settlers brought their commercial competence to their new home and played a prominent part in English trade. The Chancery Rolls for the next twenty years are full of licences for them to trade in Bordeaux, Bayonne, Brittany or elsewhere in France, and to bring the wine they bought to England. 'There seems little doubt that many of them managed to repair their fortunes' in their country of adoption.[65]

Nevertheless, Margery James argued that in all probability this advantageous situation did not last very long. Two important factors were in operation. Firstly, with the changed politics after the accession of Louis XI, the return of the migrants was being encouraged to revitalize the economy of Bordeaux and to re-populate the place. If the emigrants were to return with their commercial skills intact, prosperity would return with them.

The Gascon immigrants were becoming increasingly resented in England, and soon decided to return without any external stimulus. There were two examples of this happening in Southampton in the decade 1475 to 1485. A Gascon called Pascau Parent had got on the wrong side of a London vintner called Robert John who had connections in Southampton, who decided to accuse him, falsely, of incurring a debt of fifty shillings in the port. John had influence there and saw to it that the foreigner Parent was found guilty. Another Gascon, Matthew Gascoyn (what else?), brought his Bordeaux wine to Southampton, and Giles Palmer and John Bolles tried to undercut his prices. Other traders bought his wine at the asking price, and then Palmer and Bolles had him accused of breaking a covenant. When this did not work, they brought another action against Gascoyn in the court of Piepowder where, because he was not franchised in the town, he did not stand a chance of winning his case.

Other cases can be cited, and Miss James emphasised the hostility between denizen traders and Gascons being a problem that had already existed for 150 years. A vigorous group of English merchants wanted to monopolize wholesale distribution of wine in their own country, as their compatriots had monopolized the carrying trade for so long before, and they resented the business acumen that the Gascons had acquired in long years of salesmanship at home on the banks of the Garonne. However, in the 1460s and 1470s, the Gascons in England were fewer in number, and no longer presented serious competition. Besides, the Gascons were no longer loyal subjects of the English crown but had become French aliens.[66]

Chapter Nine

Disintegration in England

While conquest and its consolidation was taking its course in Guyenne, the governance of England was in process of falling apart. Henry VI had a different agenda from his father and insufficient personal authority to give direction to nobles struggling amongst themselves for the power which should have belonged only to him.

In England, as much as in France, a principal expectation of a medieval monarch was that he should provide strategic leadership in time of war. Henry VI, once emerged from the cocoon of his regency, did not do this during a period when relations between the two kingdoms which were his to rule alternated between a state of open warfare and precarious truces. His uncle Bedford had represented English military leadership as a member of the royal family, but he had died in September 1435. Henry VI now and again talked of leading a military expedition to Calais or Guyenne, but he never went, nor would the members of his council been confident if he had.

Another expectation of medieval kingship was as the efficacious source of justice. The reign of Henry VI was deficient in this respect, and the result was violent internecine strife between certain magnates and the gentry in their retinues in several parts of England.[1] Before his illness in mid-1453, it is on record that Henry VI did have a hands-on approach to justice in specific cases. When there was a revival in 1451 of the dispute during which Thomas Courtenay, Earl of Devon, attacked the Earl of Wiltshire and Baron Bonville of Chewton Mendip[2] in armed raids on Bath and on Taunton, the king was 'very angry with them for disturbing the peace'[3] and had them arrested during a royal progress in Devon and Somerset. After his protracted coma, he acted against these two antagonists in person again in 1456[4] which suggests that his earlier intervention lacked efficacity. Other examples of the breakdown of central justice are represented in the letters by and to the Paston Family.[5]

There were over-mighty subjects, as the staunch Lancastrian chief justice Sir John Fortescue called them, and there was, above all, the less than-mighty king, despite his appearing often enough in person among the judges in circuits of oyer and terminer which were meant to bring disputes to their conclusion. The extreme case of this was the first battle of St Albans where York's faction put an end to Somerset's, and took the king prisoner while preserving the appearances of his supremacy afterwards. Disintegration of justice was observable after the loss of Normandy, Anjou, Maine, Bordeaux and Bayonne, and then, again, on the killing fields of the civil war.

*   *   *

In the late 1440s, Henry VI was taking the initiative in a policy of peace with Charles VII's France in association with the Earl of Suffolk, his principal minister. When the extended truce of Tours was broken in 1449 the English in Normandy were short of resources to fight a full-scale war in a time of acute economic crisis, made worse by war with the Hanseatic League. The Duke of Somerset, as military commander, surrendered Rouen on 29 October after a siege of only three weeks, and its fall involved the loss of other strongholds which were not even under attack at the time.

In December 1449, Sir Thomas Kyriell was ready with men-at-arms and archers but the crown jewels had to be pawned to pay for them, and west country landowners were begged by the king to provide shipping to transport them to Normandy. The executors of Cardinal Beaufort's will made loans out of his estate, and Suffolk lent nearly £3,000 himself.[6] Financial incapacity led to military disorder. By then, Suffolk was being blamed for all these reverses of Fortune's wheel.

John Talbot (Earl of Shrewsbury since 1442) had been captured and held hostage at Rouen when Charles VII took it, and Somerset had fled. Other nobles besides the Duke of York were still prepared to maintain the fiction that the king was not to blame for these disasters, and who else was there to be held responsible but Suffolk, despite the reluctance he had expressed when the king chose him to lead the peace embassy in 1444?[7] Even before the fully fledged failure of the defeat at Formigny on

15 April 1450, it was Suffolk who was to be scapegoated in advance for all that was soon to come about as a result of the king's own policy initiative.[8]

The setting for Suffolk's humiliation was the Parliament that met at Westminster on 6 November 1449. Suffolk himself drew attention to the way in which slanderous verses were being circulated against perceived corruption, an example of which was the way a shipowner from Dartmouth, Robert Wennyngton, and two royal officials from the county of Kent had misappropriated ships provided to guard the seas against acts of privateering by Hanseatic, Dutch and Flemish ships on English traders in the Channel that had made the economic crisis in the south-east of England far worse.[9]

Harfleur fell to the French on the last day of 1449, and fear that they would invade England was genuine. Suffolk was arrested on 29 January and held in the Tower of London. Members of the House of Commons devised the impeachment bill brought in on 7 February by the Speaker and were supported by the new chancellor, Cardinal Kemp, Archbishop of York. A large number of lords proposed that the matter be referred to judges for their learned advice. However, the king himself intervened to suspend proceedings. Suffolk was released after six weeks. Bishop Adam Moleyns of Chichester, who had been forced to give up his post of keeper of the privy seal by the parliament hostile to all who had engineered the truce of Tours, had been murdered at Portsmouth on 9 January 1450 by a mob of Kyriell's soldiers when he attempted to settle their arrears of pay before they embarked for Normandy. Rumours grew that, as he lay dying, Moleyns had accused Suffolk of treasonable action.[10]

The eight charges in the bill of impeachment against Suffolk showed what it was that country gentlemen objected to in the public conduct of the steward of the king's household and would amount to treasonable activity if proved to be true. Their address to the king maintained that he

falsely and traitorously hath imagined, compassed, purposed, forethought, done and committed divers high, great and horrible treasons against your most royal person, the crowns of your realms of England and France, your duchies of Guyenne and Normandy, and your old inheritance of your counties of Anjou and Maine, the estate and dignity of the same, and the universal wealth and prosperity of all your true subjects of your said realms, duchies and counties ...[11]

The charges were distortions of the facts, but they were widely believed already.

On 7 March, Suffolk was brought again before the king and the lords in the parliament chamber to hear new charges which had been drawn up by the Commons. He was not sent back to the Tower of London, but held in the Jewel Tower in the palace of Westminster and given a copy of the charges so as to familiarize himself with them. After four days, he was on his knees before the king in the lords' presence to claim that he was innocent of anything treasonable in his peace negotiations.

Suffolk began to prepare his defence against charges which concerned his relations with Charles VII and the French courtiers. Details were presented by his opponents about estates that had been transferred from dispossessed English military settlers to French *seigneurs* in Normandy and in Gascony. The king's revenues had been depleted by unwise grants blamed upon Suffolk, and it was alleged that he and French officials had profited financially from such corrupt dealing. There was a factual basis for all this, but it was often given a 'spin' to make his actions treasonable.

An act of resumption took back into the crown's possessions lands that had been granted away and the income thus recovered for the king's permanent resources should allow the king to 'live of his own', not depend upon the granting of taxation which should be reserved for exceptional circumstances. When the act was passed in the session at Leicester in May 1449, the money raised was to be used for the army's arrears of wages. This was humiliating to the crown, but necessary in the financial crisis that was being universally felt.[12]

The precision of the charges against Suffolk caused the king to intervene on his behalf once more. On 17 March he summoned the lords who were in London to attend on him in private with Suffolk present. On the king's orders, Chancellor Kemp dismissed some of the charges. Henry VI took Suffolk under his own protection and out of parliament's reach. There had been two bills brought to parliament, one of attainder and the other of impeachment, and the king was protecting Suffolk against both. Of the lords and bishops present at this audience, there were several who owed their positions to Suffolk's patronage.

Suffolk was blamed for the disasters going on in Normandy as English garrisons were being taken piecemeal, even if the final defeat at Formigny was still a month in the future. Hostility towards Suffolk intensified and when, on the night after the audience, he was being spirited away to one of his manors in Suffolk, his entourage was set upon by a mob of Londoners on the road.

After a fortnight, the parliament was adjourned to meet later at Leicester in safer Lancastrian territory, and the king took it upon himself to announce that Suffolk was to be exiled from the realm for five years beginning on 1 May, but was forbidden to go to France 'or any other of the king's territories'. He set sail from Ipswich to go to the Low Countries with a safe-conduct from Duke Philip of Burgundy.

He was in a little flotilla of ships, and one of them went ahead to see if it were possible to break his journey at Calais. This ship's master betrayed his position to the captain of the ship *Nicholas of the Tower* who siezed Suffolk off the coast of Dover on 2 May. The sailors gave him the appearance of a trial, put him in a small boat, where his neck was placed on the gunwhale and his head cut off with a rusty sword. His body and head was found on Dover beach, and lay in a church for a month until the king in person ordered his burial at Wingfield College in Suffolk.[13]

His killing could not be traced to any particular individual or group,[14] but it was an expression of the intense popular reaction to news of the finality of the French victory at Formigny on 15 April, when Clermont defeated Kyriell, for which Suffolk was blamed. The king protected him because it was his own policy that Suffolk had tried to implement.

Scapegoating Suffolk didn't work. Recent historians have commented, 'the death of William de la Pole, Duke of Suffolk, in March 1450 initiated a new and prolonged political crisis from which the House of Lancaster and the kingship of Henry VI never recovered',[15] and 'The fall of Suffolk was the fall of the king himself.'[16] Henry VI's loss of Suffolk can be seen as the moment when rejection of the dual monarchy offered to the English by the opportunism of Henry V in the treaty of Troyes became inevitable. Henry VI's reign was crippled by what his father had arranged with Queen Isabeau and Philip of Burgundy in 1420 by means of an accord that was more of a contract for incessant warfare than a treaty for peace.[17]

With Suffolk gone, the crown accepted the Leicester Parliament's reform programme. All crown lands granted away since the beginning of Henry VI's reign save those made to the queen and the new royal colleges at Eton and Cambridge were to be resumed (though the king did not allow grants to members of his household to be taken from them). The crown's debts and arrears had reached £372,000. The current annual cost of the royal household was £24,000 and the normal revenues of the crown only £5,000. The commons proposed that after an act of resumption the king could at last 'live of his own'. Resumed land, customs and royal estates ought to provide £11,000 a year. However, such progress as was being made in financial retrenchment was brought to an end by the outbreak in Kent of Jack Cade's rebellion. The parliament ended abruptly on 6 June.[18]

*   *   *

One account of the rebellion written close in time to the events of the summer and autumn of 1450 was included in '*John Benet's Chronicle*'. The identity of its original compiler 'is a matter for guesswork', and what the chronicler wrote was incorporated into a commonplace book kept by a Bedfordshire clergyman whose name it bears and who is known to have died in 1474.[19] It tells us that 'Men of Kent rose and elected themselves a very brave and discreet captain who called himself John Mortimer (because he claimed affinity with the Duke of York[20]), who collected fifty thousand followers.'[21] On 11 June, they came to Blackheath near Deptford and the king gathered troops from all over England at Clerkenwell to make war against 'the captain'.

Jack Cade's own proclamation says what the rebellion was about: 'It is to be remedied that the false traitors will suffer no man to come into the king's presence for no cause without bribes where none ought to be had, nor any bribery about the king's person, but that every man might have his coming to him to ask him grace or judgement in such case as the king might give.' The false traitor was named as Suffolk who is accused in the proclamation of murdering the Duke of Gloucester at the Bury parliament. Because of Suffolk's false counsel,

The king has lost his law, his merchandise is lost, his common people is destroyed, the sea is lost, France is lost, the king himself is so set that he may not pay for his meat nor drink and he owes more than ever any king of England ought, for daily his traitors about him, where anything should come to him by his laws, anon they take it from him.

The rebellion was about false counsellors, and the men of Kent were offering an alternative in all loyalty to the king, if the proclamation is to be believed.[22]

The king sent Cardinal Kemp, the Chancellor, the archbishop of Canterbury and the Duke of Buckingham to meet the captain. The captain informed them of his grievances and asked for them to be made 'into statute law for the future'. He stayed at Blackheath for eight days, waiting for the king's response, 'and not intending any damage or spoliation to the king or to the realm'. On 18 June, the king led 20,000 'well-armed men' to Blackheath, only to find that the captain 'who did not wish to resist the king's advance if possible', had left on 17 June for Sevenoaks. A knight and a gentleman, both called Stafford, caught up with the men of Kent, and were killed by them[23] along with forty other men. The rest of the Staffords' detachment took flight. The king, the lords and the members of their army were 'greatly afraid'.

This skirmish turned a revolt into a rebellion because it let Cade and his men see that they could be a force against the government. Cade took Sir Humphrey Stafford's expensive brigandine, 'smitten full of gilded nails,' and his gilded spurs, which he wore for the time he had left to live as a sign of his acquired prowess and gentility.[24] Some of the royal retainers saw what rebels could do in these circumstances and their loyalty wavered to the extent that some of them deserted. Soldiers recently returned from Normandy after piecemeal defeats were taken into the king's household, and fermented dissent among the other troops. To avert the deleterious effects of this, they were formed into a single unit under an experienced commander, Lord Scales, who installed himself in the Tower of London.[25] The king and his council decided that speedy repression was the only way to reassert their authority. This reaction only stiffened the resolve of Cade and his followers to resist in armed combat.[26]

There was discontent among the king's retainers who had not been in Normandy at all. They threatened to leave his service if named 'traitors' among the king's officials were not deprived of their positions. There were violent attacks against their houses in London.[27] The king was at Greenwich when he was told about this and he allowed the arrest of Lord Saye, formerly Sir James Fiennes, veteran of Agincourt and close associate of Suffolk in the royal household, thinking he would be safe in the Tower. The king appeared 'to have vacillated and then panicked'. He summoned Saye to attend upon him, but the constable, the Duke of Exeter, responsible for the Tower, refused to let him out.[28]

The king withdrew to Berkhamstead Castle, avoiding the Londoners by going a good part of the way by boat. He then went on to Kenilworth, while the bishop of Salisbury (William Ayscough, who had officiated at his Titchfield wedding to Queen Margaret) was murdered near Frome. By the end of June, the captain was back at Blackheath, and 11,000 sympathizers came to Mile End on the eastern edge of London. He joined them and moved into London 'where he was welcomed by the citizens', despite one of the aldermen having his property 'despoiled', after which he took lodgings in Southwark at the White Hart. Because the king was no longer in London, Cade made a move to take the city in early July.

The lord mayor of London held a court at the Guildhall to bring named extortioners to trial 'in order to pacify the captain and the men of Kent'. The captain re-entered London by the bridge, took the unpopular sheriff of Kent, William Crowmer, who was Saye's son-in-law,[29] from the Fleet prison and had him and another man beheaded at Mile End, displaying their severed heads at Cheapside. Lord Saye himself was brought from the Tower of London, tried by the Guildhall court, and also beheaded, after which the captain 'despoiled his body'. Two other victims fell while he returned across the river to Southwark taking Saye's corpse with him, tied to his saddle.

The captain had broken his promise of non-violence. Lord Scales and Matthew Gough were sent to attack him on London Bridge, and 'about forty'[30] on the king's side, including Gough himself, were killed. The men of Kent lost 200 slain, though Cade replenished his ranks by opening the Marshalsea prison, calling the inmates to assist him. Then the king's 'charter of general pardon', formerly refused, was re-offered to Cade, in the name of John Mortimer, at the queen's insistence, without paying the customary fee,[31] and a meeting to discuss terms was held at a church in Southwark between Cade and negotiators led by William Wayneflete and the two archbishops, Kemp and Stafford, who remarked upon Cade's 'courage, educated speech and transparent intelligence'.[32] The men of Kent and Essex went off home. John Benet's text says that the offer was accepted by many of the rebels from Kent before they left. But Cade himself did not accept it and intended to go, via Dartford and Rochester, to Queensborough castle, which he was prevented from entering and made his way to Sussex, loading the booty he had taken to go by ship from Rochester. Government agents seized it there and sold it back to the wealthy Londoners whose property it was in any case.

Cade – no longer Mortimer – was denounced as a traitor, and a good price put on his head. The new sheriff of Kent – his name was Alexander Iden[33] – went after him. He and two esquires caught the captain on 12 July at Heathfield, not far from where the revolt began,[34] and were bringing him back to London, but he died from his wounds on the way. His body was taken to be identified in Southwark, and it was quartered and beheaded at Newgate, the head being displayed on London Bridge.

Jack Cade was dead but he wouldn't lie down. His reputation was still causing concern for the authorities as much as two years later.[35] Disturbances in counties far removed from Kent involving violence and plundering involved recollections of the revolt he had led. Soldiers returning home after Formigny aggravated the disturbances that continued, particularly in London, where Lord Scales took over their supervision for a while, but they went to where Lord Saye had been buried at Greyfriars and desecrated his tomb. Others also, when they returned with Somerset at the beginning of August insulted the coats of arms of Suffolk and of Saye. They broke into the Tower of London to take weapons. They prevented Henry VI from going to Eton where he wanted to celebrate the feast of the Assumption on 15 August.[36]

* * *

The Duke of York returned from Ireland two months after the suppression of the revolt and 'a direct connection between the two events may be discounted, despite later assertions to the contrary.'[37] Nevertheless, the next stage of political disintegration in England leading to the wars of the Roses began with his arrival in London at the beginning of October 1450.

He immediately became the symbolic focus for resentment against the royal household in an increasing number of violent incidents.[38]

Henry VI evidently feared that York was returnng from Ireland long before the end of his ten-year term of office there to challenge his right to the throne. The duke was prevented from landing on the Welsh coast until he came ashore in his own domains near Denbigh. Plots against the king were being laid at York's door, even to the extent that, when the king himself was waylaid at Stony Stratford on his way to the Leicester parliament, his assailant claimed that the Duke of York would come from Ireland to deal with traitors who would be present at his destination. It was later claimed that York had, indeed, been inciting revolt in Kent. Other, more miscellaneous, claims were being made around the murders of Bishop Ayscough, Lord Saye and others. 'There was every reason why Henry should fear York's return.'[39]

*   *   *

If Cade's rebellion was protest from below, then York's criticism of the ineffectiveness of the king's advisers, in particular of the Duke of Somerset, was protracted protest from above: a series of machinations involving court circles, noble affiliations, and Queen Margaret, particularly when she had at last provided the heir to the throne. The myth had long persisted that the dispute, and then the war between the red rose of Lancaster and the white rose of York had begun in 1399 with the deposition and murder of Richard II by Henry Bolingbroke, Duke of Lancaster. But it has been argued that 'the emergence of two factions grouped under the representatives of these two royal lines in the second half of the fifteenth century was an entirely new development.'[40] York, when he returned from Ireland in 1450 did not intend to challenge Henry VI for the crown, but demanded good government by the removal of corrupt members of the royal household, something already begun in the judgement and subsequent murder at sea of 'the wicked duke'[41] of Suffolk, and by the activity of Cade and his supporters in disposing of Lord Saye and Bishop Ayscough.

York had been part of the expedition to France for the coronation of Henry VI in Paris in 1430 when he was nineteen, and he was the stop-gap lieutenant in France after Bedford's death, returning to Rouen once again in 1441 with fuller powers, remaining until the successful negotiation of the truce of Tours – without opposing the peace policy favoured by the king. From the time of his appointment as lieutenant in Ireland on 30 July 1447, he was a loyal member of the Lancastrian establishment and did not see that appointment in terms of exile. Nor did he see his withdrawal from Normandy and replacement by John Beaufort, Duke of Somerset, as criticism of his conduct as lieutenant in France and Normandy.

Rumours of Somerset's misgovernment circulated and were soon transformed into public charges of mismanagement and favouritism over payments to officers in government circles, instigated by Adam Moleyns, bishop of Chichester, the lord privy seal. Furthermore, York did not resent his replacement in France by Edmund Beaufort, Duke of Somerset, despite his opposition to the latter's elder brother's disastrous expedition to Cherbourg in 1443, nor did he oppose Suffolk's journey to France which ended in the betrothal of Marguerite of Anjou to the king. It was a relief to him not to be near the centre of decision-making when Le Mans was given up in 1448, or when Fougères was seized with government approval in the following year – the event which led Charles VII to renounce the truce of Tours.[42]

Once back in Westminster, York took pains to clear himself of any treasonable implications by making a whole-hearted declaration of his loyalty to Henry VI, and this was possibly the result of advice given to him at Shrewbury by John Talbot and his son Lisle who three years later died together at Castillon.[43] Nevertheless, charges were brought against members of his circle of associates. Sir William Oldhall, Sir William Ashton and John Framlingham, were charged with having plotted Henry VI's death because he had agreed to sell out his two kingdoms to Charles VII. This was in the context of the charge York made in September 1452 against Somerset of abandoning Rouen too easily. Somerset blamed Oldhall for Cade's rebellion, and pointed back behind him to York. Before that happened, Somerset had taken Suffolk's place in the king's household, despite his vulnerability after the loss of Normandy, and this choice by the king involved the perceived rejection of York, who had become heir-apparent to the throne after Gloucester's death five years earlier. Another stage in governmental disintegration had been passed. It was followed by all the tensions created by the alliance between the Duke of Somerset and the royal household, and these were the result of the king's own decision. York was a dangerous threat to Somerset's position at the king's side.

York arranged to meet the king at Westmnster to present what was tantamount to a public manifesto. The king did not accept it and substituted an agenda promising a more transparent form of government in due time. York left to move about the country, colluding with the Duke of Norfolk about nominees for the shire elections that were soon to take place. The king and his household took counter-measures of a similar kind. Somerset himsef crushed a further rising in Kent. There was disorder in London between factions for York and for the royal household.[44] Early in 1452, the Duke of York decided upon definitive political action to rid the king of the Beaufort faction personified by Somerset and to assert his own credentials as heir presumptive to the still childless king.

Bordeaux had surrendered to Charles VII on 10 June 1451, and Calais was being threatened by Philip of Burgundy in the winter of 1451–52. York was also gathering support in the country, represented by that given him by the Earl of Devon and Lord Cobham who held west country lands. The publication of his correspondence with the king in the previous two years had brought him considerable popular support.

York began a new campaign with a statement issued from Ludlow on 9 January declaring once more that he whole-heartedly supported Henry VI. If he had a royal agenda it was as the king's legitimate successor, not as his replacement. He asked John Talbot, Earl of Shrewsbury, who had been head of his military operations in Normandy and who stood high in national estimation, and the bishop of Hereford, who had strong links with the court, to report to the king that he was faithful and true in his loyalty to him. He also wrote to the town of Shrewsbury on 3 February, specifically blaming Somerset for the loss of Normandy and Guyenne and the menaces now being presented to Calais, and for actually encouraging the king's enemies. He claimed that his own proposals would have put things right, but Somerset had effectively blocked their application and, moreover, plotted his undoing and deprivation of his heirs. He sought an armed force from the townsmen of Shrewsbury that would accept his command in a march southwards.

Henry learned about this from John Talbot and took his own measures in one of the few situations in which he was to exhibit personal leadership. He tried to conciliate York by sending Thomas Kent, who had replaced Bishop Moleyns as lord privy seal, to consult with York at Ludlow, but he was rebuffed by the duke. York ignored other measures taken by the king, and began to move towards London, which made the king return there also. This gave an unavoidable impression that York was intending to depose the king. The king tried again to conciliate the duke by sending William Wayneflete and Henry Bourgchier to intercept him for further discussion, which had no more success than Thomas Kent's mission.

On the king's instructions, the mayor and aldermen of London did not allow York to enter the capital and he took up a position in his own lands at Dartford. The king reached London soon afterwards. Both sides were well stocked with armaments and their forces were (over-)estimated at 20,000 each. But the only nobles who actually brought their armed retinues to support the duke were Devon and Cobham, with 6,000 each, although York had artillery pieces in seven ships on the Thames nearby, and had set up bastilles and bulwarks. High ranking emissaries rode back and forth between the king at Blackheath and York at Dartford until the king agreed to accept York's petition against Somerset and promised to keep him in the Tower while an enquiry should be held. An accord to this effect was made between the king and York in person at Blackheath on 2 March.

York's charges against Somerset were specific: he had replaced his own efficient officers by others less able, neglected to keep the duchy of Normandy's defences in good order, deprived English soldiers of their wages and given away the lands held by English military settlers in Anjou and Maine. He had surrendered to the French before he had exhausted all possibilities of counter-attack, and was undermining the morale of the defenders of Calais ever since Cherbourg had fallen. All this had allowed Charles VII to turn his attention without opposition towards Bordeaux and Bayonne.

York, Devon and Cobham knelt before the king and presented their petition but when they went into the royal tent, they found Somerset himself, evidently still at liberty. York was disarmed, escorted to London by an armed force that included Somerset himself, and held under house arrest at Baynard's Castle, his London house, for two weeks. After that, he was brought to St Paul's Cathedral where he once again swore allegiance to Henry VI and that he would never resort to rebellion again but, if he had grievances, would use the due processes of law. Three days later he had no option but to conclude an agreement with Somerset in the sum of £20,000 that they both would abide by an arbitration to be made between them. York knew he could no longer count on the men of Kent and was allowed to return to Ludlow.

The Earl of Shrewsbury (not the gentlest of leaders of punitive forces as we have seen before) went to subdue the remaining Kentish rebels, particularly one John Wilkins, and more than twenty heads were left to rot on London Bridge. There was further resistance in Kent until the king issued a general pardon as he had tried to do two years earlier in the case of Cade's supporters with only those who were involved in murdering Bishops Moleyns and Ayscough exempted from it. After a few months, judicial commissions of oyer and terminer were ordered in the parts of the country subject to York's influence, in some of which the king himself took part. Another sign of the king's increased self-confidence was a knighting ceremony held in the Tower on 5 January 1453 for the king's half-brothers Edmund and Jasper Tudor, now Earls of Richmond and Pembroke respectively. Also knighted were the Earl of Salisbury's two sons, Thomas and John Neville, among others who represented support towards York and Lancaster alike.

Action was taken against York's principal supporter Sir William Oldhall, who had lost most of his property in Normandy, but who was maintained in sanctuary by the dean of St. Martin-le-Grand in London, despite all Somerset attempts to bring him out for trial. Somerset even took over Oldhall's house at Hunsdon in Hertforshire, and had him attainted by the Commons on 24 May 1453. York lacked the support of other magnates or of knights of the shire in parliament, the Londoners did not support him, nor entirely did the men of Kent.

Parliament was prorogued on 2 July until 12 November, and Chancellor Kemp drew attention to the length of the arduous session that had just been concluded, and the king's own remarks at the prorogation were very brief. He had attended the long session in person, and it can be speculated that he was feeling the pressure upon himself even before he heard the news of Castillon, especially after news arrived of disturbances in Yorkshire. Furthermore, he presided over a council meeting at Sheen on 21 July to deal with disputes between the Duke of Somerset and Richard Neville, Earl of Warwick, about possessions in south Wales. Henry was personally involved in this because it was he who recently granted these lands to Somerset whereas they had been held by Warwick since 1450. Warwick was maintaining castles against Somerset's attempts to take them over. Henry VI ordered Warwick to hand them over to Lord Dudley, but there is no certainty that he complied. By the end of July, Henry was on his travels again, this time to Kingston Lacy in Dorset, and then on to the hunting lodge at Clarendon, near Salisbury in Wiltshire. It was there that he heard about Castillon and, whether or not it was this news that brought it on, his depressive stupor began and lasted for the next eighteen months, during which time he knew nothing of Cardinal Kemp's dying on 22 March, nor of the safe delivery on 13 October (four days after Charles VII finally took Bordeaux) of a son to Queen Margaret who was to be his heir.[45] There were certain rumours circulating about the child not being Henry's son, but these were and are usually regarded as malicious falsehoods – one could even conjecture that anxiety about what was being said contributed to the king's collapse. Then came the defeat and death of Shrewsbury, so recently active in this affair, at Castillon on 17 July, of which news arrived in England in early August.

In our time the realization of the extent to which stress can be debilitating has tended to replace the unlimited admiration of stalwart resistance towards personal weakness. As we have noticed, there was plenty of stress for Henry VI after the truce of Tours broke down in 1449. Things went inexorably wrong for the English in Normandy and then in Gascony while the magnates in England disputed with each other, and legal administration broke down under a system where patronage now counted more than justice, normally supposed to be the prerogative of the king's majesty of which princes, prelates, politicians and people were meant to be in awe. There is nothing written that heads of state are immune from post-traumatic stress disorder.

Henry VI gave a fair appearance of being in control after York had gone back to Ludlow, but there had been undeniable undercurrents of criticism at a popular level at least since 1442 when a yeoman in Farningham in

Kent said that 'the king was a lunatic as his father was' (did he mean his grandfather?) and bought a pardon from the king. Thomas Carver, bailiff to the abbot of Reading, was put in prison when he was heard to find fault with the king's capacity to govern. Carver went on to make an odious comparison with the Dauphin Louis who was the same age as Henry. Henry commuted his sentence when he was condemned to death for treason. In 1450, a yeoman at Brightling in Sussex had said in the hearing of others on market day 'that the king ... would of times hold a staff in his hands with a bird on the end, playing therewith as a fool, and that another king must be ordained to rule the land, saying that the king was no person to rule the land'. All this provides 'a contemporary link with the Yorkist picture of the "simple" king'. When the king fell into his severe melancholic state in 1453, the immediate reaction of contemporaries was to think of curses and necromancy. It was said that some Bristol merchants had been consulting books of sorcery in July (an effect of fears for the Bordeaux wine trade?) and someone confessed to casting a spell over the king's cloak at the same time.[46]

There was a Dutchman at Ely who named his fighting cocks after Henry VI and Philip of Burgundy 'and expressed delight when the latter won'. Now, after Cade's rebellion and York's challenge to Somerset at Dartford, the questioning of Henry's intelligence came more into the open. Abbot Whetehampstead of St. Albans said that the king was 'half-witted in the affairs of state'. Others asserted that the king's appearance was that of a child. Another Dutchman gave his opinion that it would be more appropriate to have a sheep on the coinage instead of a ship. 'Such comments reflected the current of opinion and perhaps were the more interesting for their repeated suggestion that the king's mnd was unbalanced. Perhaps the breakdown in 1453 was less a bolt from the blue than it was made out to be.'[47]

In the conditions of government which resulted from the king's illness and not knowing how long it was going to last or whether it would be fatal, members of the council, including the Bordelais, Dean Pey de Tasta of Saint-Seurin, now settled permanently in England in the king's service, had soon to take steps to fill the void of responsibility.[48] Now that there was a Prince of Wales and Somerset was his godfather, York was no longer heir presumptive, and no longer seen as a threat to national stability. The king's collapse changed everything for him.[49]

The king was now incapable of defending Somerset who had dominated the political scene since Dartford, as he had tried to defend Suffolk four years before. York was free once more to proceed against his adversary.[50] Once he was in London, he reasserted his former charges against him made at the time of his Dartford adventure through the good offices of his associate, the Duke of Norfolk: Normandy and Gascony had been lost through Somerset's treasonable acts. York gained a declaration from the council under the great seal on 21 November that all men were free to associate with him. He then alleged that the king, the queen and Somerset had given orders that he ought to be avoided on pain of royal displeasure. Two days later, Somerset was committed to the Tower of London, while York's associate, the Earl of Devon, was freed from Wallingford Castle to replace him on the council.

As soon as Somerset was in the Tower, he took over as many lodgings as he could in the streets around it for his servants and supporters, and deployed a network of spies in other noble households. York's faction surrounded themselves with their armed retainers. The Speaker of the House of Commons, Thomas Thorpe, was working against York.[51] Norfolk attempted to have Somerset convicted for treason, but the Commons did nothing to have him arraigned.

The death of Cardinal Kemp on 22 March galvanized English politics.[52] The Lords sent a deputation to the king, but he was still in his non-communicative state, so they had to appoint a new chancellor themselves. The Lords chose York as Protector of the Realm and Chief Councillor, and it can be deduced that this happened 'because Kemp was no longer there to stop it'.[53] His powers were to be personal and concerned with the defence of the realm against its enemies or rebels. Richard Neville, Earl of Salisbury, York's close associate, was chosen as chancellor. On 3 April there was an act of Parliament that York should be Protector so long as it pleased the king or until the Prince of Wales was old enough to assume power. This effectively meant that if he were to get out of line, the council could dismiss him.

So long as the king was ill, York was able to provide the semblance of stability. His 'one enduring achievement in a campaign to reform the

lethargic Lancastrian regime and to secure his own political ascendancy'
was the protection of Calais, presumed as Charles VII's next target after
Normandy and Gascony. Another danger was that, since Somerset
had been captain of Calais in 1451 his lieutenants who were still there
might try to spring him from the Tower. So York guaranteed the loans
amounting to 12,000 marks to the Calais staple merchants which would
enable a further loan to them to pay the garrison which needed to be
kept loyal to him as Protector. He was unable, however, to prevent their
mutiny which Viscount Bourgchier was sent to calm. York assumed the
captaincy himself, but he never gained access before his first protectorate
was terminated by the king's recovery. His role was restricted to 'reacting
to, rather than dictating, events' but his personal concerns and political
survival dominated his actions.[54]

While the king was incapacitated, the queen began to emerge, once
she had a more official position as the mother of the heir to the throne.
A letter from John Stodeley to the Duke of Norfolk, written in London
on 19 January 1454, reports on the factions drawing up behind York
and Somerset, despite the latter's arrest.[55] But, more importantly, it
reports that the queen had devised a plan to give herself regent's powers
for so long as the king might be incapacitated and was submitting it to
Parliament.

'The queen has made a bill of five articles desiring those articles might
be granted. The first is that she desires to have the whole rule of this
land; the second is that she may appoint the chancellor, the treasurer,
the privy seal and all other officers of this land ... that the king should
appoint; the third is that she may give all the bishoprics of this land and
all other benefices that belong to the king's gift; the fourth is that she
may have sufficient livelihood assigned to her for the king and the prince
and herself.'[56] Stodeley did not know what the fifth article was. However,
there was no precedent for a queen regent in England, even if there was in
France in the case of Blanche of Castille for Louis IX over two hundred
years before, and the letter seems to have been written before York was
proposed as protector.[57]

Around Christmas 1454, the king regained his senses. Somerset was
released (did the queen have a role in that?) to be reinstated as the king's
principal minister and, once the king was presiding over council meetings

again, York gave him his resignation. York and Somerset submitted their dispute to arbitrators with a recognisance of 20,000 marks (though no award seems to have been made), and Somerset was again captain of Calais. Salisbury was no longer chancellor. York and the Nevilles (Salisbury and his son Warwick) had gone to their estates by March 1455 to contemplate their next moves, provoked by some 'unmistakable signs of victimisation' by the Lancastrian royal family.[58]

There was to be a Parliament at Leicester, and their loyalty was to be discussed at it. They had not been invited to the planning meeting at Westminster beforehand. They decided on their own agenda, the same one as at Dartford three years before: to take up arms in support of Somerset's dismissal. They began their advance south to London from Yorkshire at the same time as the court party was beginning its journey to the midlands. The king was to advance towards St Albans to collect reinforcements to guard his journey to Leicester, and commanded York, Salisbury and the Duke of Norfolk, who had joined them, to disband their force. Once both sides were near St Albans, the king sent the Duke of Buckingham, newly appointed as constable of England, to negotiate. The Yorkists were adamant that Somerset be handed over to them, perhaps to be put on trial. York wanted to act before the king's reinforcements could arrive from Hertfordshire. The king kept aloof from discussion, but while it was still going on, early in the morning on 22 May, Warwick began the fighting in the streets of St Albans.

The king and his lords went into the street too. After his banner had been unfurled, York and the others would be traitors if they lost the battle. There was violent fighting and Somerset and Northumberland were killed, along with nearly a hundred others. The king was wounded in the neck, Buckingham and Dorset were wounded and then taken prisoner. The Earl of Wiltshire ignominiously fled. King Henry took refuge in a tanner's house, where York and the Nevilles came to him and knelt before him. The king accepted this reassurance and went with them into the Abbey to stay in the precincts overnight. Credit for York's victory was attributed to Warwick, but it has been asserted that 'St Albans was not the first battle of the civil war. York was fighting to be rid of Somerset.'[59] York's biographer asserts that it was the king's naïvety that led him to stand by Somerset whom he should have had the political sense discreetly to dismiss after Dartford. That was why York 'waylaid him at St Albans'.[60]

York had brutally applied military superiority to his dispute with Somerset, which gave him the success which his earlier attempts at Westminster in 1450 and Dartford in 1452 had not, despite the ships on the river laden with cannon and ammunition. His opponents at St Albans had not foreseen a fight, and many of them did not have any armour with them.[61] Half an hour of actual fighting achieved what he wanted. Somerset was dead. The king was in his power. The only risk was that the king might have been killed and then he would have been a regicide.

The next day saw the Yorkists in London with Warwick carrying the king's sword. On Whit Sunday, the king wore his crown in St Paul's Cathedral, 'which he would only receive from the Duke of York', that is, not from the archbishop of Canterbury. The king withdrew to Windsor, and York to Hertfordshire. The only office York received immediately for himself was the honorific one of Constable, replacing Buckingham. His associates, however, did profit from their victory: Salisbury received property from the unfortunate Lord Camoys, who had done his best to defend Bordeaux so recently, and the Percy family had rewards that would 'keep them in line'. Financially speaking, the Nevilles and the Bourgchier family profited the most, especially since Viscount Bourgchier was now treasurer, while his brother was archbishop of Canterbury.[62]

There was a need for a parliament to stabilize the new situation. Writs were issued at the end of May, and, when it met on 9 July at Westminster, it could be seen that the Commons were 'marginally disposed' towards York. Since he had shown all reverence towards the king's majesty, there was a large attendance of peers in the Parliament and, whether they were at St Albans or not, they were glad to join him in a fresh act of homage. But the divisions among the assembled lords remained, and, in this respect, the disintegration continued despite the 'superficial normality' that was developing.[63] The autumn saw more armed disturbances and there was need for someone to act in the king's name to provide the authority which the king himself was not exerting. When Parliament reassembled the Commons refused to take any decisions unless a Protector were appointed, and the issue was decided upon, turning the clock back, as it were, to 1454. York began his second protectorate.

The Queen was looking for ways in which she might assure her husband's and son's position – to say nothing of her own – by exerting her own influence in the royal household. Her bid to obtain a regency from Parliament while the king was incapacitated had failed, but she decided to seek other ways of taking action. She had potential influence over the king's decisions inasmuch as his mind was not now so enfeebled, but this could only be exercised in private between the two of them. There was no overt political rôle for a medieval queen in England. Besides, courtiers shied away from the dangerous precedent of another French queen: Isabella, the consort of Edward II, a century before. For a while at least, Margaret maintained her subordinate rôle in supporting her husband's authority, even if his actual power was ineffective.

York's second protectorate came to an end over the question of resumption of rentable lands that the king had granted away in order to allow him to 'live of his own' raised in petitions from the house of Commons. A letter from John Bocking to Sir John Falstolf in the Paston collection says that the queen was 'a grete and strong-labourit woman [who] sparith noo peyne to due hire thinges to an intent and conclusion to hir power'[64] in exempting herself from such resumptions over properties that had been made over to her and the Prince of Wales. Grants made by the king for his educational foundations at Eton and Cambridge were also to be respected. However, certain among the lords exerted themselves towards the same end for themselves. So, if the king's right to grant exemptions was challenged, then his authority could be also challenged, and 'the holder of authority could be replaced.'[65] The most recent precedent for such action was only fifty-six years in the past and there were enough people still about who remembered it with horror.

Almost all the lords opposed a second version of the Commons' petition that the king's rents should be resumed. Benet's *Chronicle* says that 'the lords went to bring the king to Parliament to persuade him to refuse a resumption.' So, on 14 January 1456 'in the king's presence, the Duke of York resigned his office, and left Parliament before it concluded.'[66] York's position was indefensible. He resigned in face of opposition from the lords. Only Warwick supported him over the resumptions.

The queen could certainly manage without him. While York was exercising his second protectorate, Margaret's unofficial position was gradually gathering strength and Bocking's comment about her represented a real situation. When the court was at Coventry, she was shown the same deference by the members of the council as they showed to the king. On at least one ceremonial occasion, the king's sword was carried before her as she processed through the city on her own. She coalesced her own following with the Prince of Wales' council from 1457 onwards and this gave her a measure of control in Wales, in the duchy of Lancaster, the Chester palatinate and the duchy of Cornwall. Members of her household were promoted to national office: William Booth became archbishop of York, and his brother Laurence keeper of the privy seal and then bishop of Durham. Close associations were formed with several magnates, like the new Duke of Buckingham, and, more noticeable for our purposes, John Talbot, the second Earl of Shrewsbury, who would die supporting her at the battle of Northampton. Moreover, appointments made in the name of the Prince of Wales, who was still a toddler, were hers. Her presence in the midlands and north-west strengthened control of the monies assigned to the prince.[67]

The aim of restoring unity remained as a priority among the lords for some time longer. There was no desire to destroy York whom they continued to respect. Queen Margaret's influence meant that he would be required to repeat his submission to the king several times until 1459, but he was restored in his Irish lieutenancy (which was meant to have lasted for ten years in any case) and he took part in the 'Loveday' organized by the king: a procession to a ceremony in St. Paul's Cathedral on 25 March 1458, regarded by historians as 'an empty reconciliation' and destined to fail.[68]

This occasion was meant to devise an accord between the Yorkists and the heirs of their victims killed at St Albans. In the procession, the king walked on his own, wearing his crown and royal robes, and the queen walked hand in hand with York. Henry was appealing for peace and harmony, the normal queenly role, but Margaret 'had not replaced him with herself' as 'the image and focus of regnal authority... . This public perception in fact reinforced Margaret's power. Since she was not – nor could be – a party to the formal agreement, her actual, though informal, power went unrestrained. In publicly agreeing to the settlement and accepting the king's award, York had in fact recognized the queen's power through the language of symbolic gesture.'[69]

Enough has been said in this chapter to give a picture of increasing disintegration resultant upon the king's ineptitude and incapacity and the consequent factional disputes. The most important consideration in these months was the emergence of Queen Margaret as the political figure she had intended to become during the king's incapacity.

Subsequently, the king's supporters and the Yorkists met at Blore Heath in Shropshire for an indecisive battle. The Yorkists regrouped and encountered the royal army again near Ludlow, after which York and his second son Rutland went to Ireland while Salisbury, Warwick and York's elder son, Edward, Earl of March, withdrew to Calais. They were attainted at the Coventry parliament. They returned and won a victory at Northampton on 10 July 1460. York claimed the throne at the Westminster Parliament in October but York, Salisbury and Rutland were killed by a Lancastrian force at Wakefield on 30 December 1460. On 3 February, March was victor at Mortimer's Cross. Margaret's forces won at the second battle of St Albans, but she was not admitted into London. The Earl of March was acclaimed king there as Edward IV, and on 31 March won the decisive battle of Towton.

The final loss of the duchy of Aquitaine was brought about by Lancastrian ineptitude eventually leading to civil war at the same time as Charles VII reorganized France and incorporated Gascony into his Valois kingdom.

Chapter Ten

Peace at Picquigny

1461 saw the battle of Towton in England and the death of Charles VII in France, and there were two new sovereigns: the bright, competent military commander Edward IV who had already showed his mettle on battlefields: 'handsome prince, among the handsome of the world, at the time when he was in all respects in command of affairs';[1] and Louis XI, 'who did not have a rival to his foresight, his suppleness, and his ardour in action. He saw things quickly, he had a generous interest, a talent for constructive delays, all that good collection of political qualities which Philippe de Commynes meant by *sagesse*.'[2]

When he was sixteen years old, Louis had compromised himself in the movement of the great feudal lords against his father, known as the *Praguerie*.[3] He had been sent away into the Dauphiné where he adopted effective measures to rule his province, creating a *Parlement* in Grenoble in 1453 and imposing innovatory economic measures. He was most noted for his love of intrigue. He was seen as always taking the opposite point of view from his father's policies. When his first wife, Margaret of Scotland, died, he re-married without his father's authorization. His new wife was Charlotte of Savoy. This and other measures he took provoked his father's wrath, and he abandoned his domain to take refuge with Philippe of Burgundy who installed him at Genappe in Brabant from where he carried on his wheeling and dealing. Despite it being a dangerous experiment after the successes of Charles VII the new reign brought about a reversal in method, policy and personnel.

The courtiers watched this ugly man, with his long nose, double chin, pot-belly and bandy legs, who had a bit of a stutter and who dressed in a bizarre manner with his gowns shorter than usual and his almost comical hats decorated with medals made of lead. He had no sense of style in the courtiers' eyes. At his coronation banquet, he took the crown off and left it on the table in front of him. The only thing kingly about him was his passion for the hunt. He had been a successful military commander, but his preference was for diplomatic solutions rather than warfare. Subtlety and bending of the truth were his strengths. He was systematic in buying people's consciences, and had total disdain for all engagements with others if they were not profitable to his purpose. He was prodigiously active, wanting to know and see everything, and carry things out himself. 'With his qualities and his defects, his strengths and his weaknesses, would this son of Charles VII complete what had already been achieved or put it in danger?'[4]

Add to these another new character, Charles, count of Charolais, son of Philip the Good, who was to inherit Burgundy on his father's death in 1467. He is Charles *Le Téméraire* in French, traditionally Charles the Bold in English, but appreciably more like Charles the Rash,[5] whose impetuous machinations in between the two kings added to the political mixture of these years. 'He took himself to be a noisy fly in the universal spider's web.'[6] In turn friend of Lancaster and then brother-in-law to York, he was 'resolved to break France and make a new kingdom of Burgundy'.[7]

*   *   *

When Charles VII died on 22 July 1461, relations with England were 'particularly delicate'.[8] The Lancastrian cause was represented by the intractable Queen Margaret, disliked in England for personifying all things French, and very suspect in a society still reeling from the social losses in Normandy and in Gascony. There were also high feelings in France about her brother, Duke John of Calabria, disputing under arms the kingdom of Naples with Ferdinand of Aragon, united with the Sforza Duke of Milan, in a war which had broken out in 1459 and was at its height in 1461.[9] Charles VII had favoured Margaret's cause in the last weeks of his life. In contrast, his heir, allied with Philip the Good of Burgundy, whose guest he had been for many years, had taken an active part in York's victory.

When war between the two roses began, Charles VII had thought of profiting from it to re-open the French war with England, gathering troops in Normandy in July 1456 for an attack on Calais.[10] But Philip the

Good's refusal to let him attack through his territory, especially since the Dauphin Louis was a guest at his court, had persuaded him against doing so. A little later on, he refused to participate in an attack upon York by the king of Scotland, claiming that his French vassals were too turbulent to leave unsupervised.[11] However, he did oppose York in support of Margaret when he sent the grand seneschal of Normandy, Pierre de Brézé, with a fleet to attack and pillage the port of Sandwich in August 1457,[12] in reprisal for which, an English fleet threatened La Rochelle and devastated the île de Ré while another took Harfleur in November.

The rout of Ludford Bridge on 12–13 October 1459 gave the Lancastrians supremacy and Salisbury, Warwick and the Earl of March took refuge in Calais, while York and his other son Rutland made for Ireland.[13] A French agent was taken prisoner by Lancaster at the battle of Northampton, 10 July 1460, but after a skirmish at Wakefield on 30 December during which York and Salisbury were killed, Queen Margaret set him free with propositions for Charles VII, who did not lend her the 8,000 écus she asked for but did give her retinue free passage into France and armed a large fleet for them. After Towton, Charles VII was afraid of what the victorious Edward IV might do. In the final weeks of his life he sent a fleet to raise Wales against Edward[14] which ravaged the Cornish coast and returned just before the king breathed his last. Edward reacted vigorously, and it seemed that war was 'inevitable and imminent'.[15]

On coming from Brabant for his coronation at Reims, Louis XI's first actions were to dismiss his father's officials and reverse most of his policies. While he was Dauphin, his policy had been Anglophobic. His first wife was Margaret of Scotland (1436), he had defended Guyenne against Lord Hungerford in 1440, and in 1443 had forced John Talbot to raise the siege of Dieppe. But subsequently, he refused to participate in his father's war. At the time of Bordeaux's rebellion in 1452, when he did offer to help, Charles VII refused. From then onwards,[16] as the Duke of Burgundy's guest, he was increasingly hostile to the king's policies, and he enthusiastically supported the house of York despite James II of Scotland's attempts to reconcile father and son.[17] He even considered taking refuge at Edward IV's court should he ever have to leave the Burgundian states.[18] Philip the Good was in cahoots with Warwick at the time,[19] and the Yorkist leaders, including the future King Edward, were refugees for a short time at the Duke of Burgundy's court. The Dauphin's troops fought alongside the Yorkists at Towton and, on the eve of his taking the throne, Louis urged Edward, then Earl of March, to invade England from France.[20]

The situation remained complicated at the moment of Charles VII's death. Lord Hungerford, the military commander in Gascony twenty years before, was now a leading diplomat for Queen Margaret and arrived in France at the head of a delegation bearing safe-conducts from the not-yet-dead king, though the real negotiator was the Duke of Somerset, travelling with him incognito. Although they landed at Eu in Normandy, avoiding Burgundian territory, they were meant to gather the count of Charolais and the Dauphin Louis to their cause. It was there that they learned that Louis XI had succeeded as King of France.

Louis was at Avesnes when he heard of their arrival, attending his father's requiem. He had the Lancastrian party arrested and revoked their safe-conducts, taking Somerset to Arques as his prisoner. Louis XI seems to have wanted to please Philip the Good whose help he needed to secure his kingdom.[21] He did not want to renew the war with England and had to pacify (*tranquilliser!*) Edward IV.

Charolais, Burgundy's heir, supported Queen Margaret however, and Philip the Good was thought to be not long for this world. So Louis XI, with his penchant for diplomatic chicanery, told the mayor of Caen to have the English delegation brought to him at Tours. When they arrived, Louis made them welcome, but he neither promised nor signed anything for them. He sent Somerset, on his way back to the Queen in Scotland, to Bruges to meet the future Duke of Burgundy, in company with a delegation of French lords. Hungerford stayed in France.

Edward IV was emboldened by this ambiguous policy to test the waters with Louis. He sent a delegation led by John Wenlock and including Pey de Tasta, former Dean of Saint-Seurin at Bordeaux, to reach Calais in mid-September. Philip the Good was in Paris, and he requested safe-conducts for the English delegation from Louis, who prevaricated so well that eventually Philip went home and met them at Valenciennes on his own turf on 8 October without safe-conducts, choosing his closest associates to negotiate with them. Their talks led to arrangements for a conference to be held at Bruges or Saint-Omer or Lille to which Louis XI would be invited to send a delegation.

Philip the Good was proposing himself as an intermediary in accordance with the Treaty which he had made with Charles VII at Arras as long ago as 1435. Louis received his invitation, but he did nothing to help the Yorkist cause at the time, preferring to prevaricate. By these 'successive oscillations' he succeeded in creating an equivocal situation 'where he pleased himself, and from which he extracted an honest benefit'.[22]

A key to understanding the way Louis XI functioned is given in the so-called War of the Public Weal which occupied him in 1465. Just as he had been at the centre of the *Praguerie,* his young brother, the Duke of Berry was being used by the great nobles as the figurehead for a rebellion against him four years into his reign. The disturbance broke out suddenly while the king was at Poitiers, and his brother left precipitately for Nantes where the Duke of Brittany was waiting for him.

Louis XI soon assembled and financed an army, while sending messages to his good towns to reassure himself of their loyalty as his father had. The Duke of Bourbon responded with a manifesto proposing that unjust taxes would be removed, and that the magnates were acting against Louis XI in response to appeals from churchmen, nobles and the poor. He named his collaborators as René of Anjou, the Dukes of Berry, Brittany, Nemours and Calabria, the counts of Armagnac, Foix, Saint-Pol, Dunois, and, especially, Philip of Burgundy's heir, the count of Charolais. The count of Dammartin, Antoine de Chabannes, condemned for treason, escaped from prison and joined in.

Louis issued his own manifesto, raising the spectre of an English invasion on the heels of internecine strife as had happened in his grandfather's time. Neverthless, sympathizers with the rebels gathered in Paris. Louis moved to Saumur, taking it from René of Anjou, who offered him support but was not believed. Others among the rebels, Foix, Nemours, Armagnac, showed similar duplicity. Greater danger emerged when the senile Philip the Good handed over the government of Burgundy to his son Charolais. Louis XI intensified his military preparations to remove Bourbon from the conflict before the other rebels could act in concert and advanced towards his regional capital Moulins, offering generous terms to his second city Montluçon on the way. The magnates made a proclamation that they had no objection to Louis reigning, but it was they who were going to rule. Armagnac's troops were advancing northwards, as devastatingly as any English *chevauchée* had ever done.

The advance to Moulins was checked by the news that Charolais had raised money for an army with which to advance on Paris. Louis gained a truce of eight days for negotiation. Charolais's march southwards was under way. Bourbon and Nemours had reached Moulins, and had received reinforcement from Burgundy ignoring the truce.

On 20 June news came to Louis XI that Bourbon, Nemours and Armagnac had met at Riom, near Clermont, so he advanced, joined by a large force from Dauphiné, towards them, and when he arrived patched up a truce with Nemours, Bourbon having gone back to Moulins. He sent word to Paris that he would be there as soon as he could cover the 230 miles from Riom. He set out and was continually attacked from behind by Bourbon's troops until he had crossed the Loire. He knew that Charolais was now approaching Paris from the north as he was from the south, but by the time he reached Orleans, the Burgundians were already near Paris. On 10 July they crossed the Seine at Saint-Cloud intending to advance to meet the king without attacking the city they knew to be well defended by Marshal Rouault. They halted at Montlhéry where they took up position along the ridge.

The king was aware of the enemy's artillery and ditches when he arrived there also, but he inspired loyalty nevertheless. The battle began in the morning of 16 July 1465. There were 22,000 Burgundians, including some English archers, against Louis XI's 14,000 including his household Scots. His mood was positive and aggressive, especially since he held a good position which Charolais had left for him to occupy. His force was mainly of cavalry, not trained in fighting on foot. He had sent orders for Marshal Rouault to leave Paris and attack the Burgundians in the rear. He expected him to arrive in mid-afternoon.

The inexperienced Charolais gave no order to advance. Louis did, however, leading the 'main battle' while Brézé and Maine rode at the wings. The Burgundians began a disorderly advance. Brézé held back while they were caught up in furrows and vines. Their archers, commanded by Saint-Pol, began to let off volleys over their heads into the French ranks. Then Brézé organized a feint before he led his cavalry into Saint-Pol's troops, losing his own life, but dispersing his opponents. Louis XI's uncle, the count of Maine, abandoned the field with Charolais breaking from his centre to go after him. The Burgundian professionals held firm however, and attacked Louis XI, turning what had seemed such a victory into an uncertain fight. The Scots saved the king from being trampled when he was thrust from his horse and, once re-mounted, he rallied his men despite Rouault's failure to appear and Maine's desertion.

Then Charolais returned to the the battlefield, and it was realized that there was to be no victor, no vanquished at Montlhéry. Louis XI's determination remained, however and he began his march to Paris.[23] He found out why Rouault had not come to support him. There had been some confusion about the order he had given, included in which was a command to hold on to Paris. This had been done and, when the Burgundians fled from the battle back across the bridge at Saint-Cloud, they were captured and held in the capital for ransom. The king was received with acclamation. He did not reprimand Rouault, nor even Maine when he arrived soon after him. Very soon he left Paris in the hands of its guardians and moved off to Normandy to raise a new army. As the men were formed into companies they were sent immediately to Paris where the army of the Princes had set about imposing a siege.

The king, the count of Maine, and Penthièvre re-entered Paris, whose south-western defences were still under siege, on 28 August, at the head of 12,000 troops and an artillery train, together with provisions of food, and he was once more acclaimed. He remained aggressively confident and constructed bulwarks in the latest Italian fashion, before conducting negotiations in person with the count of Saint-Pol leading to a truce, after which he countered the princes' terms with his own. Berry was offered the counties of Brie and Champagne, and others were offered cash settlements – a prelude to the king's later actions with another enemy. He took the risk of a meeting on the right bank of the Seine where Charolais and Saint-Pol were backed by a great force of arms and he had none but a few attendants. He began the process of detaching Charolais from the other princes.

The Princes had taken Pontoise, and then Rouen. They now had Normandy, France's richest province, and Louis XI decided that the dukedom should, despite his earlier reluctance, be given to his brother Berry. Charolais was to have Picardy and the towns of the Somme that Louis had bought back from Philip the Good, and the settlement brought Burgundy's lands to within nearly fifty miles of Paris itself. Saint-Pol would have the well-paid post of Constable of France.

A perpetual truce was then proclaimed and the treaty of Conflans embodied officially what had been agreed informally on 5 October. Bourbon, Brittany, Nemours and Armagnac were also dealt with singly and offered lavish pensions. An agreement was promulgated in another treaty. Peace broke out and Louis accepted the need for a gesture towards his opponents' claim for public well-being in the form of a Council of Thirty-Six, to hear complaints and make reforms which he soon transformed to his own purposes. Bourbon had the governorship of eastern France, Nemours of Roussillon in the south-east. The rest had to be content with pensions, and Armagnac with a pardon. John of Anjou (Calabria) was much enriched. The king had separated out the members of the League, and he had won by appealing to their self-interest.[24]

Looking at Louis XI's methods at the outset of his 22-year reign is enough to give an insight into his manner of conducting military diplomacy which would continue. The twists and turns of his relations with Lancastrians and Yorkists were convoluted, so we will fast-forward to the time of Edward IV's victory at Tewkesbury. The re-enthroned king of England was looking for a cause to unite public opinion behind him. Edward IV needed to make capital out of his successful generalship already demonstrated at Barnet, where Warwick, after he had changed sides, was killed, and at Tewkesbury itself where Henry VI's son perished.

* * *

It seems right to see how the early years of Louis XI's reign affected the recently acquired French province of Guyenne. The first thing to notice is a change of seneschal. Louis XI turfed out his father's ministers and close allies and replaced them with his own long-term associates. So Olivier de Coëtivy was out of favour for some years, losing some of his valuable lordships until the more mature king realised the value of his half-sister's husband and compensated him with the lordship of Rochefort, trusting him to do local errands in the Saintonge, like stopping the masons who were constructing the new bell-tower on the priory church of Saint-Eutrope at Saintes from escalating their estimated costs as the work went on.[25]

The English traders, who still made their way to Bordeaux in small numbers, remained restricted by the rules imposed by Charles VII, registering their arrival at Soulac before they entered the Gironde Estuary, enduring long waits, and having to call in at Blaye to unload their cannon and other weapons. Once at Bordeaux, they were under close surveillance from the municipal police: ships' captains and traders could only have lodgings ashore in certain designated hostels, and they could not appear in the street or on the quays before seven in the morning or after five in the evening. If they went out of the town to go to winetastings in the country, they had to have specific permission of the *jurade* and be accompanied by members of the watch. These restrictions had the reasonable effect that most English traders did not think going to Bordeaux would be worth their while.

From Edward III's time onwards, there had been two free trade fairs every year at Bordeaux, each lasting sixteen days, which drew a large number of participants. Charles VII had suppressed the tax-exemptions that went with them, and the fairs had ceased to be viable. Similar conditions obtained at Libourne and Saint-Emilion as well. So, in 1462 when Louis XI made his royal progress as the new king, he found an economic desert in the towns on the banks of the Garonne and the Dordogne. Guyenne had lost a third of its inhabitants, the port of Bordeaux was void of shipping, and no traders were working on the quays. The tax revenue had fallen from 60,000 livres before the French conquest to barely half that sum. Landowners had stopped planting vines. Manufacture of swords and spear-points, a flourishing enterprise in the middle ages, shrank to nothing by the end of the fifteenth century. Ribadieu found a lament in the requests of the *jurats* of Saint-Emilion that 'before the war, there were two or three thousand hearths and people of all social strata, but now there are barely 200.' Departmental archives showed that the areas around Marmande and Sainte-Foy were regarded as depopulated in consideration of all the uncultivated land in them; the proprietors who were liable to taxes there were summoned to appear before the seneschal's tribunal at Agen. The people who lived near formerly prosperous Sarlat refused to pay certain taxes in 1463 'on account of being in an uninhabited land'.[26]

Louis XI had done something toward ameliorating these conditions by his letters of pardon – *abolition* – to various towns in the Guyenne, granting a reduction of taxes on wines sold to foreigners from twenty-five sous on each barrel to eighteen, and abolishing his father's taxes for defence (except those which were raised to equip the contingent of free-archers). He abolished the charges on perishable goods. He aimed at re-establishing the two annual free markets by extending them to three weeks each. In 1464, he re-established all the former customs, privileges and liberties of Bordeaux.[27]

There is a progressive accumulation of ordinances and letters patent issued by Louis XI between the time of his royal progress of 1462 and the Picquigny treaty of 1475 addressed to officials in Bordeaux concerned with conditions in the Bordelais. The topics addressed include certain of the functions of a *Parlement* as a court of appeal being transferred from Paris to Bordeaux (1463), the opening of the port of Bordeaux to English traders (1463), free entry of all foreigners into the port (1465), the regulation of debts incurred at the port by English traders (1466), suppression of taxes on the Bordelais wine harvest (1466), regulations for accountants and other officials, to suppress corrupt practices in the port (1467 and 1469), exempting the Bordelais (including residents in the god-daughter towns) from work-service on the Hâ and Trompette fortresses (1469), authorising a tax for naval defence at Bordeaux (1469), confirming and modifying privileges (1470), rules for foreigners spending money in Bordeaux (1472), exemption of the Bordelais from providing transport costs for free-archers (1474), regulation of money-supply (1474) and rate of exchange (1475).[28]

Louis XI exerted himself to entice back those who had left Guyenne after the conquest, whether of 1451 or 1453, telling emigrants and those banished to England that they were welcome to return so long as they made an oath of submission. That let those who had had large possessions in Aquitaine hope that they could return to enjoy them. The relations or friends whom the exiles had left in Gascony went to see Louis XI and told him that the *seigneurs* banished in 1453 were not at all lacking in the fidelity which they owed to Charles VII; if they had broken their oath, it had been against themselves, forced upon them by the English, or provoked by force of circumstance.[29]

We have already benefited from the anecdotal powers of the Abbé Baurein, the antiquarian who before the Revolution of 1789 worried the clergy in the diocese of Bordeaux with his questionnaires about the past in their parishes because they thought they were a ruse by the Archbishop to increase control over them. He told this story about the relations and friends of Jehan de Lalande, knight, son of another knight called Jehan de Lalande, who, when Talbot came into the Bordelais with a great number of English men and ships and entered the lands of Jehan the father, the Lalande family supported Talbot to save their property, as did nearly all the nobles in the locality. When Bordeaux surrendered in 1453 and the English were obliged to return home, they went with them on account of the fear that they would have been severely treated by Charles VII. They had, since then, remained in England but they resented the way they were treated by their hosts, particularly the Lalandes' son, who was itching to return. One of these two Lalandes, seeing that his presence irritated the Londoners, had been appointed mayor of Bordeaux by Henry VI in 1461,[30] a post which, of course, it was impossible to take up so, in the year after, he received important grants from the king of England in the vicinity of Calais. Louis XI restored Lalande the younger to La Brède, and those among the banished who wanted to come home received back their lands and chateaux regardless of his father's grants to his senior officers.[31]

Baurein also related that it was the count of Kendal, the chaptal de Buch's son, who had pleaded Lalande's cause to get back his lordship of La Brède.[32] His self-respect would not let him plead his own cause. It was the king that made the first move in Kendal's own reinstatement in Guyenne. He had passed several years in England since 1452 as a wool merchant on his wife's lakeland property and was no longer young. He accepted the invitation.

The sire of Anglade had been another punished for supporting Talbot, imprisoned in the Châtelet in Paris for eight years in poverty and misery. He was released by Louis XI upon a petition in which he explained his presence at Castillon. He and his ancestors had loyally taken sides with the English until 1451, but in 1452, as soon as Talbot had taken Bordeaux, Jehan d'Anglade, as a true subject of Charles VII and a man faithful to his oath, had gone to put himself at the disposal of the Duke of Bourbon, the king's brother, governor of Guyenne, then established at Libourne, who had been ordered to watch English movements in the Entre-deux-Mers. He made his own movements known to the duke, not directly, but by a third party. He himself came to the duke a little later with new information, but he found the duke gone and the French evacuated from the town. 'Thus troubled, he went back to his family home at Anglade, itself situated in the Entre-deux-Mers.' By a strange coincidence, on the night he arrived there, an Englishman called Charnot arrived, accompanied by other Englishmen, who ordered him in the name of Henry VI to let them into his house. Anglade refused them entry from the Saturday after Talbot's retaking of Bordeaux until the Thursday following, when Captain Charnot returned and repeated his demands. Anglade saw that there was nothing for it but to give up his house, and took his place under the banner of King Henry.

This story could be challenged at several points. Anglade was well known for having taken part with those who had summoned Talbot into Guyenne, and it was possible to say that, if he had given himself up to the Duke of Guyenne, he had nonetheless been seen in action in 1453 against Charles VII's men in raising the siege of Chalais, which was not far away from his home. But Louis XI, who had a good memory, had not kept in mind any of this bad evidence against him. He exonerated him from every penalty, and re-established him immediately in his family's inheritance.[33]

Gaillard de Durfort, the defender of Blanquefort in 1453, was another of the landowners who were reinstated by Louis XI. He took longer to come home than the others. He served Edward IV as governor of Calais, and he was sent as his ambassador to Charles the Bold in 1470 to restrain him from attacking France prematurely and to take him his order of the Garter.[34] He was also given command of a force that invaded Brittany. He landed at Brest in 1472 with two thousand archers. The attack failed and he eventually surrendered, was recalled to Guyenne and recovered all his lands.

*   *   *

Edward IV's victory at Tewkesbury on 4 May 1471 was a shock to Louis XI who had not expected it at all, having supported Edward of Lancaster and Queen Margaret. However, with Prince Edward and Henry VI dead, and Queen Margaret humiliated by Edward IV, Louis had to accommodate himself to the effects of the white rose's victory. He had also lost Warwick, killed at the battle of Barnet who, before he changed sides against Edward IV, had represented the Anglo-French accord at Westminster.

On the other hand, Charles the Bold ordered a celebration of Edward's triumph. He had forged diplomatic links with Naples, from which the house of Anjou had been excluded, and with Aragon in signing the Treaty of Saint-Omer on 1 November 1471.[35] Edward IV, once re-established in England, claimed to be on excellent terms with the king of Castille despite that king's adherence beforehand to Henry VI. The Duke of Brittany was allied with England and Aragon, and was involved in intrigues with Gaston IV of Foix and in favour of Jean V of Armagnac, at that time exiled in Castille. Edward IV also wanted to set the magnates of the Midi against Louis XI around the person of the king's brother, Charles of France, recently appointed Duke of Guyenne instead of Normandy. There was from now on a new imbalance in western European politics after the Lancastrian disaster tilted against Louis XI. He had hoped to dismember the Burgundian state by sharing it with Lancastrian England if Tewkesbury had gone the other way. Now the threat of dismemberment was being made against France by the coalition of which Charles the Bold and Edward IV were the principals.[36]

Edward IV needed to be what Henry VI had not been: a successful military commander against France. This was what led him to revive the dual monarchy presented in the Treaty of Troyes more than 50 years before by a conquest for which he would be the commander-in-chief. Edward IV's sister Margaret had married Charles the Bold on 3 July 1468, and common policy between the king and the duke was to be expected. Edward renewed a thirty-year truce with Duke Francis II of Brittany, agreeing to send troops into his duchy against France. Moreover, he actively made preparations for a fleet to be acquired.

In parallel, Charles the Bold made his own preparations, on the basis of the accord with England and the treaty of Saint-Omer with Naples and Aragon. Nevertheless, he continued his negotiations with Louis XI, to the extent of marrying his daughter Mary to Louis's brother Charles,

Duke of Berry, who was also Duke of Normandy for a little while but had then (1469) been persuaded to accept Guyenne and La Rochelle instead. Louis had thought of offering him the provinces of Champagne and Brie, but having these would have brought him too close to Burgundy's intrigues.

The Duke of Guyenne died at the fortress of Hâ in Bordeaux[37] on the night of 24–25 May and this event galvanized Edward IV into actively entering into the coalition of Louis XI's enemies.[38] He was by then experiencing a certain stability. There was no Lancastrian in a position to challenge him and he had made truces with the Scots. It was said that Charles the Bold had offered the county of Eu to Edward once he had conquered Normandy, whereupon Louis XI ordered Admiral de Bourbon to establish an armed presence there. Then it was rumoured that the English would land in Brittany or try to reclaim Guyenne.

Edward IV announced in the Parliament that assembled on 7 October 1472 that he intended to recover his kingdom of France and asked for supply for the expedition he intended to prepare.[39] His request was greeted with enthusiasm but there were restrictions on Parliament's agreement. He had asked for 118,000 pounds stirling to pay the wages of 13,000 archers for a year. Precautions were taken to assure the lords and commons that the money raised in a special income tax of a tenth would actually be spent on a real expedition, that he would actually leave the comforts of his castles and cross the English Channel at the head of his army. The money would be returned to those who had contributed it if Edward IV had not left England by September 1474. This deadline was extended by two years since, by February 1475, only a third of the required sum had been collected.[40]

Louis XI was soon preparing himself against the eventuality of an English invasion. He made peace with Francis II of Brittany – after he had made an armed attack on him – by an accord signed on 1 January 1473, by which the duke would give him back the county of Montfort and provide him with a pension of 30,000 *livres tournois* each year. Charles the Bold agreed to extend the truce he had made with Louis XI until 1 April 1474. So there was time to make defences ready against Edward IV.

By the time Louis XI had to confront Edward IV and Duke Charles, he was in a position to command quick access to the finances that would be necessary whatever form that confrontation might take. His two opponents signed the treaty of London on 24 July 1474 and prepared to invade France. Edward IV intended to embark with his enormous army on 1 July 1475 and Duke Charles committed himself to support the English with a force of 10,000 men at least.[41]

Rumours circulated that the English would choose to land in the south-west, and an attack on Bayonne was expected. Cargoes of wheat from Poitou for four ships were transported there and to Blaye and Bordeaux. The count of Comminges, governor of Bayonne, Bordeaux and Blaye received his orders, and he equipped Bayonne with six hundred lances by April 1475, and Bordeaux took in 164 veteran soldiers, each with three fighting men. The castles of La Trompette and Hâ received artillery pieces. Louis XI ordered companies from far off Roussillon to be brought to reinforce Guyenne, and overall command of the province was unified. The now ageing Dunois was in command of Poitou, Touraine and Maine, put in a state of readiness in April. The reserves were mobilized at the beginning of May. Repairs to fortifications were carried out in Normandy at various places. Special provision was made for the fortification of Dieppe, and an entirely new castle was constructed at La Hougue.

As early as 26 December 1474 there was a rumour of an English squadron off Mont Saint-Michel and archers were sent into Lower Normandy. The scare was groundless, but a fund was established for feeding the 24 guard-dogs at Mont Saint-Michel. On the Contentin peninsula, commissioners called up one in ten labourers for coastal defence. So by April/May 1475 all the coast of the Atlantic and the Channel was in a state of readiness.[42]

*   *   *

Duke Charles hired Italian cavalry and a corps of English archers. Foreign troops formed a third of his effectives but their numbers were much fewer than Louis XI had at his disposal. He wanted to test the capabilities of this new force by supporting the Archbishop of Cologne against his revolting cathedral chapter in the town of Neuss on the Rhine. He was still there in person when Edward IV began his invasion of France.

To keep Duke Charles interested in his great enterprise, Edward IV proposed co-operation on a commercial level as well as a military one: a Burgundian money market in England and an English one in Burgundy, and a wool market in Northumberland, from which Flemish merchants could export English fleeces. He expressed impatience with Charles's military adventure at Neuss, especially since in August 1474, after the fruitless siege had lasted more than a year, the Emperor Frederick declared war on Burgundy, and invited the German princes to join a league against the duke.[43]

When truces expired on 1 May 1475, Louis XI sent troops into Burgundy and Franche-Comté in order to take advantage of the duke's involvement at Neuss, and to make Edward IV think twice about invading France if he saw his ally crushed in a pre-emptive strike. Several Burgundian strongholds in Picardy capitulated. Then Louis XI was led to believe that the English had already landed in Normandy and withdrew with part of his force to investigate the truth of the report, only to find his own fleet returning from its patrolling. He strengthened the artillery capability of the Norman ports. A new fleet was readied for further Channel patrols. In his absence, the army of Picardy disbanded itself.

The first English contingents landed in Calais at the end of May, under harassment by the French fleet, after which the arrival of the transports went smoothly.[44] Edward himself seemed in no hurry to leave his creature comforts, and he reached Calais only on 4 July.

The array was certainly meant to impress, being led by the king in person accompanied by the Dukes of Clarence, Gloucester, Norfolk and Suffolk, the Earls of Ormond, Northumberland and Arundel, Anthony Woodville, the queen's brother, the lords Boyd, Scrope, Ferrers, Stanley, Hastings, Howard, and Grey of Ruthyn.

Even archers were on horseback. There was powerful artillery, and they had an enormous plough pulled by fifty horses to dig trenches. All the components for encampments had been brought over, and there was a pre-fabricated wooden house with leather roof coverings for the king's immediate retinue.[45] There was a civilian contingent too: the bishop of Lincoln, Thomas Rotherham, the Chancellor; the Chaplain, John Gunthorp; the Dean of the Chapel Royal, William Dudley, accompanied in song by four lay clerks and five choirboys. There was John Coke, a

Doctor of Laws and and eight public notaries. Other needs were met by two medical doctors and seven surgeons, with eight assistants.[46]

The Garter Herald was sent from Dover in advance to find Louis XI in Normandy and give him Edward IV's challenge. Louis refused it but rewarded the herald with substantial sums of money, lengths of velvet cloth and promise of more gratuities for him if there should be a subsequent agreement between the two kings.

To prevent the English living off the land Louis XI destroyed the crops between the Somme and the towns of Hesdin and Arras inland from Calais. He assigned nine hundred lances to defend Dieppe and had the town of Eu burnt down. The total French strength was 2,000 men-at-arms and 4,000 archers. But, in case the English went straight for the île de France, arrangements were made for Beauvais to be well supplied with wheat and the streams of Thérain drained to deny drinking water to the invaders. The Paris reserves were dispersed throughout the area as defenders.[47]

Edward IV began the breakout from Calais in early July 1475. Duke Charles abandoned the siege of Neuss and made his way north to Calais with no more than a small escort. Some of the English regarded him as a traitor to their cause. He suggested that the English should cross Burgundian territory as far as Peronne, then go via Saint-Quentin and Laon to Reims. The Burgundians would crush René of Lorraine who had declared for Louis XI, and then proceed through the county of Bar to join the English in Champagne, whose capital, of course, was Reims and it was coronation at Reims that made kings in France, so Edward IV went along with this plan. He and the duke were at Saint-Omer on 19 July. They went on a sort of lap of honour which even included two nights at Agincourt. When the troops reached Doullens a great review lasting three days was arranged in the presence of Edward and Charles together.

Louis XI made his way to Beauvais where he invoked the aid of Our Lady of Peace and promised the dean 3,000 livres for her shrine should the English be defeated. He sent officers in haste to carry out defence works at Reims. Deep ditches were dug all around the town at right angles, and each bourgeois family there would pay for a *coulverine*, following the example of their successful counterparts at Neuss.

Then Edward IV marched to the Somme, and camped near Peronne. Louis XI ordered Doullens to be destroyed once the English had left and moved from Beauvais to Compiègne, to strengthen the fortresses of Picardy. Edward IV had little confidence in his allies. François II of Brittany professed friendship but was carrying on underhand negotiations with Louis XI. Duke Charles after all, refused to allow the English forces to enter towns along the Somme, Peronne in particular. This meant that the English army in the Somme valley would find nowhere to spend the winter. In this resourceless region previously devastated by the French, Edward regretted the luxuries that he usually enjoyed in London. English burgesses came to his camp to inspect how he was using the subsidies they had granted him and found their existence painful. The captains received no booty in return for their efforts. Illusions were soon lost.[48]

Edward IV was beginning to think that a good settlement between him and the king of France would be preferable to the trials of a campaign that was already turning out badly. Even before he arrived at the Somme he had sent Ireland King of Arms to find Louis XI, who had given him a secret audience lasting two hours and a present of 200 *écus* in gold. Edward IV became convinced that Louis XI would make an arrangement with him that would allow him to meet the costs already incurred by this expedition.

The English captured a gentleman's valet from Louis XI's household. In accordance with custom, as the first prisoner to be taken, he was freed. Lord Howard and Lord Stanley each gave him a gold *noble*, and asked him to convey their respectful greetings to his king. Louis XI sent for and questioned him. He chose a different valet called Merindot, known as a conversationalist, as his messenger in return. Philippe de Commynes persuaded the man to present himself to the King of England wearing a herald's uniform made out of a trumpeter's banner. He came from a La Rochelle family and Commynes promised him a job as a tax-collector on the île de Ré for afterwards.

Merindot found himself in the King of England's presence and delivered his message: the King of France desired to live in peace with England and offered an honourable peace. Edward IV welcomed the proposal. Safe-conducts were exchanged for ambassadors and meetings arranged. The pretend and secret 'herald' was given four gold *nobles* by the English and sent back to Louis XI. The ambassadors of both sides met together at a village close to Amiens with surprising rapidity the next day. Louis XI succeeded in excluding Charles of Burgundy and François II of Brittany from any discussions.

At the negotiations on 14 August 1475, the English side opened by making the usual claim to the throne of France, or at least possession of Normandy and Guyenne. The French recognized this as the formality it had become. The King of France proposed to pay 75,000 *écus* to the King of England within fifteen days to cover the costs of his expedition. When he had received this sum, Edward IV would leave French territory, leaving hostages behind with Louis XI until he had withdrawn the greater part of his army to England. A truce would then be signed along with a commercial treaty. There would be secret clauses specifying friendship between the two sovereigns, obliging each one to aid the other in case of a revolt by their subjects. Louis would pay Edward an annual sum of 50,000 *écus* during his lifetime and he would marry the dauphin at his own expense to one of Edward's daughters, allowing for a dowry of 60,000 *livres* a year.

Louis XI was offering to pay the King of England to go away. Perhaps what he was doing lacked the dimension of glory, and was not in the chivalric tradition of the high middle ages, but he knew that Duke Charles had refused the shelter of the town of Peronne for the winter to his ally, and he wanted to secure Edward IV's agreement to his proposal before the duke could return. He also knew how unreliable the count of Saint-Pol was likely to be and, with the attitude of the feudal magnates as it was, a new episode of the War of the Public Weal was a strong possibility. With no English soldiers on his soil, Louis XI would be able to minimize that threat. What had to be done had to be done quickly.[49]

Edward IV was certainly not averse to the proposal and soon managed to persuade English captains to accept cash payments instead of unlikely ransoms for French prisoners. The English negotiators went to pass the night at Compiègne as the guests of Admiral de Bourbon, and the next day went to the Abbey of Our Lady of Victory near Senlis to be welcomed by Louis XI himself. The conditions for a truce were drawn up and oaths were exchanged. The two kings met in person near Amiens.

On 19 August, the Duke of Burgundy arived in haste from Luxembourg, burst in on Edward IV at the Saint-Christ English camp and asked him to his face if what he had been told about this agreement was true.

King Edward told him what had happened – a truce for nine years had been arranged, and Burgundy and Brittany were to be included in it. The duke had no intention of taking part in it. He angrily said that he had not brought the English king over to help him, but in order that he could recover what was rightfully his. For his part, he would only accept the truce three months after King Edward's army had left France. With that, he left and went back to Luxembourg.[50]

Louis XI was more than satisfied that such a rift had occurred in the coalition against him and set about raising the money he had offered to Edward IV by sending his chancellor and financier-general to take out a loan from the secretariat of the *Parlement* and from the town of Paris who advanced the sum required until All Saints Day (1 November). The financier-general himself rounded up the figure to the sum required from his personal fortune. Louis sent a message to the chancellor reminding him that above the sum promised to the English king, other payments to his courtiers would also be necessary.

Louis arrived in Amiens on 25 August, and the English army was on the right bank of the Somme. Cartloads of good wine were sent to Edward, and tables were set out at the gates of Amiens with lavish dishes on them. He ordered the town taverners not to make his former enemies, now valued guests, pay for anything. When nine thousand of them turned up to benefit from this generosity, it was Edward who stationed archers at the gates to keep the townspeople safe from his troops who were out of their faces.[51]

Although beginning his career as a member of the Burgundian admnistration, for the last three years Commynes had been trusted member of Louis XI's circle of intimate friends.[52] All modern commentators base their accounts on Philippe de Commyne's memoirs so, for the meeting arranged to finalize the Franco–English treaty itself, we shall go direct to the source.[53]

When his king decided to make the final treaty face to face with Edward IV, Commynes was sent with others, French and English, to find a suitable meeting place on the river. They decided that the best place would be Picquigny, nine miles from Amiens where there was a strong castle, though they could not choose the castle itself since the Duke of Burgundy had burnt it down. The Somme flowed through open country there. Orders were given for a strong and wide bridge to be constructed, and the French provided the carpenters and materials. In the middle of the bridge something like a lion's cage was to be provided, made out of trellis. A man could easily push his arm through the gaps in it. The top of the structure was covered with boards in case it rained, despite it being August. Up to a dozen people could get under it on either side, but no one could pass the trellis to reach the other end of the bridge. A boat with two oarsmen was provided as a ferry for those who would need it.

This arrangement was chosen because of the memory of how Charles VII had become implicated in the murder of John the Fearless on the bridge at Montereau in 1419. This time there would be no wicket gate that could be opened, and any handshaking desired would be achieved through the gaps in the trellis. Louis XI told the story to Commynes when he gave him his instructions.

So, on 29 August 1475, the meeting took place. Louis XI arrived first with about eight hundred men-at-arms. The English army was already drawn up on the other side of the river with a large contingent of cavalry. Commynes was one of the twelve men Louis had with him, and had been asked to dress like the king as often happened. The king of England arrived on the other side of the barrier via the causeway, also well attended by his brother Clarence, Northumberland, Hastings, his chamberlain, the chancellor Thomas Rotherham, and others. Four of them were dressed in cloth of gold like their king, who himself wore a large velvet cap decorated with a fleur-de-lys in jewels. Commynes observed that he noticed that Edward IV was fatter than when he had last seen him.

The kings embraced each other through the trellis, they exchanged deep bows and greetings, with Edward speaking in French, and then Thomas Rotherham, bishop of Lincoln and chancellor of England, prophesied that a great peace was about to be made. Letters sent by King Louis to King Edward that concerned the proposals were opened. A missal was brought and a fragment of the True Cross, on which both swore to keep what had been mutually promised: a truce to last for nine years sealed by marriage alliances.

Then King Louis, talking for the sake of talking (as French people say), jokingly invited Edward to come to Paris to dine with the ladies, offering to give him the Cardinal of Bourbon as a confessor to absolve him from any sins he might commit, '*car il sçavait bien que ledict cardinal estoit bon compagnon*'.[54]

Afterwards, alone with only Commynes, the kings discussed without coming to any decision what they would do if the Dukes of Burgundy or Brittany did not accept the treaty. Edward would abide by whatever Duke Charles decided for himself, but asked Louis not to make war on the Duke of Brittany because 'in his hour of need he had never found such a good friend.'[55] Louis went to Amiens and Edward to his camp, for which Louis XI had provided all the candles. As they rode away, Louis told Commynes that he did not really want the king of England to accompany him to Paris: he had paid him to leave France and only once he had gone would he be able to keep up the desired appearances of friendship.[56]

At a time when something of the spirit of chivalry still persisted, many were shocked to see Louis XI drawing up accounts as if he were a trader in gold ingots. On both French and English sides there were malcontents who complained at the king being so generous with his gifts. Edward IV's brother, Richard, Duke of Gloucester (the future Richard III), received crockery and good horses.[57] There seemed to be no limit to Louis XI's generosity with the tax revenue from his towns, and several influential English noblemen received pensions, being no more adverse to taking them than their king had been to receive what he labelled as his 'tribute'.

Commynes tells the story of a Gascon *gentilhomme* whom he had known for a long time previousy called Louis de Bretelles who served King Edward and who was unhappy about the peace. Commynes asked him how many battles the king of England had won and Bretelles answered that he had personal knowledge of nine of them. He added that he had lost only one – this one, shame for which was more important than the honour Edward had gained from the other nine.

When Commynes reported this conversation to King Louis, the king remarked that Bretelles was a scoundrel ('*un très mauvais paillard*'), and he needed to be stopped from airing his opinions. To do this, the king asked Bretelles to dinner with him, and tried to bribe him to remain in France instead of going back to England. This was of no avail, and so the king gave him 1,000 crowns, cash in hand, and made him a promise to foster the interests of his brothers who were his subjects. Commynes added that he himself had a word in Bretelles's ear after dinner, to the end that he would put himself out to encourage friendship between the two kings.[58]

When Henri Ribadieu wrote about this incident, he identified this Louis de Bretelles with Louis de Berthais who had emigrated to England from Bordeaux immediately after the first conquest in 1451 and had returned the next year as an equerry in Talbot's army referring to 'the hardly chivalric rôle he played on the day after his arrival in Bordeaux in helping Arnaud Bec to take de Coëtivy prisoner in a garden'.[59]

Ribadieu went on to mention another Louis, this time *de Brutailhs*, who received at another time several Gascon manors from Henry VI. So it is possible that the seigneur of Gamarde, Auribat and Campet between Marsan and Dax – worth eighty livres sterling a year – was Commynes's acquaintance of long standing who objected to the treaty of Picquigny. The Gascon seigneur took Louis XI's thousand *écus* but he remained in the service of the English crown after the peace.[60]

*   *   *

When the day's business had been completed, the king invited three or four of his intimates to his own quarters in Amiens to relax a little, and Paul Murray Kendall relates an anecdote from what took place.[61] Louis XI was afraid that he would say something derogatory to the English in public that would get back to them. Thinking himself alone with close friends, and amused by the thought, he said, 'My father chased the English out of France by force of arms, but I managed it with a few venison pasties and some good wine!'[62]

But then, to his horror, he realized that someone else had come into the room. This was another Gascon, one who had established himself in the wine trade in London and whose wife was English. He had come to seek the king's permission to take a certain quantity of wine from France without paying the customary dues. Louis XI gave him his permission, but only if he returned home directly to Gascony. He did not want him repeating what he had heard him say to his English clients. To make sure that he couldn't, the king immediately put him under guard to be escorted to Bordeaux. He was allowed to bring his wife to join him there, but not to go to London himself. He had to send his brother to fetch her.[63]

* * *

The meeting on the bridge resulted in a series of legal deeds dated at Amiens and the English camp. The treaty of Picquigny has sometimes been considered as the legal end of the Hunded Years War, but it actually registered no more than a truce which was the first of these deeds. All hostilities between the contracting parties were to cease until sunset on 29 August 1482. The English could reside in France and trade without safe-conducts during this time, provided they were not accompanied by more than a hundred armed men. The taxes imposed upon them since 1463 were no longer to apply. The French in England would be treated correspondingly.

* * *

After the treaty of Picquigny had been signed and Edward IV paid by Louis XI to go home, English traders were permitted to come freely once again to Bordeaux without a safe-conduct – conditions made precise in royal letters dated 8 January 1476. Not only were the English allowed to go into Bordeaux to purchase wines, but wherever they wished in Guyenne. They did not have the monopoly any more, but by then they did not want it: English traders had found other interests, *autres chats à fouetter,* or, since they were no longer on French soil, other fish to fry.

Bibliography

Printed Primary Sources

Archives departementales de la Gironde (A.D.G.).

Archives departementales de la Charente-Maritime (A.D.C-M.).

Archives historiques du département de la Gironde, (A.H.G.) 1859–1933, https://gallica.bnf.fr/ark:12148. This Collection includes the *Livre des Brouillons* kept in its original form on vellum in the *Archives Métropole de Bordeaux*. Many of the documents in the collection were destroyed in a fire in a former archives building in 1862 and, subsquently, intensive work of printing and cataloguing of what remained took place under the direction of *érudits* like Henri Barkhausen during the Third Republic. The *Livre des Brouillons* is of the utmost importance because it contains the original draft of documents now lost which were written by the secretary for the time being to the *jurade* and the Council of Thirty. The original document may be consulted, but there is also the printed volume (1867) available in the *Salle de Lecture*.

Basin, Thomas, *Histoire de règnes de Charles VII et de Louis XI*, Tome 1, ed., J. Quicherat, Paris, 1855.

Beckynton, Thomas, Secretary to King Henry VI and [subsequently] Bishop of Bath & Wells, *Official Correspondence of*, ed., George Williams, Vol 2, London 1872, Cambridge, 2012.

Benet, John, *Chronicle, 1399–1462, An Engish Translation with New Introduction*, Alison Hanham, Basingstoke & New York 2016.

Blacman, John, *Memoir of King Henry VI*, ed., M.R. James, Cambridge, 1919.

Bourgeois de Paris, Journal d'un, de 1405 à 1449, ed., Colette Beaune, Paris 1990.

Chartier, Jean, *Chronique de Charles VII, roi de France*, ed., Vallet de Viriville, 2 Vols, Paris, 1858. http://gallica,bnf,fr/ark:/12148/btp6k277120 and 27713b

Chastellein, Georges, *Oeuvres*, 8 vols, Baron Joseph de Kervyn de Lettenhove, Brussels, 1863–1866.

Clercq, Jacques du, *Mémoires de*, 3 vols, ed., Baron Frédéric de Roffenberg, Brussels, 1823, (Google Books).

Commynes, Philippe de, *Memoirs of the Reign of Louis XI 1461–1483*, ed & trans, Michael Jones, Harmondsworth, 1972.

—— ed., Joseph Calmette, 2 Vols. Paris, 1925.

—— ed., with Life and Notes, Andrew R. Scoble, 2 Vols, London, 1856.

—— *The Universal Spider, The Life of Louis XI of France*, Translated and edited by Paul Kendall, London, 1973.

Escouchy, Mathieu d', *Chronique*, ed., Gaston du Fresne de Beaucourt, 3 Vols, Paris 1863–1864.

Leseur, Guillaume, *Histoire de Gaston IV, comte de Foix*, 2 Vols, ed., Henri Courteault, Paris, 1893.

Letters and Papers Illustrative of the wars of the English in France during the reign of Henry the sixth king of England, ed., The Rev. Joseph Stevenson, 2 Vols., London, 1864.

Louis XI, *Lettres choisies*, ed., Henri Dubois, Paris, 1996.

Monstrelet, Enguerrand de, *Chronicle*, ed., Louis Douët-d'Arcq, 2 vols, Paris, 1857–1862.

Parliament Rolls of Medieval England, eds., Chris Given-Wilson, Seymour Phillips, Mark Ormrod, Geoffrey Martin, Anne Curry & Rosemary Horrox, Woodbridge, 2005. http://www.british-history.ac.uk

Recueil des Privileges accordé à la ville de Bordeaux par Charles VII et Louis XI, ed., Marcel Gourion, Bordeaux, 1938.

Roye, Jean de, *Journal connu sous le nom de Chronique scandaleuse*, ed., Bernard de Mandrot, Paris, 1894.

Stowe, John, *Three Fifteenth Century Chronicles, with historical memoranda by John Stowe, the antiquary, and contemporary notes of occurrences written by him in the reign of Queen Elizabeth*, ed., James Gairdner, London, 1873, Hardpress Classics.

Vergil, Polydore, *Three Books of English History comprising the reigns of Henry VI, Edward IV and Richard III*, ed., Sir Henry Ellis, London 1844. BiblioBazaar Reproduction Series.

Wavrin, Jehan de, *Recueil des Chroniques et Anchiennes Istories de la Grant Bretagne, à Present nommé Engleterre*, Vol 5, 1447–1471, eds., Sir William and Edward L.C.P. Hardy, London, 1891, Cambridge 2012.

Secondary Sources
(The place of publication is London unless otherwise indicated.)

Allmand, Christopher, *The Hundred Years War; England and France at War c.1300–c.1450*, Cambridge 1988.

—— *Henry V,* 1992.

Balasque, Jules, *Etudes Historiques sur la ville de Bayonne*, Volume 3, Bayonne, 1875. Barker, Juliet, *Agincourt; The King, the Campaign, the Battle*, 2005.

—— *Conquest; The English Kingdom of France in the Hundred Years War.* 2009.

Baurein, Jacques, *Variétés bordelaises, ou essai historique et critique sur la topologie ancienne et moderne du Diocèse de Bordeaux*, 6 Vols, Bordeaux, 1784.

Beaucourt, Gaston Du Fresne de., *Histoire de Charles VII*, 6 Vols, Paris, 1881–1891, http:gallica.bnf/ark:/12148/bpt6k54011226

Blay de Gaix, Gabriel-François de, *Histoire militaire de Bayonne, Tome Ier, De l'Origine de Bayonne à la mort de Henry IV,* Bayonne, 1899.

Bochaca, Michel, *Les Marchands bordelais au temps de Louis XI; Espaces et reseaux de relations économiques*, Bordeaux, 1998.

—— *Le Banlieue de Bordeaux; Formation d'une jurisdiction municipale suburbaine (vers 1250–vers 1550)*, Strasbourg, 1997.

—— *Villes et organisation de l'espace en Bordelais (vers 1300–vers 1550)*, Paris, 2015.

—— and N. Foucherre, *La Construction des châteaux du Hâ et de la Tropeyte*, in Anne-Marie Cocula et Michel Combet, *Château et Ville: actes des rencontres d'archéologie et d'histoire de Perigord, les 28, 29 et 30 septembre 2001*.

—— *Le règlement des litiges commerciaux entre bourgeois et étrangers: les jurisdictions compétentes pour 'fait de marchandises' à Bordeaux du milieu du XVe au milieu du XVIe siècle, Annales de Bretagne et des Pays de l'Ouest*, 2010. http://abpo.revues.org/1007

Boutrouche, Robert, *La Crise d'une société; seigneurs et paysans du Bordelais pendant la Guerre de Cent Ans*, Paris, 1947.

Bove, Boris, *Le Temps de la Guerre de Cent Ans*, Paris, 2009.

Brissaud, D., *Les Anglais en Guyenne*, Paris, 1875.

Burne, A.H., *The Agincourt War*, 1956.

Calmette, Joseph, *Louis XI, Jean II et la Révolution Catalane*, Paris, 1903. Classic Reprint.

—— and G. Périnelle, *Louis XI et L'Angleterre (1461–1483)*. Paris, 1930.

—— *Les Dernières Etapes du Moyen Age Français*, Paris, 1944.

—— *Chute et Relèvement de La France sous Charles VI et Charles VII*, Paris, 1945.

Carpenter, Christine, *The Wars of the Roses; Politics and the Constitution in England c.1437–1509*, Cambridge, 1997.

Carus-Wilson, E.M., *Medieval Merchant Venturers, Collected Studies*, 1967.

Castor, Helen, *Blood & Roses, The Paston Family and the Wars of the Roses*, 2004.

—— *She-Wolves, The Women who Ruled England before Elizabeth*, 2011.

—— *Joan of Arc, A History*, 2015.

Contamine, Philippe, *Charles VII, Une vie, une politique*, Paris, 2017.

—— *La Guerre de Cent Ans*, 9e Edition, 2010.

Corbin, Raimond, *Histoire du Dernier Archevêque Gascon, Pey Berland et du pays bordelais au XVe siècle*, Bordeaux, 1888, declared in the public domain by the *Bibliothèque national de France*, http://gallica.bnf.fr and re-published by *Les Editions Pyrémonde(Princi Negue)*, Monein, 2006.

Curry, Anne, *The Hundred Years' War 1337–1453*, Oxford and New York, 2002.

—— and Michael Hughes, ed., *Arms, Armies and Fortifications in the Hundred Years War*, Woodbridge, 1994.

—— *The Battle of Agincourt; sources and interpretations*, Woodbridge, 2000.

—— with Peter Hoskins, Thom Richardson, & Dan Spenser, *The Agincourt Companion*, 2015.

Des Garets, Marie-Louyse, *Le Roi René; un artisan de la Renaissance française au XVme siècle*, Paris, 1946.

De Vries, Kelly, and Robert Douglas Smith, *Medieval Military Technology*, Toronto, 2012.

—— Ed., *Medieval Warfare 1300–1450*, London and New York, 2010.

Dockray, Keith, *Henry VI, Margaret of Anjou and the Wars of the Roses from Contemporary Chronicles, Letters and Records*, revised edition, 2016.

—— *Henry V,* Stroud, 2004.

Dodd, Gwilym, ed., *Henry V; New Interpretations*, York, 2013.

Drouyn, Léo, *Bordeaux vers 1450, Description topographique*, Bordeaux,1874, re-published, *Les Editions Pyrémonde(Princi Negue)*, Monein, 2009.

—— *La Guienne Anglaise, Histoire et description des villes fortifiées, forteresses et châteaux construits dans la Gironde pendant la domination anglaise*, Bordeaux, Paris, 18--, re-published http://www.hardpress.net

Dunn, Diana, *War and Society in Medieval and Early Modern Britain*, Liverpool 2000.

Favreau, Robert, *Histoire de l'Aunis et de la Saintonge, Vol II, Le Moyen Age*, La Crèche, 2004.

—— *La Praguerie en Poitou, Bibliothèque de l'école des chartes, Tome 129, 1971, No, 2 pp. 277–301.*

Favreau, Robert, Régis Rech et Yves-Jean Riou, *Bonnes Villes du Poitou et de pays charentais (XIIe-XVIIIe siècles)*, Poitiers, 2002.

Fouché, Charles, *Taillebourg et ses Seigneurs*, Chef-Boutonne, 1911.

Garnier, Robert, *Dunois le bâtard d'Orléans 1403–1468*, Paris, 1999.

Gascon Rolls Project, www.gasconrolls.org

Goodman, Anthony, *John of Gaunt; The Exercise of Princely Power in Fourteenth-Century Europe*, 1992.

Green, David, *The Hundred Years War; A People's History*, New Haven and London, 2015.

Green, Vivien, *The Madness of Kings; Personal Trauma and the Fate of Nations*, Stroud 1993.

—— *The Later Plantagenets*, 1955.

Griffiths, R.A., *The Reign of King Henry VI*, 1981.

Grummitt, David, *Henry VI*, Abingdon and New York, 2015.

—— *A Short History of the Wars of the Roses*, London and New York, 2013.

Harriss, Gerald, *Shaping the Nation, England 1360–1461*, Oxford, 2005.

Harris, Robin, *Valois Guyenne; A Study of Politics, Government and Society in Late Medieval France*, Woodbridge and Rochester NY, 1994.

Hicks, Michael, *Bastard Feudalism, Overmighty Subjects and Idols of the Multitude during the Wars of the Roses*, History, Vol. 85, No. 279 (July 2000), pp. 386–403.

—— *The Wars of the Roses*, New Haven and London, 2010.

Jacob, E.F., *The Fifteenth Century 1399–1485*, Oxford, 1961.

James, Margery Kirkbride ed., Elspeth M. Veale, *Studies in the Medieval Wine Trade*, Oxford, 1971.

Johnson, P.A., *Duke Richard of York 1411–1460*, Oxford, 1988.

Jones, Michael and Malcolm Vale, ed., *England and her Neighbours 1066–1453, Essays in honour of Pierre Chaplais*, London and Ronceverte, 1989.

Keen, Maurice, *English Society in the Later Midde Ages 1348–1500,* 1990.

—— *Chivalry,* New Haven and London, 1984.

—— *Nobles, Knights and Men-at-Arms in the Middle Ages,* London & Rio Grande, 1996.

—— *The End of the Hundred Years War: Lancastrian France and Lancastrian England,* in *England and Her Neighbours, 1066–1453, Essays in Honour of Pierre Chaplais,* ed., Michael Jones and Malcolm Vale, London & Ronceverte WV, 1998.

Kendall, Paul Murray, *Louis XI, '… the universal spider …',* 1971.

—— Trans, and ed. *Philippe de Commynes The Universal Spider, The Life of Louis XI of France,* 1973.

Kleineke, Hannes, *Edward IV,* 2009.

Lavaud, Sandrine, *Une communauté enracinée; les Anglais à Bordeaux à la fin du Moyen Age, Revue de Bordeaux et de la Gironde,* No.1, 2002, pp.

—— *Bordeaux et le vin au Moyen Age. Essor d'une civilisation,* Bordeaux, 2003.

Marchegay, Paul, *La Rançon d'Olivier de Coëtivy, seigneur de Taillebourg et sénéchal de Guyenne, 1451–1477,* Les Roches-Baritaud, 1877.

—— *Lettres de Marie de Valois, Fille de Charles VII et Agnès Sorel à Olivier de Coëtivy, seigneur de Taillebourg, Son Mari, 1458–1472,* Les Roches-Baritaud (Vendée), 1875.

Maurer, Helen E., *Margaret of Anjou, Queenship and Power in Late Medieval England,* Woodbridge, 2003

McFarlane, K.B., *England in the Fifteenth Century,* ed., G.L.Harriss, 1981.

—— *Lancastrian Kings and Lollard Knights,* Oxford, 1972.

Minois, Georges, *Charles VII; un roi shakespearien,* Paris 2005.

—— *La Guerre de Cent Ans,* Paris, 2008.

—— *Charles Le Téméraire,* Paris, 2015.

Oman, Charles W., *Warwick the Kingmaker,* 1893.

Oxford Dictionary of National Biography, online version, https://www.oxforddnb.com.

Pardessus, J.M., *Table chronologique des Ordonnances des rois de France de la troisième race,,* Vol XVII, Paris,1847. Google Books.

Pépin, Guilhem, ed., *Anglo-Gascon Aquitaine; Problems and Perspectives,* Woodbridge, 2017.

Pérotin Yves, *Les Chapitres bordelais contre Charles VII, Annales de Midi, revue archéologique, historique et philosophique de la France méridioniale, Tome* 63, No. 13, 1951, pp. 33–42.

Perroy, Edouard, *La Guerre de Cent Ans,* Paris, 1945.

Peyrègne, A., *Les émigrés gascons en Angleterre (1453–1485), Annales de Midi, Tome* 66, No.26, 1954, pp. 113–128, doi: 10.3406/anami. 1954.5987

Pollard, A.J., *John Talbot & The War in France 1427–1453, 1983,* Barnsley, 2005.

—— *Warwick The Kingmaker; Politics, Power and Fame,* New York, 2007.

Renouard, Yves (dir,) *Bordeaux sous Les Rois d'Angleterre,* Bordeaux, 1965.

——— *Histoire Médiévale d'Aquitaine, Tome I, Institutions et Relations Franco-Anglaises, Tome II, Vin & Commerce du vin de Bordeaux*, Cressé, 2005–2011.

——— *Le Grand commerce du vin au Moyen Age, Revue historique de Bordeaux et de la Gironde,* i 1952, pp. 5–18.

——— *Les Conséquences de la Conquête de la Guyenne par le roi de France pour le commerce des vins de Gascogne, Annales du Midi,* Tome 61, No. 1–2, 1948, pp. 15–31. doi: 10,3406/anami. 1948.5637

Ribadieu, Henri, *Histoire de la conquête de La Guyenne par les Français,* Bordeaux, 1866. This work has been declared as being in the public domain by the *Bibliothèque national de France* and the text is available in full at http://gallica.bnf.fr . In 1990, the identical text was republished by *Les Éditions Princi Negre,* Belein Beliet, with the addition of a Preface by Christian Coulon to make it more readily available to readers who prefer the printed page.

——— *Les Châteaux de la Gironde,* Bordeaux, 1856, declared in the public domain by the *Bibliothèque national de France,* http:gallica.bnf.fr and republished by *Editions Pyremonde/Princi Negue,* Monein, 2009.

Ross, Charles, *Edward IV,* London 1974, new edition, New Haven and London,1997.

Sablon du Corail, Amable, *Louis XI; Le joueur inquiet,* Paris, 2015.

Samaran, Charles, *La Maison d'Armagnac au XVe siècle et les dernières luttes de a Féodalité dans la Midi de la France,* Paris, 1908. Primary Source Edition.

——— *Comment une des filles de Jean IV d'Armagnac faillit d'être reine d'Angleterre (1442–1443), Revue de Gascogne,* Jan 1901. *Persée.*

Seward, Desmond, *A Brief History of The Hundred Years War,* 1978.

Storey, R.L. *The End of the House of Lancaster,* Gloucester, 1986.

Sumption, Jonathan, *Trial by Battle, Trial by Fire, Divided Houses, Cursed Kings; The Hundred Years War I–IV,* 1999–2015.

Vale, M.G.A.,*The Last Years of English Gascony, 1451–1453,* T.R.H.S., Series 19 (1969).

——— *English Gascony 1399–1453; A Study of War, Government and Politics during the later stages of the Hundred Years' War,* Oxford, 1970.

——— *War & Chivalry, Warfare and Aristocratic Culture in England, France and Burgundy at the end of the Middle Ages,*1981.

——— *Charles VII,* Berkeley and Los Angeles, 1974.

——— *La Fin de la guerre de Cent Ans vue par les Anglais, Cahiers Art et Science 8, 1453, revue annuelle,* Bordeaux, 2004, pp. 173–205.

——— *The Ancient Enemy, England; France and Europe from the Angevins to the Tudors,* New York, 2007.

——— *Henry V, The Conscience of a King,* New Haven and London, 2016.

——— *A Fifteenth Century Interrogation of a Political Prisoner,* Bulletin of the Institute of Historical Research, xlii, 1970, wiley.com/doi

Watts, John, *Henry VI and the Politics of Kingship,* 1996.

Wolffe, Bertram, *Henry VI,* 1981.

Appendix

Further Information on Images

1. The principal towns, localities and rivers are shown in a Gascony much
   reduced by 1399 from the large area proposed by Edward III's negotiators
   and momentarily accepted by France in 1360. The low-lying landscape is
   dominated by the river system.
2. The coronation of Henry V, bas-relief from the king's chantry chapel in
   Westminster Abbey, © The Dean and Chapter of Westminster Abbey. The
   mystical nature of the kingship which Henry envisaged is represented here,
   but it proved impossible, despite the compliance of some French seigneurs in
   Normandy, Anjou and Maine, to extend it into the dual monarchy of England
   and France as stated in the treaty of Troyes which he signed with the Duke of
   Burgundy and the compliant Charles VI in 1420, two years before his death.
3. The Founder's Statue, © the Provost and Fellows of Eton College, portrays
   Henry VI at his most regal, engaged in what he regarded as his priority in
   the Lancastrian formula of government: facilitating education based on the
   Christian faith sustained against contemporary Lollardy.
4. The Adoration of the Magi, attributed to Jean Fouquet from the Hours
   of Etienne Chevalier, MS 71 Musée Condé at Chantilly, reproduced by
   permission (© *Bibliothèque national Francaise, Department de rèproduction*) is
   a much more kindly portrait of Charles VII than the other attributed to the
   same artist in the Louvre. Here he offers his triumphs to the Christ-child,
   attended by his Scottish bodyguard in the uniforms which they wore when
   he paraded with them through Rouen in 1450 – not being present in person
   when Dunois paraded through Bordeaux a year later.
5. Pey Berland's Tower and St. Andrew's Cathedral at Bordeaux, lithograph
   realized by Lemercier of Paris from a drawing by Léo Drouyn for Alexandre
   Ducourneau, *Histoire nationale des Déparetements de France – Gironde*, 1845.
   © Les Éditions de l'Entre-deux-Mers, coll., *Léo Drouyn, les albums de dessins*.
   During a period of recession and invasion, when no one else in Bordeaux
   was able to commission building projects, the Archbishop saved the town's
   stonemasons from becoming de-skilled by the construction of this tower
   with its elaborate design and ornamentation (R. Corbin, *Histoire du dernier
   archeveque gascon*). The figure of the Virgin Mary which now surmounts it is
   an addition post 1845.
6. The castle of Quatre-Sols at La Réole, eastern facade, eau-forte by Léo
   Drouyn for La Guienne militaire, 1861, © Les Éditions de l'Entre-deux-

Mers, coll., *Léo Drouyn, les albums de dessins.* This immense structure was besieged by Charles VII in person in 1442 but on that occasion, he was not able to take it and, after his lodgings in La Réole caught fire, he left to spend Chritmas at Montauban.

7. The castle at Blanquefort, *eau-forte* by Léo Drouyn for *Choix des types les plus remarquables au moyen-âge dans le département de la Gironde*, 1846. © Les Éditions de l'Entre-deux-Mers, coll., *Léo Drouyn, les albums de dessins.* This fortress was the property of Gaillard de Durfort, who defended it against the count of Clermont and then escaped to lend his aid to Camoys in the defence of Bordeaux. It had also been the focus of the Bordeaux militia's defeat in the *male journade* on 1 November 1450.

8. Edward IV's invasion route was meant to take him to Reims for his French coronation. He made his way to the towns on the River Somme which had been ceded to Burgundy by Charles VII in 1435. Edward's alliance with Charles the Bold went sour when the duke did not provide substantial military support and refused him entry to Peronne as winter quarters.

Notes

Introduction

1. Ralph V. Turner, *Eleanor of Aquitaine, Queen of France, Queen of England*, New Haven and London, 2009, pp, 104–122.
2. Yves Renouard, *Bordeaux sous Les Rois d'Angleterre*, Bordeaux, 1965, pp. 24–30.
3. *Ibid.*, p, 225.
4. Renouard, p. 61.
5. *Ibid.* pp. 64–65.
6. Sandrine Lavaud, *Une communauté enracinée; les Anglais à Bordeaux à la fin du Moyen Age, Revue de Bordeaux et de la Gironde*, No.1, 2002 pp. 35–48.

Chapter 1

1. Yves Renouard, *Bordeaux sous les rois d'Angleterre Bordeaux*, 1965, p. 413. E.F. Jacob, *The Fifteenth Century 1399–1485*, Oxford, 1961, pp. 11–27.
2. Jonathan Sumption, *Trial by Fire, The Hundred Years War II*, p. 445–448.
3. M.G.A. Vale, *English Gascony*, Oxford, 1970, p. 53.
4. Ibid., p. 43.
5. Christopher Allmand, *Henry V,* London, 1992, p. 55.
6. Vale, p. 53.
7. Jonathan Sumption, *Cursed Kings, The Hundred Years War IV*, London, 2015, p.200.
8. *Ibid.*, p. 210.
9. Allmand, *Henry V,* p. 12.
10. Leo Drouyn, *La Guienne Anglaise*, Bordeaux, Paris, 1860, p. 301.
11. Sumption, IV, pp. 210–214.
12. Renouard, pp. 415–417.
13. Sumption, IV, pp. 217–220.
14. J.H. Shennan, *The Parlement of Paris*, Stroud, 1998, pp. 161–162.
15. Joseph Calmette, *Les Dernières étapes du Moyen Âge Français*, Paris, 1944, pp 34–35.
16. Froissart, *Chronicles*, Trans., Geoffrey Brereton, London, 1978, pp. 395–396.
17. V.H.H. Green, *The Madness of Kings, Personal Trauma and the Fate of Nations*, Stroud, 1993, pp.72–86.
18. Philippe Contamine, *Charles VII, une vie, une politique*, Paris 2017, p. 30, my translation.

19. Calmette, *Moyen Âge Français*, pp. 67–81.
20. Allmand, pp. 48–49.
21. Ed., F.W.D. Brie, London 1906 & 1908, Vol II, p. 271. www.dartmouth.edu
22. K.B. McFarlane, *Lancastrian Kings and Lollard Knights*, Oxford, 1972, p. 110.
23. Allmand, p. 54.
24. Juliet Barker, *Agincourt The King, the Campaign, the Battle*, London, 2006, p. 21
25. Vale, pp. 62–66.
26. Philippe Contamine, *Charles VII, Une vie, une politique*, Paris, 2017, pp. 28–33.
27. Sumption, IV, p. 366. See also K.B. McFarlane, *Henry V, A Personal Portrait*, in *Lancastrian Kings and Lollard Knights*, p. 124.
28. Contamine, pp. 29–32.
29. Allmand, pp. 66–70. Sumption IV, pp. 370–372.
30. Sumption, IV, pp. 374–384.
31. Allmand, pp. 72–74.
32. Jenny Stratford, *'Par le special commandement du roy'. Jewels and Plate Pledged for the Agincourt Expedition*, in *Henry V, New Interpretations*, ed. Gwilym Dodd, York, 2013, pp. 163 & 168.
33. Allmand, pp. 74–78.
34. *Ibid*, pp. 78–82.
35. To name two recent studies, essential for understanding the events: Anne Curry, *The Battle of Agincourt, Sources and Interpretations*, Woodbridge, Rochester NY, 2000 & 2009. and Juliet Barker, *Agincourt, The King, The Campaign, the Battle*, London, 2005.
36. Barker, *Agincourt*, p. 222.
37. *Ibid.*, pp. 221–223.
38. Jules Michelet, *Histoire de France*, Paris, 1840, *Tome* VI, p. 20.
39. Barker, *Agincourt*, pp. 237 & 239.
40. *Ibid.*, pp. 244–247.
41. *Ibid.*, p. 247.
42. *Ibid.*, p. 261.
43. *Cursed kings, The Hundred Years War IV*, London, 2015.
44. *Henry V, The Conscience of a King*, New Haven and London, 2016.
45. *The London Review of Books*, 19 May 2016, p. 29.
46. *La Guerre de Cent Ans*, Paris, 1945, p. 9. Keith Dockray, *Henry V*, pp. 11 & 68.
47. *Ibid.*, p. 205. My translation and my emphasis.
48. Michelet found this phrase in the monk of St Albans, Thomas Walsingham's, Chronicle.
49. Jules Michelet, Histoire de France, Tome VI, Paris, 1840, pp. 37–38. See also Anne Curry, *The Battle of Agincourt, Sources and Interpretations*, p. 166.

50. *Lancastrian Kings and Lollard Knights*, p. 126.
51. *Ibid.*, pp. 129–131.

Chapter 2

1. Helen Castor, *Joan of Arc, A History*, London, 2014, pp. 36–40. Of the many accounts of this event, this one is particularly poignant.
2. Philippe Contamine, *Charles VII, Une vie, une politique*, Paris, 2017, pp. 28–34.
3. Maurice Keen, *Nobles, Knights and Men-at-Arms in the Middle Ages*, London & Rio Grande, 1996, pp.235–238.
4. Gwilym Dodd, *Agincourt: Henry's Hollow Victory*, in *History Today*, 10 October 2016.
5. Juliet Barker, *Conquest*, p. 88.
6. *Ecclesiastes* 10, 16.
7. *Conquest*, p. 88.
8. *Henry VI and the Politics of Kingship*, Cambridge, 1996, p. 31.
9. Michael Hicks, *The Wars of the Roses*, New Haven and London, 2012, pp. 15–26.
10. Henry V, Act 4, Scene 2.
11. David Grummitt, *Henry VI*, London, 2015, p. 29.
12. *Ibid.*, p. 15.
13. *Ibid.*, pp. 16–18.
14. *Ibid.*, p. 20.
15. *Ibid.*, p. 27.
16. *Henry V, The Conscience of a King*, New Haven and London, 2016, p. 172.
17. Grummitt, *Henry VI*, p. 64.
18. *Ibid.*
19. *Ibid.*, p. 65.
20. *Ibid.*, pp. 66–67.
21. *Ibid.*, p. 67.
22. Beaucourt, Vol I, p. 241 & Vol II, p. 55.
23. Beaucourt Vol 1, p. 243.
24. Grummitt, p. 68.
25. Michael K Jones, *The Battle of Verneuil (17 August 1424): Towards a History of Courage (2002)*, *War in History*, 9, pp. 375–411, in Kelly de Vries, Ed., *Medieval Warfare, 1300–1450*, London & NY, 2016. Google Books (which does not permit more precise pagination for quotations).
26. Beaucourt, Vol II pp. 60–61.
27. Beaucourt, Vol II pp. 60–61.
28. Juliet Barker, *Conquest, The English Kingdom of France in the Hundred Years War*, London, 2009, reprinted 2010, p. 78.
29. Beaucourt, Volume II, p. 64.
30. The phrase was coined by Alfred H. Burne, *The Agincourt War*, London, 1956, reprinted Ware, 1999, p.196. It is also Juliet Barker's title for her chapter on the events in *Conquest*, London, 2009, reprint 2010, pp. 76–92.

31. Beaucourt's words
32. Michael K. Jones, *Op. cit.*
33. *Hétéroclite* : the word is used by Georges Minois.
34. *Journal d'un bourgeois de Paris de 1405 à 1449. Texte original présené et commenté par Colette Beaune*, Paris, 1990, p. 211–212.
35. Michael K. Jones, *Ibid.*
36. Minois, *Charles VII*, pp. 192–194. Grummitt, *Henry VI*, p. 69.
37. Barker, *Conquest*, pp. 79–80.
38. Michael K. Jones, *Ibid.* Google Books.
39. Barker, *Conquest*, p.80.
40. Boris Bove, *Le Temps de la guerre de cent ans 1328–1453*, Paris, 2009, p. 460. A *salut* was worth 1.10 *livres tournois*.
41. Grummitt p. 68 and Jones, *op. cit.*
42. Grummitt, pp. 68–69.
43. Barker, *Conquest*, p. 81.
44. *Ibid.*, p 83.
45. *Ibid.*
46. V.H.H. Green, *The Later Plantagenets*, London, 1955, pp. 299–301 from which are taken all but one of the phrases between quotation marks in homage to a respected teacher.
47. Barker, *Conquest*, p. 85.
48. *Ibid.*, p. 86.
49. R.A. Griffiths, *Henry VI*, p. 73.
50. Grummit, p. 58.
51. R.A. Griffiths, *Henry VI*, p. 73.
52. C.L. Kingsford, ed., *The Chronicles of London*, 1905, cited by Griffiths., p. 77.
53. Griffiths, p. 78.
54. *Ibid.*, p. 79.
55. *Ibid.*, p. 81.
56. Barker, *Conquest*, p. 88.
57. *Ibid.*
58. *Ibid.*, p. 92.

Chapter 3

1. Barker, *Conquest*, pp. 95–97.
2. Helen Castor, *Joan of Arc, A History*, London, 2009, pp. 77–86.
3. *Ibid.*, p. 28.
4. *Ibid.*, pp. 69–70.
5. *Ibid.*, p. 90. M.G.A. Vale asserted that the Anjou family's involvement 'would be impossible to prove.' *Charles VII*, Berkeley and Los Angeles, 1974. p. 50.
6. Castor, pp. 97–133.
7. *Journal d'un Bourgeois de Paris de 1405 â 1449*, Paris, 1990. p. 266.
8. Castor, pp. 153–164.

9. Grummitt, *Henry VI*, pp. 74–79.
10. Grummitt, *Henry VI*, pp. 74–79.
11. Bove, pp. 446–448.
12. Grummitt, *Henry VI*, pp. 94–97.
13. Malcolm Vale, *Henry V, The Conscience of a King*, New Haven and London, 2016, pp.144–145 & 177–178.
14. Donald Matthew, *The Norman Monasteries and their English Possessions*, Oxford, 1962.
15. I owe this observation to Dr. Robert W. Dunning, formerly Somerset County Archivist.
16. Bertram Wolffe, *Henry VI*, pp. 142–143.
17. *The Nobility of Later Medieval England, Oxford, 1973*, p. 284.
18. Grummitt, p 108.
19. R.A. Griffiths, *The Reign of King Henry VI*, London, 1981, p. 275.
20. *Ibid.*, p. 277.
21. Bertram Wolffe, *Henry VI*, London, 1981, p. 92.
22. Wolffe, pp. 154–159.
23. Charles Samaran, *La Maison, d'Armagnac au XVe siècle et les dernières luttes de la féodalité dans le midi de la France*, Paris, 1908, p. 78. Nabu Public Domain Reprints.
24. *Archives Historiques de la Gironde, Tome* 16, 1878, p. 243.
25. Samaran, p.79, n.1.
26. This episode is well documented in English sources: Nicholas Harris Nicholas, ed., *A Journal by one of the Suite of Thomas Beckyngton ... during an embassy to negotiate a marriage between Henry VI and a daughter of the count of Armagnac, A.D. 1442*, London 1828 (Google Books), and George Williams, ed., *Official Correspondence of Thomas Beckynton*, Vol. 2, Cambridge, 2012, re-published from The Rolls Series, London 1872. For an assessment of Thomas Beckynton himself, see Robert W. Dunning, *Oxford Dictionary of National Biography*, online edition *ad loc.*
27. Charles Samaran, *Comment une des filles de Jean IV d'Armagnac faillit d'être reine d'Angleterre (1442–1443)*, *Revue de Gascogne*, January 1901, pp. 376–387. Persée.
28. *Ibid.* p. 384.
29. *Henry VI and the Politics of Kingship*, Cambridge, 1996.
30. *The Wars of the Roses, Politics and the Constitution in England, c1437–1509*, Cambridge, 1997, p. 115. See also Grummitt, *Henry VI*, pp. 103–107.
31. Wolffe, p. 123.
32. Ribadieu, pp. 140–142.
33. Ribadieu, pp. 137–138.
34. www.gasconrolls.org/en/edition/calendars/C61_126/document/html, No. 27. 22 August 1436.
35. www.gasconrolls.org/en/edition/calendars/C61_127/document/html, No. 81. 15 July 1437 (Ribadieu's note says 5).

36. Ribadieu. p. 140.
37. *Ibid.*, p. 142.
38. *Official Correspondence of Thomas Beckynton, Secretary to King Henry VI and (afterwards) Bishop of Bath and Wells*, Vol 2, Ed., George Williams, 1872, re-published, Cambridge, 2012, pp. 186–190.
39. Ribadieu, p. 151.
40. *Official Correspondence*, pp. 191–193.
41. Ribadieu, p. 154.
42. *Ibid.*, p. 195.
43. *Ibid.*, pp. 156–157 (my translation). Ribadieu had contacted the Bodleian Library at Oxford for this document., cited as Ashm. Ms. 789, fol. 179.
44. *Ibid.*, p. 159.
45. *Ibid.*, pp 155–161.
46. *Ibid.*, p. 163.
47. Beaucourt, *Charles VII*, Vol III, pp. 232–246.
48. Wolffe, p. 190.
49. *Ibid.*, pp. 269–174.
50. Marie-Louise des Garets, *Un Artisan de la renaissance française au XVme siècle, Le Roi René*, Paris, 1946, p. 131.
51. Helen E. Maurer, *Marguerite of Anjou, Queenship and Power in Late Medieval England*, Woodbridge, p. 19.
52. Gerald Harriss, *Shaping the Nation, England 1360–1461*, Oxford, 2005, pp. 178–179.
53. R.A. Griffiths, *The Reign of Henry VI*, Stroud, 1981, p. 486.
54. *Ibid.*, pp. 326–328.
55. Griffiths, pp. 486–489 and Maurer pp. 19–22.
56. Griffiths, pp. 492–494.
57. Maurer, p. 33.
58. *Ibid.*, p. 11.
59. Griffiths, pp. 494–495.
60. *John Benet's Chronicle 1399–1461*, ed., & trans., Alison Hanham, Basingstoke and New York, 2016, p. 23.
61. Barker, *Conquest*, p. 346
62. Barker, *Conquest*, p. 337.
63. *Ibid.*, p. 358.

Chapter 4

1. Maurice Keen, *Nobles, Knights and Men-at-Arms in the Middle Ages*, London amd Rio Grande, 1996, p. 234.
2. Georges Minois, *Charles Le Téméraire*, Paris, 2015, pp. 19–20.
3. Boris Bove, p. 448.
4. Gaston du Fresne de Beaucourt, *Charles VII, Tome III, Le Reveil du roi*, Paris, 1885, pp. 69–70.

5. Buch was his lordship situated near the Bassin d'Archachon to the south-west of Bordeaux.

6. Robert Boutruche, *La Crise d'une société, Seigneurs et paysans du Bordelais pendant la Guerre de Cent Ans*, Paris, 1947, p. 399.

7. *Ibid.*, p. 400.

8. Denys Joly d'Aussy, *Bulletin de la Société des Archives Historiques XIV, 1894, La Saintonge pendant la guerre de Cent Ans*, p. 388.

9. www.gasconrolls.org C61_129, N° 64. M.G.A.Vale, *English Gascony*, p. 108.

10. Robert Favreau, *L'Histoire de l'Aunis et de la Saintonge, Vol II, Le Moyen Age*, La Crêche, 2014, p. 349.

11. *Arch. Comm. de Saint-Jean d'Angély*, CC8, cited by Favreau.

12. Boutruche, *Crise*, p. 400.

13. Ribadieu, *Conquête*, p. 128.

14. Boutrouche, *Crise*, p. 400.

15. *Ibid.*, p. 401.

16. These cover seven pages of close print in Beaucourt, *Charles VII*, Vol II: pp. 402–409.

17. Hippolyte Dansin, *Etude sur le gouvernement de Charles VII*, Strasbourg, 1856, pp. 41–45.

18. Robert Favreau, *La Praguerie en Poitou, Bibliothèque de l'Ecole des Chartes*, 1971, *Livraison* 2, p. 285. www.persee.fr.

19. Jean Chartier, *Chronique de Charles VII, roi de France, Vol I*, ed., Vallet de Viriville, 1858, p. 258.

20. Peter H. Wilson, *The Holy Roman Empire; A Thousand Years of Europe's History*, London, 2016, p. 99.

21. Favreau, *Praguerie in Poitou*, p. 278.

22. Favreau, *Saintonge*, p. 349.

23. Robert Garnier, *Dunois, le bâtard d'Orléans (1401–1468)*, Paris, 1999, p. 230.

24. G. Clémont-Simon, *Un Capitaine de routiers sous Charles VII, Jean de La Roche, Revue des questions historiques*, July 1895, pp. 41–42, www.gallica.bnf.fr.

25. Beaucourt, *Charles VII*, Vol III, pp. 116–120.

26. George Minois, *Charles VII, Un roi shakespearien*, Paris, 2005, pp. 396–397.

27. *Ibid.*, p. 398.

28. See also Beaucourt, *Charles VII*, Vol III, pp. 123–135.

29. Jean Chartier, *Chronique de Charles VII, roi de France*, Ed., Vallet de Viriville, Paris, 1858, Tome I, pp. 254–255.

30. Favreau, *Praguerie en Poitou*, pp. 291–292.

31. *Ibid.*, p. 296.

32. Robert Favreau, Régis Reich et Yves-Jean Rioux, Eds., *Bonnes Villes du Poitou et des pays charentais*, Poitiers, 2002, p. 408.

33. Favreau, *Praguerie in Poitou*, p. 292.

34. Beaucourt, *Charles VII*, Vol III, pp. 126–127.
35. E.g., by Bernard de Rosier, Provost of the church in Toulouse, a King's Counsel and one of Lomagne's enthusiastic supporters.
36. *La Chronique d'Enguerrand de Monstrelet*, Ed., L. Douët-d'Arcq, Paris, 1861, Vol V, p. 414.
37. Georges Minois, *Charles VII*, p. 402.
38. Beaucourt, *Charles VII*, Vol III, p. 134.
39. *Ibid.*, pp. 170–171.
40. *Ibid.*, p. 133.
41. *Ibid.*, pp. 131–132.
42. Christine Carpenter, *The Wars of the Roses, politics and the constitution in England, c1437–1509*, Cambridge, 1997, p. 96.
43. Boris Bove, *Le Temps de la Guerre*, pp. 451–452.
44. Kelly DeVries & Robert Douglas Smith, *Medieval Military Technology*, Toronto, 2012, p. 159. Boris Bove, *Le Temps*, p. 452.
45. Bove, *Ibid*.
46. Barker, *Conquest*, p. 359.
47. Guillaume Leseur, Histoire de Gaston IV, comte de Foix, Ed.. HenriCourteault, Vol I, Paris, 1893, Classic Reprint, pp. 120–128.
48. Monstrelet, Tome II, p. 25, & *Preuves de la Chronique de Mathieu d'Escouchy*, p. 15.
49. Favreau, *Praguerie en Poitou*, p. 293.
50. Charles Samaran, *La Maison d'Armagnac au XVe siècle et les dernières luttes de la féodalité dans la Midi de la France*, Paris, 1908, Primary Source Edition, p. 46.
51. *Ibid*.
52. *Ibid*.
53. *Ibid.*, pp. 62–63.
54. *Ibid.*, p. 65.
55. *Ibid.*, pp. 71–73.
56. *Chronique*, Ed., Douet d'Arc, Paris, 1857, pp. 292–293.
57. *Ibid*.
58. Samaran, p, 74.
59. *Ibid.*, p. 75, and *Pièce justificative* N°3, p. 368.
60. *Ibid.*, p. 76.
61. *Ibid.*, p. 78.
62. *Ibid.*, pp. 89–90.
63. *Ibid.*, p. 90, n.1.
64. Beaucourt, *Charles VII*, Vol III, p. 225.
65. Samaran, *Maison*, p. 90.
66. *Ibid.*, p. 92.
67. *Ibid.*, pp. 93–99.

Chapter 5

1. R.A. Griffiths, *The Reign of King Henry VI*, pp. 510–511.
2. M.G.A. Vale, *Charles VII*, 1974, pp. 118–119.
3. B.de Mandrot, *Louis XI et le drame de Lectoure*, Revue historique (Paris), 1888, pp. 241–242, www.Gallica.
4. Gaston Fresne de Beaucourt, *Histoire* de Charles VII, Tome V, *Le* Roi *victorieux*, Paris, 1890, p. 40, n. 1.
5. *Ibid.*, p. 45, n. 2.
6. *Ibid.*, p. 45.
7. *John Benet's Chronicle 1399–1462, An English Translation with a New Introduction*, ed. Alison Hanham, Basingstoke and New York, 2016, p. 30.
8. Beaucourt V, p. 43.
9. Ribadieu, *Conquête*, p. 173.
10. *Ibid.*
11. Jean Chartier, *Chronique de Charles VII*, Ed., Vallet de Viriville, Paris, 1858, Tome II, p. 242.
12. Ribadieu, *Conquête*, p. 175. *Jean Chartier, Chronique de Charles VII, Ed.*
13. Raymond Corbin, *Histoire du dernier archevêque gascon, Pey Berland, et du pays bordelais au XVème siècle.*
14. Nicholas Harris Nicholas, *Journal of a Member of the suite of Thomas Beckington*, London, 1828, p. 201.
15. Corbin, *ibid.*, provides details, pp. 136–137. A more general account is found in Chartier, p. 247.
16. Corbin, *ibid.*, p.140.
17. *Ibid.*, pp. 139–140, and Boutruche, *Crise*, p. 406.
18. *Ibid.*, p.140.
19. *Ibid.*, p. 138.
20. Jean Glenisson, *La Reconstruction agraire en Saintonge méridionale au lendemain de la guerre de Cent ans*, Revue de la Saintonge et de l'Aunis, 1975, p. 65.
21. Chartier, II, pp. 249–253.
22. *Ibid.*, pp. 255–260.
23. Corbin, *Pey Berland*, p. 141.
24. Chartier II, pp. 255–260.
25. Corbin, Pey *Berland*, pp. 141–142.
26. Georges Minois, *Charles VII*, p. 643.
27. A.H.G., Vol X, N°36, p. 79.A
28. Yves Renouard, *Bordeaux sous les Rois d'Angleterre*, Bordeaux, 1965, p. 27.
29. *Registres de la Jurade, Tome III*, 8 January 1407, cited by Sandrine Lavaud.
30. Sandrine Lavaud, *Bordeaux et le Vin au Moyen Age*, Luçon, 2003, pp. 99–101. Forton's will is archived as ADG 3 E 0807 f° 49, dated April 1445.
31. A.H.G., *Tome* LVI, 1925–27, pp. 34–38.
32. R.A. Griffiths, *Henry VI*, p.529.

33. *Ibid.*
34. British History Online: http://www.british-history.ac.uk/no-series/ parliament-rolls-medieval/march-1453 Introduction.
35. *Benet's Chronicle*, p. 32.
36. Ribadieu, pp. 217ff.
37. *Ibid.*, p. 219.
38. Corbin, *Pey Berland*, p. 145.
39. Ribadieu, p. 224, and Corbin, *Pey Berland*, p. 145.
40. Ribadieu, p. 226.
41. *Ibid.*, p. 232.
42. *Livre des Bouillons*, fol. 142, v° (see Bibliography).
43. *Ibid.*, fol. 141 v°.
44. Ribadiau, p. 235.
45. *Ibid.*
46. *Ibid.*, p. 236.
47. *Ibid.*
48. *Ibid.*, p. 237. The full text of the treaty is given by Jean Chartier, Vol II, pp. 279–291. The treaty embodies all that Charles VII wrote in a letter to the citizens of Bordeaux from Saint-Jean d'Angély, dated 20 June 1451, BnF Dupuy I [1.1 ark:/12148/CC883885] N° 153. Thanks are due to Mme Véronique Martin, at the time *responsable du site de Jonzac des Archives départementales de la Charente-Maritime*, for her transcription of the king's letter.
49. Jules Balasque, avec la collaboration de E. Deleurens, *Etudes Historiques sur la ville de Bayonne*, Tome III, Bayonne, 1875, p. 468.
50. *Ibid.*, p. 474.
51. *Ibid.*, p. 479.
52. *Ibid.*, p. 483.
53. See also M.G.A. Vale, *English Gascony*, pp. 133–135.
54. *Balasque-Dulaurens.*, p. 488.
55. Ribadieu, p.169. In reprisal for the act of treason, Henry VI's council deprived Beaumont of his lordship of Curton in the Entre-Deux-Mers and gave it to the *Jurade* of Bordeaux who had asked for it, the better to defend themselves from attack. www.gasconrolls.org, C61_137, N°4. See also Guilhem Pépin's introductory note to this roll.
56. *Ibid.*, p. 189.
57. Balasque-Dulaurens, pp. 491–492.
58. *Ibid.*, p. 493, citing *Archives de Bayonne*, AA 1, p. 356.
59. *Ibid.*, p. 496.
60. *Ibid.*, p. 497.
61. *Ribadieu*, p. 255.
62. Balasque-Dulaurens, p. 497.
63. Balasque-Dulaurens says there were twelve pinnaces and one warship.

64. Guillaume Leseur, *Histoire de Gaston IV, Comte de Foix*, Ed., Henri Courteault, Paris, 1893, pp. 206–213.
65. *Ibid.*, Vol I, p. 214, where also n. 2 says that the account of the cross in the sky is also given in the *Preuves* of Mathieu d'Escouchy, not in full daylight but at seven in the morning, citing a letter from Foix and Dunois to the king.
66. Balasque-Dulaurens, p. 499.
67. Leseur, Vol I. pp. 218–219.
68. *Joan of Arc, A History*, London, 2015. p. 20.

Chapter 6
1. Yves Renouard, *Bordeaux sous les rois d'Angleterre*, p. 513.
2. Corbin, *Pey Berland*, p. 283.
3. Ribadieu, p. 253. Jehan de Wavrin, *Receuil des Chroniques et anchiennes istoires de La Grant Bretaigne à présent nommé Engleterre*, ed., William and L.C.P. Hardy, London, 1891, Reprint, Cambridge, 2012, Vol 5, p. 185.
4. *Ibid.*, p. 257.
5. Ribadieu, pp. 258–259.
6. *Histoire des règnes de Charles VII et de Louis XI*, Ed., J. Quicherat, Paris, 1855–1859, pp. 257–258.
7. www.gasconrolls.org *ad loc.*
8. Beaucourt, *Charles VII*, Tome V, pp. 262–263
9. Chartier, Tome II, p. 330.
10. *Ibid.*, p. 331.
11. *Histoire des règnes de Charles VII et de Louis XI*, Ed., J. Quicherat, Tome I, Paris, 1855–1859, p. 260.
12. *The Last Years of English Gascony, 1451–1453*, T.R.H.S., Series 19 (1969), p.126.
13. *Conquête*, p. 269.
14. *Charles VII, Tome V,* pp. 263–264.
15. *La Crise*, p. 408.
16. *Bordeaux sous les rois d'Angleterre*, p. 515.
17. M.G.A. Vale, *Last Years*, pp. 126–127.
18. *Ibid*
19. John Watts, *Henry VI and the Politics of Kingship*, p. 287n, 288, 319n, 347n, 350n.
20. Vale, *Last Years*, p. 127 (citing A.D.G., G 1160, f° 88v and *La Cartulaire de l'Eglise Collégiale de Saint-Seurin*, Ed, J. Bruteils, 1897, p. xxxvii). See also Robin Harris, *Valois Guyenne*, Woodbridge and Rochester NY, 2005, p. 9.
21. See below.
22. A.J. Pollard, *John Talbot and the War in France,1427–1453*, Barnsley, 2005, (R.H.S., 1983), pp. 65–70.
23. Joseph Stevenson, *Letters and Papers illustrative of the wars of the English in France*, Vol 2, Part II, p. 589. Forgotten Books.

24. See below.
25. Vale, *Last Years*, p. 124.
26. http://www.britishhistory.ac.uk:rymer-foedera:vol ll/ pp. 303–318 and www.gasconrolls.org, C61_139, N° 17.
27. *Variétés bordelaises*, Tome II, pp. 361–363.
28. Marcel Gourion, *Receuil des Privilèges accordés par Charles VII et Louis XI*, Bordeaux, 1938, N°VI, p. 46.
29. Vale, *Last Years*, p. 138, and *A Fifteenth Century Interrogation of a Political Prisoner*, B.I.H.R., 1970.
30. A.H.G., Tome XII, 1870, p. 343.
31. Michael Hicks, *The Wars of the Roses*, New Haven and London, 2012, pp. 49–55.
32. Joseph Stevenson, *Letters and Papers*, Vol 2, Part II, pp. 379–482.
33. John Watts, *Henry VI*, pp. 294–296.
34. http/www.british-history.ac.uk/no-series/parliament-rolls-medieval/march-1453
35. R.A. Griffiths, *Henry VI*, p. 391.
36. Boutrouche, *La Crise*, p. 409n.
37. Joseph Stevenson, *Letters and Papers*, Vol 2, Part II, pp. 486–494. Forgotten Books.
38. I am indebted to Mr Tom Edlin who teaches history at Westminster School for information on this topic.
39. Boris Bove, *Le Temps de la Guerre de Cent Ans, 1328–1453*, Paris, 2013, pp. 465–470.
40. M.G.A. Vale, *Charles VII*, pp. 127–134, Beaucourt, *Charles VII*, Tome V, pp. 85–133 & 426–433 and Edouard Perroy, *La Guerre de Cent Ans*, Paris, 1945, pp. 290–291.
41. Jean-Yves Ribault, *The Palace of Jacques Coeur*, Paris, 2008, *passim*.
42. Beaucourt, *Charles VII*, Tome V, pp. 268–269.
43. Beaucourt, *Supplément aux preuves de Mathieu d'Escouchy*, p. 33.
44. Beaucourt, *Charles VII*, Tome V, p. 270.
45. *Ibid.*, pp. 271–272.
46. A.J. Pollard, *John Talbot*, p. 127, citing *Chronique*, ed., de Beaucourt, Tome II, 1864, pp. 34–35.
47. *Ibid.*, citing Jean de Bueil, *Le Jouvencel, texte établi et annoté par Léon Lecestre*, Paris, 1887, p. 296.
48. Ribadieu, p. 299, based on Thomas Basin, Tome I, p. 265.
49. *Conquête*, p. 312.
50. *Charles VII*, pp. 604–605.
51. *Mémoires de J. du Clercq*, Ed., Frédéric, Baron Roffenberg, Tome II, Brussels, 1823, Livre III, pp 152–161 (Google Books).
52. Malcolm Vale, *War and Chivalry*, London, 1981, p. 76.
53. Kelly de Vries & Robert Douglas Smith, *Medieval Military Technology*, Toronto, 2nd Edition, 2012, pp. 85–86.

54. A.J. Pollard, ONDB, Oxford, online edition, 2008, http://www.oxforddnb. com/view/article/26932

55. A.J. Pollard, *John Talbot, the War in France 1427–1453*, R.H.S., 1983, and Barnsley, 2005, p. 123.

56. *Ibid.*, p. 138, n36.

57. Beaucourt, *Charles VII*, Tome V, p. 276.

58. See also Lt-Col. Alfred H. Burne, *The Agincourt War*, London,1956, re-issued, Ware, 1999, pp. 331–342.

59. A.J. Pollard, *John Talbot*, p. 138.

60. Philippe Contamine, *Charles VII, une vie, une politique*, Paris, 2017, p. 307.

61. *Ibid.*, pp. 307–308.

62. I owe this sentence to Mr Tom Edlin.

63. David Grummitt, *Henry VI*, Abingdon and New York, 2015, p. 170.

64. A.F. Pollard, *John Talbot*, pp. 122–124.

65. K.B. McFarlane, *England in the Fifteenth Century, Collected Essays*, London, 1981, pp. 23–43, though modified by others since then.

66. See Helen Castor, *Blood and Roses, The Paston Family and the Wars of the Roses*, London 2004.

67. *War and Chivalry*, London,1981, p. 162.

68. *Ibid.*, p. 161.

69. '*Jamais, dit-il, je n'oyrai messe, ou j'aurai aujourd'hui rué jus (jeté à terre) la compagnie des Français qui est là-bas dans ce parc devant moi.* ' Ribadieu, *Conquête*, pp. 296–297.

70. A.J. Pollard, *John Talbot*, pp. 133–134.

71. *Chronique*, Vol II, p. 7.

72. A.J. Pollard, *John Talbot*, p.126. See also Sean McGlynn, *By Sword and Fire, Cruelty and Atrocity in Medieval Warfare*, London, 2008, p. 216, and the discussion in Maurice Keen, *Chivalry*, New Haven and London, 1984, pp. 224–237.

73. A.J. Pollard, *John Talbot*, p. 129, author's italics.

74. M.G.A. Vale, *Last Days*, p. 132, and see Beaucourt, Tome V, p. 262.

75. *Ibid.*

76. www.gasconrolls.org, C61_139, 31 Henry VI, N°66.

77. Jacques Baurein, *Variétés bordelaises, ou essai historique et critique sur la topologie ancienne et moderne du Diocèse de Bordeaux*, 1784, Tome I, pp. 206–207.

78. Ribadieu, pp. 275–277.

79. A. Peyrègne, *Les Emigrés gascons en Angleterre* (1453–1485), *Annales de Midi*, Tome 66, N° 26, 1954, p. 115, n.20.

80. Ribadieu, p. 272.

Chapter 7

1. Ribadieu, p. 333.

2. *Ibid*

3. See Léo Drouyn, *Bordeaux vers 1450, description topographique*, Livre I, Bordeaux 1871, re-issued 2009, and the two volumes of his topographical engravings, *Léo Drouyn et Bordeaux*, Saint-Quentain-de-Baron, 2011.

4. Camille Favre, *Introduction biographique au Jouvencel*, Paris, 1887, pp. ccvi-ccvii.

5. Beaucourt, *Charles VII*, Tome V, p. 278.

6. Barker, *Conquest*, p. 362.

7. www.gasconrolls.org C61_139, N° 66

8. Ribadieu, p. 335.

9. Marcel Gourion, *Recueil des privilèges accordés à la ville de Bordeaux par Charles VII et Louis XI*, Bordeaux, 1938, Annexe, pp. 177–182.

10. *Ibid.*, p. 178.

11. R.A. Griffiths, *Henry VI*, p. 352.

12. Ribadieu, p. 337, citing Chartier, p. 269.

13. Ribadieu, p. 340.

14. Guillaume Leseur, *Histoire de Gaston de Foix*, Tome II, p. 26.

15. Ribadieu, p. 344. Ribadieu's account of the siege and capitulation of Bordeaux leans heavily upon the *Chronique de Mathieu d'Escouchy*, the continuator of Monstrelet, cited by him as de Coucy.

16. *Ibid.*, p. 342; Beaucourt, *Charles VII*, Tome V, p. 281.

17. Ribadieu, *Conquête*, p. 347.

18. Ribadieu, p. 350.

19. *Ibid.*, p. 351.

20. *Ibid*, p. 352, citing Jean Chartier.

21. *Ibid.*, p. 353.

22. *Registres du Parlement de Paris*, cited by Dom Devienne, *Histoire de Bordeaux*, p. 549

23. *Ibid.*

24. A.H.G., Tome II, *Livre des Privilèges*, pp. 243–256.

25. Ribadieu, p. 355.

26. *Ibid.*, p. 356.

27. Marcel Gourion, *Recueil*, pp. 183–184.

28. Ribadieu, p. 358.

29. *John Benet's Chronicle 1399–1462, An English Translation with a New Introduction*, Alison Hanham, ed., Basingstole and New York, 2016, p. 35.

30. Ribadieu, p. 377.

31. Ribadieu, p. 377.

32. *Ibid.*, p. 378 and n.2.

33. Vale, *Last Years*, p. 129.

34. www.gasconrolls.org, C61_139, N°69.

35. *Ibid.*, preamble.

36. On 17 February 1454, Charles VII had given his small lordship in the Landes at Trau to Gerard of Albret. (Ribadieu, p. 382.)

37. Ribadieu, pp. 379–382. Boutruche, *Crise*, p. 413.
38. A.H.G., 1888, pp. 365–366.
39. Robin Harris, *Valois Guyenne*, p. 110.
40. Michel Suffran, *Le Guide du Bordelais*, Besançon, 1991, pp. 96 and 396.
41. Michel Bochaca and N. Fouchère, *La Construction des châteaux de Hâ et de Tropeyte*, in Anne-Marie Cocula and Michel Combet, *Château et ville : actes et rencontres d'archéologie et histoire en Perigord, les 28, 29 et 30 septembre 2001*, Bordeaux, 2002, pp. 53–64.
42. Marc Seguin, *Jonzac* à la *fin du Moyen* Âge, *Revue de Saintonge et Aunis*, XXXVII, 2011, p. 61.
43. J.M.Pardessus,*Table chronologique des Ordonnances des rois de France de la troisième race* Vol XVII, Paris,1847, p.439. Google Books.
44. A.D.C-M., E262
45. Robin Harris, *Valois Guyenne*, Woodbridge and Rochester NY, 1994, p. 100.
46. Robin Harris, *Valois Guyenne*, Woodbridge and Rochester NY, 1994, p. 26.
47. A.H.G., Tome V, *Livre des coûtumes*, Ed., Henri Barkhausen, N° 23, pp. 642–680.
48. Ribadieu, *Conquête*, *Préface*, p. xi.
49. Yves Perotin, *Les Chapitres bordelais contre Charles VII*, *Annales de Midi. Revue historique, archéologique et philologique de la France méridionale, Tome* 63, N° 13, 1951, p.34ff. www.persée.fr.
50. www.gasconrolls.org, 61_139, N° 18.
51. Henri Barkhausen, ed., A.H.G., Tome XII, 1870, pp. 342–343.
52. Perotin, *Chapitres*, p. 36.
53. *Ibid*.
54. *Ibid.*, p. 37.
55. Vallet de Viriville, *Histoire de Charles VII, Tome* III, p. 328.
56. Ribadieu, pp. 420–421.
57. Perotin, *Chapitres*, p. 38.
58. Gourion, *Recueil*, p. 84.
59. Perotin, *Ibid*.
60. *Ibid*
61. *Ibid.*, p. 39.
62. *Ibid*.
63. A.H.G., Vol XI, p. 396.
64. Perotin, *Chapitres*, p. 40.
65. A.H.G., Tome IX, pp. 227–231, 303–305 & 309–310 (Minutes of the *Grands Jours*).
66. Perotin, *Chapitres*, p. 41.
67. Ibid., p. 41.
68. *Harris, Valois Guyenne*, p. 96.
69. *Ibid.*, p. 97.
70. See above, pp. 51–55.
71. Helen Castor, *Joan of Arc, A History*, pp. 222–242.

Chapter 8
1. Beaucourt, *Charles VII*, Tome I, pp.228–230.
2. *Ibid.*, Tome II, pp. 395–397.
3. Harris, *Valois* Guyenne, p. 28.
4. Pierre Prétou, *The Subjection of the Landes and Southern Aquitaine by the king of France (1441–1463)*, in Guilhem Pépin, *ed.*, *Anglo-Gascon Aquitaine, Problems and Perspectives*, Woodbridge, 2017, p.175.
5. *Ibid.*, pp. 178–179.
6. Illustration 4.
7. Prétou, *Subjection*, pp. 176–177.
8. *Ibid*
9. Joseph Stevenson, *Letters and Papers Illustrative of the Wars of the English in France During the Reign of Henry VI, King of England*, Vol I, p. 343.
10. Robin Harris, *Valois Guyenne*, p. 28 &n.
11. Stevenson, *ibid.*, cited in Prétou, *Subjection*, p. 173.
12. Prétou, *ibid.*, p. 180.
13. Robin Harris, *Valois Guyenne*, p. 25.
14. Ribadieu, p. 401, nn. 1 & 2.
15. Paul Marchegay, *La Rançon d'Olivier de Coëtivy, extrait de la* Bibliothèque de *l'Ecole des Chartes*, Vol XXXVIII, 1877, pp. 5–6, 21–23 & 24–25, ADC-M Br 5219, cited by Robin Harris, Valois Guyenne, p. 27.
16. Marchegay, *Rançon*, p. 21.
17. *Ibid.*
18. Gourion, *Recueil*, p. 65.
19. Henri Barkhausen, ed., A.H.G., Tome IX, pp. 81–83.
20. *Lettres de Marie de Valois, fille de Charles VII et Agnès Sorel, à Olivier de Coëtivy, Seigneur de Taillebourg, son mari, 1458–1472*, Les Roches Baritaud, 1875, ADC-M, Br 5219.
21. Beaucourt, *Charles VII*, Tome VI, pp. 432–434, which leans on Marchegay's two publications.
22. Sandrine Lavaud, *Bordeaux et le vin au Moyen Age*, Luçon, 2003, pp. 165–180.
23. *Ibid.*, p. 209.
24. A.H.G. IX, N°. 24., pp. 680–685.
25. Christine Carpenter, *The Wars of the Roses*, Cambridge, 1997, p. 105.
26. E.M. Carus-Wilson, *The Effects of the Acquisition and of the Loss of Gascony on the English Wine Trade*, B.I.H.R., XXI, N°. 63, 1947, reproduced in *Medieval Merchant Venturers, Collected Studies*, London & New York, 1954, p.271ff. This section leans heavily upon this article.
27. A.H.G. XXXVIII, pp. 223–228, cited in Carus-Wilson, *Effects*, p. 273, n. 2.
28. Carus-Wilson, *Effects*, p. 274.
29. *Ibid.*, pp. 274–275.
30. *Ibid.*, p. 276.
31. *Ibid*, p. 277, citing A.H.G. IX pp. 447ff.
32. Prétou, *Subjection*, p. 180.

33. Carus-Wilson, *Effects*, pp. 274–278.

34. *Les Conséquences de la conquête de la Guyenne par le roi de France pour le commerce des vins de Gascogne*, Annales de Midi, Tome 61, 1948, pp. 15–31.

35. M. Gourion, *Recueil des privilèges accordés à la ville de Bordeaux par Charles VII et Louis XI*, Bordeaux, 1938, p. 20.

36. *Ibid.*, p. 25, cited by Renouard, *Conséquences*, p. 20.

37. Renouard, *Conséquences*, p. 21.

38. *Ibid.*, citing E. Power and M. Postan, *Studies in English Trade in the XVth Century*, London, 1933, pp. 1–28 & 321–360.

39. Renouard, *Conséquences*, p. 22. His authority is M. Gouron, *L'Amirauté de Guyenne*, Paris 1938, p. 113. The details are different from those given by Miss Carus-Wilson, above, p. 18.

40. *Ibid.*, pp. 22–23.

41. A.H.G.,Tome IX, p. 404.

42. *Conséquences*, p. 23.

43. *Ibid.*, p. 24.

44. *Ibid.*

45. Gourion, *Recueil*, p. 123.

46. *Ibid.*, pp. 123–124.

47. E.g., Théophile Malvezin, *Histoire du commerce de Bordeaux depuis les origines jusqu'au nos jours*, Bordeaux, 1892, Vol II, pp. 19–22. www.gallica.bnf.fr

48. Gourion, *Recueil*, pp. 106–107.

49. Renouard, *Conséquences*, p. 25.

50. *Ibid.*

51. *Ibid.*, p. 26.

52. www.gasconrolls.org C61_144.

53. Renouard, *Conséquences*, p. 27.

54. *Ibid.*, p. 28.

55. *Ibid.*

56. Samaran, *La Maison d'Armagnac*, pp. 164–174.

57. Renouard here cites Calmette & Périnelle, *Louis XI et l'Angleterre*, pp. 91–92 & 106.

58. Renouard, *Conséquences*, p. 30.

59. See also : A. Peyrègne, *Les Emigrés gascons en Angleterre (1453–1485)*, *Annales du Midi*, Tome 66, N°. 26, 1954, pp. 113–128.

60. Gourion, *Recueil*, pp. 73–75.

61. *Studies in the Medieval Wine Trade*, Oxford, 1971, p. 85.

62. *Ibid.*

63. www.gasconrolls.org, *ad loc.*

64. *Ibid.*

65. James, *Wine Trade*, p. 86.

66. *Ibid.*, pp. 86–88.

Chapter 9

1. Michael Hicks, *Bastard Feudalism, Overmighty Subjects and Idols of the Multitude during the Wars of the Roses*, History, Vol 65, No. 279, (July 2000), p. 389. http://www.jstor.or/stable/24424946

2. As Sir William Bonville, he had been seneschal of Gascony between 1443 and 1445 and would be appointed to that office again in 1453 when it was too late.

3. Hanham, ed., *Benet's Chronicle*, p. 32.

4. Michael Hicks, *The Wars of the Roses*, New Haven and London, 2012, pp. 98–99.

5. See Helen Castor, *Blood and Roses, The Paston Family and the Wars of the Roses*, London, 2005, Chapter Three.

6. Barker, *Conquest*, p. 392.

7. *Ibid,*, p. 316

8. Grummitt, Henry VI, pp. 151–155.

9. *Ibid.*, p. 152.

10. Grummitt, p. 152.

11. *Parliamentary Rolls*, V, 177, cited in R.A. Griffiths, p. 679.

12. R. L. Storey, *The Fall of the House of Lancaster*, pp. 76–77.

13. R.A. Griffiths, *Henry VI*, pp. 676–684. *John Benet's Chronicle 1399–1462*, ed., and trans., Alison Hanham, London and New York, 2016, pp. 26–27.

14. *Ibid.*, p. 684, n.85.

15. David Grummitt, *Henry VI*, p. 158.

16. John Watts, *The Politics of Kingship*, p. 254.

17. Gwilym Dodd, *Agincourt: Henry's Hollow Victory*, in *History Today*, 10 October 2016.

18. G.L. Harriss, *Shaping the Nation, England 1360–1461*, Oxford, 2005, p. 619.

19. *John Benet's Chronicle 1399–1461, An English Translation with New Introduction*, Alison Hanham, Basingstoke and New York, 2016, *Introduction*, p. 2. The account of Cade's rebellion offered here is peppered with quotations from this source, pp. 27–29, unless noted as being from elsewhere.

20. *The Brut or Chronicles of England*, ed., Friedrich W.D. Brie, London, 1906, p. 517.

21. This is one of the 'often wild' estimates of the number of men of Kent involved that Griffiths refers to, p. 619.

22. *A proclamation made by Jacke Cade, Capytayn of ye Rebelles in Kent*, in *Three Fifteenth-Century Chronicles with Historical Memoranda by John Stowe*, ed. James Gairdner, London, 1880, pp. 94–103.

23. Also found in *The Brut or Chronicles of England*, p. 517.

24. Brut, p. 518.

25. Griffiths, p. 613.

26. *Ibid.*, p. 612.

27. *Ibid.*
28. *Ibid.*
29. *Ibid.*
30. Griffiths concludes from other sources that it was 'several hundred' that were killed there, p. 615.
31. Griffiths, p. 620.
32. *Ibid.*, p. 619.
33. Brut, p. 519.
34. Griffiths, p. 616.
35. *Ibid.*, p. 643.
36. *Ibid.*, p. 646.
37. *Ibid.*, pp. 617–618.
38. *Ibid.*, p. 648.
39. P.A.Johnson, *Duke Richard of York 1411–1460, Oxford, 1988*, pp. 78–81.
40. R.L. Storey, *The End of the House of Lancaster*, New Edition , Gloucester, 1986, p. 4.
41. Benet's Chronicle consistently calls him that: ed., Hanham, p. 26 seven times.
42. *Oxford Dictionary of National Biography*, John Watts, *Richard of York (1411–1460)*: doi: 10.1093/ref:odnb/23503
43. Johnson, p. 81.
44. *Ibid.*, pp. 82–86.
45. Wolffe, pp. 268–270.
46. Storey, pp. 34–35 & 136.
47. Vivian Green, *The Madness of Kings, Personal Trauma and the Fate of Nations*, Stroud, 1993, p. 63.
48. Johnson, p. 136.
49. Griffiths, pp. 693–700. *John Benet's Chronicle*, pp. 32–33
50. Johnson, p. 124.
51. Wolffe, pp. 276–277.
52. Johnson, p. 133.
53. *Ibid.*, p. 134.
54. Griffiths, pp. 730–738.
55. Helen E. Maurer, *Margaret of Anjou, Queenship and Power in Late Medieval England*, Woodbridge, 2003, p. 100.
56. J. Gairdner, *The Paston Letters, London, 1904,* Vol II, pp. 295–299.
57. *Parliament Rolls of Medieval England*, ed. Chris Given-Wilson, Seymour Phillips, Mark Ormrod, Geoffrey Martin, Anne Curry & Rosemary Horrox, Woodbridge, 2005, Introduction to 1453 Parliament. http://www.brtish-history.ac.uk/no-series/parliament-rolls-medieval/march-1453 (page numbers not vouchsafed online).
58. Griffiths, pp. 740–741.
59. Johnson, p.157.

60. *Ibid.*
61. Michael Hicks, *Wars of the Roses*, New Haven and London, 2012, p. 111.
62. Johnson, pp. 155–159.
63. *Ibid.*, p. 167.
64. Gairdner, *Paston Letters*, III, p. 75 cited by Maurer, *ibid.*
65. Maurer, p. 128.
66. *Benet's Chronicle*, pp. 37–39. Johnson, p. 173.
67. Diana E.S. Dunn, *Margaret of Anjou (14301420) ONDB*, 2004, http://www.oxford.dnb.com/view/article/18049, pp. 6–7.
68. Storey, p. 185, and Wolffe , p. 312.
69. Maurer, p. 157

Chapter 10
1. Philippe de Commynes, *Memoires*, Ed., Bernard de Mandrot, Tome II, p. 90, cited by J. Calmette & G. Perinelle, *Louis XI et L'Angleterre*, Paris, 1930, p. vi, n.1 (Henceforth Calmette).
2. Calmette, p. vii and n.3.
3. See above.
4. Joseph Calmette, *Moyen Âge Français*, Paris, 1944, pp. 133–136.
5. Michael Jones, *Philippe de Commynes, Memoirs, the Reign of Louis XI 1461–83*, Harmondsworth, 1972, uses this appellation thoughout his translation.
6. Calmette, p. viii.
7. *Ibid.*, p. vii.
8. *Ibid*, p. 1.
9. *Ibid.*, p. 2.
10. Charles W. Oman, *Warwick the Kingmaker*, London and New York, 1893, p. 68.
11. Beaucourt, Vol V, p. 140.
12. Chastellain, III, pp. 347–352.
13. Charles Ross, *Edward IV*, New Haven and London, 1997, p. 21.
14. Beaucourt, Volume VI, pp. 372 & 337n.
15. Calmette, pp. 2–3 n.5.
16. *Ibid.*, p. 3 n. 1.
17. Beaucourt, Volume V, pp. 140–144.
18. Calmette, p. 3, citing Olivier de La Marche.
19. Beaucourt, Volume VI, pp. 259–260.
20. Thomas Basin, *Histoire des règnes de Charles VII et de Louis XI*, ed., J. Quicherat, Paris, 1855, Tome I, pp 301–304, cited by Calmette.
21. Calmette, p. 8, & n. 1.
22. *Ibid.*, p. 10.
23. Paul Murray Kendall, *Louis XI*, London, 1971, pp. 179–207.
24. Ibid., pp. 210–227.
25. Charles Fouché, *Taillebourg et ses seigneurs*, Chef-Boutonne, 1911, p. 213.

26. Ribadieu, p. 437.
27. *Ibid.*, pp. 439–440.
28. Marcel Gourion, *Recueil des Privileges accordé à la ville de Bordeaux par Charles VII et Louis XI*, Bordeaux, 1938, pp. 119–169.
29. Ribadieu, p. 442.
30. www.gasconrolls.org C61_143, No. 51.
31. Baurein, *Variétés bordelaises, Tome IV,* p. 247; Ribadieu, pp. 442–443.
32. *Ibid.*, IV pp. 249–251.
33. Ribadieu, pp. 443–445.
34. Jean de Wavrin, *Recueil des chroniques et anciennes histoires de La Grand Betagne à présent nommé Angleterre, Tome II*, p. 399, cited by Ribadieu, pp. 445–446 and notes.
35. Joseph Calmette, *Louis XI, Jean II et la révolution catalane*, Toulouse, 1903, p. 319.
36. Calmette, p. 144.
37. Leseur, *Life of Gaston IV of Foix*, Volume II, p. 261, n. 2.
38. Calmette, p. 150.
39. *Ibid.*, p. 154.
40. Amable Sablon du Corail, *Louis XI, Le joueur inquiet*, Paris , 2015, p.363. Charles Ross, *Edward IV*, New Haven and London, 1974, pp. 207–213.
41. *Ibid.*, p. 384. Charles Ross, *Edward IV*, New Haven and London, 1997, p. 210.
42. Calmette, pp. 191–193.
43. Sablon, p. 389.
44. Calmette, pp. 179–182.
45. *Ibid.*, pp. 183–184.
46. *Ibid.*
47. *Ibid.*, pp. 184–186.
48. Calmette p. 192.
49. Ross, p. 230. *Mémoires de Philippe de Commynes*, ed., Calmette, Vol II, Paris, 1925, pp. 39–45.
50. Philippe de Commynes, *Memoirs : the Reign of Louis XI 1461–83*, Translated with an introduction by Michael Jones, Harmondsworth, 1972, p. 251.
51. Calmette, pp. 193–199.
52. Joel Blanchard, *Commynes n'a pas 'trahi': pour en finir avec une obsession critique*, Revue du Nord, 2009/2 (No. 380), pp. 327–360. Cairn info.
53. *Commynes*, trans., Michael Jones, pp. 255–262, *Philippe de Commynes, Mémoires*, édités par Joseph Calmette, Tome II, Paris 1925, pp. 57–62, & *Philippe de Commynes, The Universal Spider, the Life of Louis XI of France*, Translated and edited by Paul Kendall, London, 1973, pp. 170–174.
54. *Commynes*, ed., Calmette, p. 66.
55. *Ibid.*, p. 67.
56. *Ibid.*,p. 68.

57. *Ibid.*, p. 67
58. *Ibid.*, pp. 70–71.
59. Ribadieu, p. 447 see above.
60. *Ibid.*, p. 448.
61. *Louis XI '... the universal spider ...'*, London, 1971, p. 351.
62. Professor Kendall presents the story again in a later book, attributing it to an interpolation in Jean de La Roye's *Chronique scandaleuse. Philippe de Commynes, The Universal Spider: the Life of Louis XI of France*, which he translated and edited, London, 1973, p.177.
63. Commynes, Jones, p. 262, & Calmette, pp. 71–72.

Index